Managing Projects
with GNU Make

Other resources from O'Reilly

Related titles Unix in a Nutshell   sed and awk
Unix Power Tools   lex and yacc
Essential CVS   Learning the bash Shell
Version Control with
    Subversion

oreilly.com *oreilly.com* is more than a complete catalog of O'Reilly books. You'll also find links to news, events, articles, weblogs, sample chapters, and code examples.

oreillynet.com is the essential portal for developers interested in open and emerging technologies, including new platforms, programming languages, and operating systems.

Conferences O'Reilly brings diverse innovators together to nurture the ideas that spark revolutionary industries. We specialize in documenting the latest tools and systems, translating the innovator's knowledge into useful skills for those in the trenches. Visit *conferences.oreilly.com* for our upcoming events.

Safari Bookshelf (*safari.oreilly.com*) is the premier online reference library for programmers and IT professionals. Conduct searches across more than 1,000 books. Subscribers can zero in on answers to time-critical questions in a matter of seconds. Read the books on your Bookshelf from cover to cover or simply flip to the page you need. Try it today with a free trial.

THIRD EDITION

Managing Projects with GNU Make

Robert Mecklenburg

Beijing · Cambridge · Farnham · Köln · Sebastopol · Tokyo

Managing Projects with GNU Make, Third Edition
by Robert Mecklenburg

Copyright © 2005, 1991, 1986 O'Reilly Media, Inc. All rights reserved.
Printed in the United States of America.

Published by O'Reilly Media, Inc., 1005 Gravenstein Highway North, Sebastopol, CA 95472.

O'Reilly books may be purchased for educational, business, or sales promotional use. Online editions are also available for most titles (*safari.oreilly.com*). For more information, contact our corporate/institutional sales department: (800) 998-9938 or *corporate@oreilly.com*.

Editor:	Andy Oram
Production Editor:	Matt Hutchinson
Production Services:	Octal Publishing, Inc.
Cover Designer:	Edie Freedman
Interior Designer:	David Futato

Printing History:

1986:	First Edition.
October 1991:	Second Edition.
November 2004:	Third Edition.

ISBN: 978-0-596-00610-5
[LSI]   [2011-02-09]

For Ralph and Buff

Table of Contents

Foreword

The make utility is an enticing servant, always there and always accommodating. Like the indispensable sidekicks found in many novels and movies, make starts out as the underappreciated supplicant to whom you throw a few odd jobs, and then gradually takes over the entire enterprise.

I had reached the terminal stage of putting make at the center of every project I touched when Steve Talbott, my supervisor and the author of the original O'Reilly classic *Managing Projects with make*, noticed my obsession and asked me to write the second edition. It proved to be a key growth experience for me (as well as a pretty wild ride) and my entry into the wonderful world of O'Reilly, but we didn't really think about how long the result would stay on the market. Thirteen years for one edition?

Enthralled in the memories of those days long ago when I was a professional technical writer, I'll indulge myself with a bulleted list to summarize the evolution of make since the second edition of *Managing Projects with make* hit the stands:

- The GNU version of make, already the choice of most serious coders when the second edition of the book came out, overran the industry and turned into the de facto standard.

- The rise of GNU/Linux made the GNU compiler tool chain even more common, and that includes the GNU version of make. As just one example, the Linux kernel itself relies heavily on extensions provided by GNU make, as documented in Chapter 11 of this book.

- The adoption of a variant of BSD (Darwin) as the core of Mac OS X continues the trend toward the dominance of the GNU tool chain and GNU make.

- More and more tricks are being discovered for using make in a robust, error-free, portable, and flexible way. Standard solutions to common problems on large projects have grown up in the programming community. It's time to move many of these solutions from the realm of folklore to the realm of documented practices, as this book does.

- In particular, new practices are required to adapt make to the C++ and Java™ languages, which did not exist when make was invented. To illustrate the shifting sands of time, the original make contained special features to support two variants of FORTRAN—of which vestiges remain!—and rather ineffective integration with SCCS.)

- Against all odds, make has remained a critical tool for nearly all computer development projects. None of make's many (and insightful) critics would have predicted this 13 years ago. Over these years, replacements sprang up repeatedly, as if dragon's teeth had been sown. Each new tool was supposed to bypass the limitations in make's design, and most were indeed ingenious and admirable. Yet the simplicity of make has kept it supreme.

As I watched these trends, it had been in the back of my mind for about a decade to write a new edition of *Managing Projects with make*. But I sensed that someone with a broader range of professional experience than mine was required. Finally, Robert Mecklenburg came along and wowed us all at O'Reilly with his expertise. I was happy to let him take over the book and to retire to the role of kibitzer, which earns me a mention on the copyright page of this book. (Incidentally, we put the book under the GNU Free Documentation License to mirror the GPL status of GNU make.)

Robert is too modest to tout his Ph.D., but the depth and precision of thinking he must have applied to that endeavor comes through clearly in this book. Perhaps more important to the book is his focus on practicality. He's committed to making make work for you, and this commitment ranges from being alert about efficiency to being clever about making even typographical errors in *makefiles* self-documenting.

This is a great moment: the creation of a new edition of one of O'Reilly's earliest and most enduring books. Sit back and read about how an unassuming little tool at the background of almost every project embodies powers you never imagined. Don't settle for creaky and unsatisfying *makefiles*—expand your potential today.

—Andy Oram
Editor, O'Reilly Media
August 19, 2004

Preface

The Road to the Third Edition

My first exposure to make was as an undergraduate at Berkeley in 1979. I was thrilled to be working with the "latest" equipment: a DEC PDP 11/70 with 128 kilobytes of RAM, an ADM 3a "glass tty," Berkeley Unix, and 20 other simultaneous users! Once, when an assignment was due, I remember timing how long it took to log in— five minutes from typing my username until I got a prompt.

After leaving school, it was 1984 before I got to work on Unix again. This time it was as a programmer at NASA's Ames Research Center. We purchased one of the first microcomputer-based Unix systems, a 68000 (not a 68010 or 20) that had a megabyte of RAM and Unix Version 7—with only six simultaneous users. My last project there was an interactive satellite data analysis system written in C with a yacc/lex command language, and, of course, make.

By 1988, I had gone back to school and was working on a project to build a spline-based geometric modeler. The system consisted of about 120,000 lines of C, spread across 20 or so executables. The system was built using *makefile* templates that were expanded into normal *makefiles* by a hand-rolled tool call genmakefile (similar in spirit to imake). The tool performed simple file inclusion, conditional compilation, and some custom logic to manage source and binary trees. It was a common belief in those days that make required such a wrapper to be a complete build tool. Several years earlier, I had discovered the GNU project and GNU make and realized that the wrapper program was probably unnecessary. I rebuilt the build system without the templates or a generator. To my chagrin, I wound up maintaining the build system for the next four years (a pattern I foolishly repeat to this day). The build system was portable to five flavors of Unix and included separate source and binary trees, automated nightly builds, and support for partial checkouts by developers with the build system filling in the missing objects.

My next interesting encounter with make came in 1996, working on a commercial CAD system. It was my job to port 2 million lines of C++ (and 400,000 lines of Lisp) from Unix to Windows NT, using the Microsoft C++ compiler. That's when I discovered the Cygwin project. As an important byproduct of the port, I reworked the build system to support NT. This build system also supported separate source and binary trees, many flavors of Unix, several varieties of graphics support, automated nightly builds and tests, and partial developer checkouts with reference builds.

In 2000, I began working in Java writing laboratory information management systems. This was one of the first really different development environments I'd worked in for many years. Most of the programmers came from a Windows background and many seemed to know Java as their first programming language. The build environment consisted almost entirely of the project file generated by a commercial Java Integrated Development Environment (IDE). Although the project file was checked in, it rarely worked "out of the box" and programmers often sat in each other's cubes working through build problems.

Of course, I began to write a build system using make, but an odd thing happened. Many of the developers were reluctant to use any command-line tool. Further, many did not have a firm grasp of such concepts as environment variables, command-line options, or an understanding of the tools used to build programs. The IDE hid all of these issues. To address these issues, the build system I was writing became more complex. I began to add better error messages, precondition checking, management of the developer's machine configuration, and support for IDEs.

Along the way, I'd read the GNU make manual several dozen times. As I looked for more material, I found the second edition of this book. It was filled with valuable material, but was sadly lacking in details of GNU make. That wasn't surprising, considering its age. The volume had stood the test of time, but by 2003 needed updating. The third edition focuses primarily on GNU make. As Paul Smith (the GNU make maintainer) writes: "Don't hassle with writing portable 'makefiles', use a portable make instead!"

What's New in This Edition

Almost all the material in this book is new. I've divided the material into three parts.

Part I, *Basic Concepts*, provides a moderately detailed examination of the GNU make features and how to use them.

Chapter 1, *How to Write a Simple Makefile*, is a brief introduction to make with a simple, but complete example. It explains the basic concepts of make such as targets and prerequisites, and covers the syntax of *makefiles*. This should be sufficient to get you going with your first *makefiles*.

Chapter 2, *Rules*, discusses the structure and syntax of rules. Explicit rules and pattern rules are covered in great detail along with old-fashioned suffix rules. Special targets and simple dependency generation are also discussed here.

Chapter 3, *Variables and Macros*, covers simple and recursive variables. This chapter also discusses how *makefiles* are parsed, when variables are expanded, and the directives for conditional *makefile* processing.

Chapter 4, *Functions*, examines the wide variety of built-in functions supported by GNU make. User-defined functions are introduced here, with numerous examples ranging from the trivial to illustrations of advanced concepts.

Chapter 5, *Commands*, explains the details of command scripts, covering how they are parsed and evaluated. Here we also discuss command modifiers, checking command exit status, and the command environment. We explore the problems of command-line limits and some ways to work around these problems. At this point, you will know all the GNU make features discussed in this book.

Part II, *Advanced and Specialized Topics*, covers larger topics, such as using make on large projects, portability, and debugging.

Chapter 6, *Managing Large Projects*, discusses many issues encountered when building large projects in make. The first topic is the use of recursive invocations of make, as well as how to implement these *makefiles* with a single, nonrecursive *makefile*. In addition, other issues of large systems are discussed, such as filesystem layout, component management, and automated building and testing.

Chapter 7, *Portable Makefiles*, discusses issues with portability of *makefiles*, primarily between various flavors of Unix and Windows. The Cygwin Unix emulation environment is discussed in some detail, along with issues arising from nonportable filesystem features and tools.

Chapter 8, *C and C++*, provides specific examples of how to separate source and binary trees and how to create read-only source trees. Dependency analysis is revisited, with an emphasis on language-specific solutions. This chapter and the next tie in closely with many issues raised in Chapter 1.

Chapter 9, *Java*, explains how to apply make to Java-based development environments. Techniques for managing the CLASSPATH variable, compiling large numbers of files, creating jars, and constructing Enterprise JavaBeans (EJBs) are introduced.

Chapter 10, *Improving the Performance of make*, begins by reviewing the performance characteristics of several make operations to provide context for how to write efficient *makefiles*. Techniques for identifying and reducing bottlenecks are discussed. The GNU make parallel jobs feature is described in some detail.

Chapter 11, *Example Makefiles*, provides two complex examples of real *makefiles*. The first is the *makefile* used to create this book. It is interesting, partly due to a fairly extreme degree of automation and partly because it applies make to a nontraditional domain. The other example consists of excerpts from the Linux 2.6 kbuild system.

Chapter 12, *Debugging Makefiles*, delves into the black art of fixing broken *makefiles*. We introduce techniques for discovering what make is doing under the covers and how to ease development pains.

Part III, *Appendixes*, includes supplemental material.

Appendix A, *Running make*, provides a reference guide to GNU make's command-line options.

Appendix B, *The Outer Limits*, explores the limits of GNU make with two unlikely capabilities: managing data structures and performing arithmetic.

Appendix C, *GNU Free Documentation License—GNU Project—Free Software Foundation (FSF)*, contains the GNU Free Documentation License, under which the text of the book is distributed.

Conventions Used in This Book

The following typographical conventions are used in this book:

Italic
> Indicates new terms, URLs, email addresses, filenames, file extensions, pathnames, and directories

`Constant width`
> Indicates source code commands, command-line options, the contents of files, or the output from commands

`Constant width bold`
> Shows commands or other text that should be typed literally by the user

`Constant width italic`
> Shows text that should be replaced with user-supplied values

Using Code Examples

This book is here to help you get your job done. In general, you may use the code in this book in your programs and documentation. You do not need to contact O'Reilly for permission unless you're reproducing a significant portion of the code. For example, writing a program that uses several chunks of code from this book does not require permission. Selling or distributing a CD-ROM of examples from O'Reilly books *does* require permission. Answering a question by citing this book and quoting example code does not require permission. Incorporating a significant amount of example code from this book into your product's documentation *does* require permission.

O'Reilly appreciates, but does not require, attribution. An attribution usually includes the title, author, publisher, and ISBN. For example: "*Managing Projects with GNU Make*, Third Edition, by Robert Mecklenburg. Copyright 2005 O'Reilly Media, Inc., 0-596-00610-1."

If you feel your use of code examples falls outside fair use or the permission given above, feel free to contact O'Reilly at *permissions@oreilly.com*.

Comments and Questions

Please address comments and questions concerning this book to the publisher:

> O'Reilly Media, Inc.
> 1005 Gravenstein Highway North
> Sebastopol, CA 95472
> (800) 998-9938 (in the United States or Canada)
> (707) 829-0515 (international or local)
> (707) 829-0104 (fax)

O'Reilly maintains a web page for this book, which lists errata, examples, and any additional information. You can access this page at:

> *http://www.oreilly.com/catalog/make3*

To comment or ask technical questions about this book, send email to:

> *bookquestions@oreilly.com*

For more information about O'Reilly books, conferences, Resource Centers, and the O'Reilly Network, see O'Reilly's web site at:

> *http://www.oreilly.com*

Acknowledgments

I'd like to thank Richard Stallman for providing a vision and the belief that it can come true. Of course, without Paul Smith, GNU make would not exist in its current form today. Thank you.

I'd like to thank my editor, Andy Oram, for his unflagging support and enthusiasm.

Cimarron Software deserves my thanks for providing an environment that encouraged me to begin this project. Realm Systems also deserves thanks for providing an environment that encouraged me to finish the project. In particular, I'd like to thank Doug Adamson, Cathy Anderson, and Peter Bookman.

Thanks to my reviewers, Simon Gerraty, John Macdonald, and Paul Smith, who provided many insightful comments and corrected many embarrassing errors.

The following people deserve thanks for valuable contributions to this work: Steve Bayer, Richard Bogart, Beth Cobb, Julie Daily, David Johnson, Andrew Morton, Richard Pimentel, Brian Stevens, and Linus Torvalds. Many thanks to the cabal that provided a safe haven in stormy seas: Christine Delaney, Tony Di Sera, John Major, and Daniel Reading.

Finally, my profound gratitude and love goes to my wife, Maggie Kasten, and our children, William and James, for their support, encouragement, and love during the last sixteen months. Thank you for sharing this with me.

## PART I

Basic Concepts

In Part I, we focus on the features of make, what they do, and how to use them properly. We begin with a brief introduction and overview that should be enough to get you started on your first *makefile*. The chapters then cover make rules, variables, functions, and finally command scripts.

When you are finished with Part I, you will have a fairly complete working knowledge of GNU make and have many advanced usages well in hand.

How to Write a Simple Makefile

The mechanics of programming usually follow a fairly simple routine of editing source files, compiling the source into an executable form, and debugging the result. Although transforming the source into an executable is considered routine, if done incorrectly a programmer can waste immense amounts of time tracking down the problem. Most developers have experienced the frustration of modifying a function and running the new code only to find that their change did not fix the bug. Later they discover that they were never executing their modified function because of some procedural error such as failing to recompile the source, relink the executable, or rebuild a jar. Moreover, as the program's complexity grows these mundane tasks can become increasingly error-prone as different versions of the program are developed, perhaps for other platforms or other versions of support libraries, etc.

The make program is intended to automate the mundane aspects of transforming source code into an executable. The advantages of make over scripts is that you can specify the relationships between the elements of your program to make, and it knows through these relationships and timestamps exactly what steps need to be redone to produce the desired program each time. Using this information, make can also optimize the build process avoiding unnecessary steps.

GNU make (and other variants of make) do precisely this. make defines a language for describing the relationships between source code, intermediate files, and executables. It also provides features to manage alternate configurations, implement reusable libraries of specifications, and parameterize processes with user-defined macros. In short, make can be considered the center of the development process by providing a roadmap of an application's components and how they fit together.

The specification that make uses is generally saved in a file named *makefile*. Here is a *makefile* to build the traditional "Hello, World" program:

```
hello: hello.c
        gcc hello.c -o hello
```

To build the program execute make by typing:

```
$ make
```

at the command prompt of your favorite shell. This will cause the make program to read the *makefile* and build the first target it finds there:

```
$ make
gcc hello.c -o hello
```

If a target is included as a command-line argument, that target is updated. If no command-line targets are given, then the first target in the file is used, called the *default goal*.

Typically the default goal in most *makefiles* is to build a program. This usually involves many steps. Often the source code for the program is incomplete and the source must be generated using utilities such as flex or bison. Next the source is compiled into binary object files (*.o* files for C/C++, *.class* files for Java, etc.). Then, for C/C++, the object files are bound together by a linker (usually invoked through the compiler, gcc) to form an executable program.

Modifying any of the source files and reinvoking make will cause some, but usually not all, of these commands to be repeated so the source code changes are properly incorporated into the executable. The specification file, or *makefile*, describes the relationship between the source, intermediate, and executable program files so that make can perform the minimum amount of work necessary to update the executable.

So the principle value of make comes from its ability to perform the complex series of commands necessary to build an application and to optimize these operations when possible to reduce the time taken by the edit-compile-debug cycle. Furthermore, make is flexible enough to be used anywhere one kind of file depends on another from traditional programming in C/C++ to Java, T$_E$X, database management, and more.

Targets and Prerequisites

Essentially a *makefile* contains a set of rules used to build an application. The first rule seen by make is used as the *default rule*. A *rule* consists of three parts: the target, its prerequisites, and the command(s) to perform:

```
target: prereq₁ prereq₂
        commands
```

The *target* is the file or thing that must be made. The *prerequisites* or *dependents* are those files that must exist before the target can be successfully created. And the *commands* are those shell commands that will create the target from the prerequisites.

Here is a rule for compiling a C file, *foo.c*, into an object file, *foo.o*:

```
foo.o: foo.c foo.h
        gcc -c foo.c
```

The target file *foo.o* appears before the colon. The prerequisites *foo.c* and *foo.h* appear after the colon. The command script usually appears on the following lines and is preceded by a tab character.

When make is asked to evaluate a rule, it begins by finding the files indicated by the prerequisites and target. If any of the prerequisites has an associated rule, make attempts to update those first. Next, the target file is considered. If any prerequisite is newer than the target, the target is remade by executing the commands. Each command line is passed to the shell and is executed in its own subshell. If any of the commands generates an error, the building of the target is terminated and make exits. One file is considered newer than another if it has been modified more recently.

Here is a program to count the number of occurrences of the words "fee," "fie," "foe," and "fum" in its input. It uses a flex scanner driven by a simple main:

```
#include <stdio.h>

extern int fee_count, fie_count, foe_count, fum_count;
extern int yylex( void );

int main( int argc, char ** argv )
{
    yylex();
    printf( "%d %d %d %d\n", fee_count, fie_count, foe_count, fum_count );
    exit( 0 );
}
```

The scanner is very simple:

```
        int fee_count = 0;
        int fie_count = 0;
        int foe_count = 0;
        int fum_count = 0;
%%
fee     fee_count++;
fie     fie_count++;
foe     foe_count++;
fum     fum_count++;
```

The *makefile* for this program is also quite simple:

```
count_words: count_words.o lexer.o -lfl
        gcc count_words.o lexer.o -lfl -o count_words

count_words.o: count_words.c
        gcc -c count_words.c

lexer.o: lexer.c
        gcc -c lexer.c

lexer.c: lexer.l
        flex -t lexer.l > lexer.c
```

When this *makefile* is executed for the first time, we see:

```
$ make
gcc -c count_words.c
flex -t lexer.l > lexer.c
gcc -c lexer.c
gcc count_words.o lexer.o -lfl -o count_words
```

We now have an executable program. Of course, real programs typically consist of more modules than this. Also, as you will see later, this *makefile* does not use most of the features of make so it's more verbose than necessary. Nevertheless, this is a functional and useful *makefile*. For instance, during the writing of this example, I executed the *makefile* several dozen times while experimenting with the program.

As you look at the *makefile* and sample execution, you may notice that the order in which commands are executed by make are nearly the opposite to the order they occur in the *makefile*. This *top-down* style is common in *makefiles*. Usually the most general form of target is specified first in the *makefile* and the details are left for later. The make program supports this style in many ways. Chief among these is make's two-phase execution model and recursive variables. We will discuss these in great detail in later chapters.

Dependency Checking

How did make decide what to do? Let's go over the previous execution in more detail to find out.

First make notices that the command line contains no targets so it decides to make the default goal, *count_words*. It checks for prerequisites and sees three: *count_words.o*, *lexer.o*, and -1fl. make now considers how to build *count_words.o* and sees a rule for it. Again, it checks the prerequisites, notices that *count_words.c* has no rules but that the file exists, so make executes the commands to transform *count_words.c* into *count_words.o* by executing the command:

```
gcc -c count_words.c
```

This "chaining" of targets to prerequisites to targets to prerequisites is typical of how make analyzes a *makefile* to decide the commands to be performed.

The next prerequisite make considers is *lexer.o*. Again the chain of rules leads to *lexer.c* but this time the file does not exist. make finds the rule for generating *lexer.c* from *lexer.l* so it runs the flex program. Now that *lexer.c* exists it can run the gcc command.

Finally, make examines -1fl. The -1 option to gcc indicates a system library that must be linked into the application. The actual library name indicated by "fl" is *libfl.a*. GNU make includes special support for this syntax. When a prerequisite of the form -1<NAME> is seen, make searches for a file of the form *libNAME.so*; if no match is found, it then searches for *libNAME.a*. Here make finds */usr/lib/libfl.a* and proceeds with the final action, linking.

Minimizing Rebuilds

When we run our program, we discover that aside from printing fees, fies, foes, and fums, it also prints text from the input file. This is not what we want. The problem is that we have forgotten some rules in our lexical analyzer and flex is passing this unrecognized text to its output. To solve this problem we simply add an "any character" rule and a newline rule:

```
            int fee_count = 0;
            int fie_count = 0;
            int foe_count = 0;
            int fum_count = 0;
%%
fee         fee_count++;
fie         fie_count++;
foe         foe_count++;
fum         fum_count++;
.
\n
```

After editing this file we need to rebuild the application to test our fix:

```
$ make
flex -t lexer.l > lexer.c
gcc -c lexer.c
gcc count_words.o lexer.o -lfl -ocount_words
```

Notice this time the file *count_words.c* was not recompiled. When make analyzed the rule, it discovered that *count_words.o* existed and was newer than its prerequisite *count_words.c* so no action was necessary to bring the file up to date. While analyzing *lexer.c*, however, make saw that the prerequisite *lexer.l* was newer than its target *lexer.c* so make must update *lexer.c*. This, in turn, caused the update of *lexer.o* and then *count_words*. Now our word counting program is fixed:

```
$ count_words < lexer.l
3 3 3 3
```

Invoking make

The previous examples assume that:

- All the project source code and the make description file are stored in a single directory.
- The make description file is called *makefile*, *Makefile*, or *GNUMakefile*.
- The *makefile* resides in the user's current directory when executing the make command.

When make is invoked under these conditions, it automatically creates the first target it sees. To update a different target (or to update more than one target) include the target name on the command line:

```
$ make lexer.c
```

When make is executed, it will read the description file and identify the target to be updated. If the target or any of its prerequisite files are out of date (or missing) the shell commands in the rule's command script will be executed one at a time. After the commands are run make assumes the target is up to date and moves on to the next target or exits.

If the target you specify is already up to date, make will say so and immediately exit, doing nothing else:

```
$ make lexer.c
make: `lexer.c' is up to date.
```

If you specify a target that is not in the *makefile* and for which there is no implicit rule (discussed in Chapter 2), make will respond with:

```
$ make non-existent-target
make: *** No rule to make target `non-existent-target'.  Stop.
```

make has many command-line options. One of the most useful is --just-print (or -n) which tells make to display the commands it would execute for a particular target without actually executing them. This is particularly valuable while writing *makefiles*. It is also possible to set almost any *makefile* variable on the command line to override the default value or the value set in the *makefile*.

Basic Makefile Syntax

Now that you have a basic understanding of make you can almost write your own *makefiles*. Here we'll cover enough of the syntax and structure of a *makefile* for you to start using make.

Makefiles are usually structured top-down so that the most general target, often called all, is updated by default. More and more detailed targets follow with targets for program maintenance, such as a clean target to delete unwanted temporary files, coming last. As you can guess from these target names, targets do not have to be actual files, any name will do.

In the example above we saw a simplified form of a rule. The more complete (but still not quite complete) form of a rule is:

$$target_1 \; target_2 \; target_3 : prerequisite_1 \; prerequisite_2$$
$$command_1$$
$$command_2$$
$$command_3$$

One or more targets appear to the left of the colon and zero or more prerequisites can appear to the right of the colon. If no prerequisites are listed to the right, then only the target(s) that do not exist are updated. The set of commands executed to update a target are sometimes called the *command script*, but most often just the *commands*.

Each command *must* begin with a tab character. This (obscure) syntax tells make that the characters that follow the tab are to be passed to a subshell for execution. If you accidentally insert a tab as the first character of a noncommand line, make will interpret the following text as a command under most circumstances. If you're lucky and your errant tab character is recognized as a syntax error you will receive the message:

```
$ make
Makefile:6: *** commands commence before first target.  Stop.
```

We'll discuss the complexities of the tab character in Chapter 2.

The comment character for make is the hash or pound sign, #. All text from the pound sign to the end of line is ignored. Comments can be indented and leading whitespace is ignored. The comment character # does not introduce a make comment in the text of commands. The entire line, including the # and subsequent characters, is passed to the shell for execution. How it is handled there depends on your shell.

Long lines can be continued using the standard Unix escape character backslash (\). It is common for commands to be continued in this way. It is also common for lists of prerequisites to be continued with backslash. Later we'll cover other ways of handling long prerequisite lists.

You now have enough background to write simple *makefiles*. Chapter 2 will cover rules in detail, followed by make variables in Chapter 3 and commands in Chapter 5. For now you should avoid the use of variables, macros, and multiline command sequences.

CHAPTER 2
Rules

In the last chapter, we wrote some rules to compile and link our word-counting program. Each of those rules defines a target, that is, a file to be updated. Each target file depends on a set of prerequisites, which are also files. When asked to update a target, make will execute the command script of the rule if any of the prerequisite files has been modified more recently than the target. Since the target of one rule can be referenced as a prerequisite in another rule, the set of targets and prerequisites form a chain or graph of *dependencies* (short for "dependency graph"). Building and processing this dependency graph to update the requested target is what make is all about.

Since rules are so important in make, there are a number of different kinds of rules. *Explicit rules*, like the ones in the previous chapter, indicate a specific target to be updated if it is out of date with respect to any of its prerequisites. This is the most common type of rule you will be writing. *Pattern rules* use wildcards instead of explicit filenames. This allows make to apply the rule any time a target file matching the pattern needs to updated. *Implicit rules* are either pattern rules or suffix rules found in the rules database built-in to make. Having a built-in database of rules makes writing *makefiles* easier since for many common tasks make already knows the file types, suffixes, and programs for updating targets. *Static pattern rules* are like regular pattern rules except they apply only to a specific list of target files.

GNU make can be used as a "drop in" replacement for many other versions of make and includes several features specifically for compatibility. *Suffix rules* were make's original means for writing general rules. GNU make includes support for suffix rules, but they are considered obsolete having been replaced by pattern rules that are clearer and more general.

Explicit Rules

Most rules you will write are explicit rules that specify particular files as targets and prerequisites. A rule can have more than one target. This means that each target has the same set of prerequisites as the others. If the targets are out of date, the same set of actions will be performed to update each one. For instance:

```
vpath.o variable.o: make.h config.h getopt.h gettext.h dep.h
```

This indicates that both *vpath.o* and *variable.o* depend on the same set of C header files. This line has the same effect as:

```
vpath.o: make.h config.h getopt.h gettext.h dep.h
variable.o: make.h config.h getopt.h gettext.h dep.h
```

The two targets are handled independently. If either object file is out of date with respect to any of its prerequisites (that is, any header file has a newer modification time than the object file), make will update the object file by executing the commands associated with the rule.

A rule does not have to be defined "all at once." Each time make sees a target file it adds the target and prerequisites to the dependency graph. If a target has already been seen and exists in the graph, any additional prerequisites are appended to the target file entry in make's dependency graph. In the simple case, this is useful for breaking long lines naturally to improve the readability of the *makefile*:

```
vpath.o: vpath.c make.h config.h getopt.h gettext.h dep.h
vpath.o: filedef.h hash.h job.h commands.h variable.h vpath.h
```

In more complex cases, the prerequisite list can be composed of files that are managed very differently:

```
# Make sure lexer.c is created before vpath.c is compiled.
vpath.o: lexer.c
...
# Compile vpath.c with special flags.
vpath.o: vpath.c
        $(COMPILE.c) $(RULE_FLAGS) $(OUTPUT_OPTION) $<
...
# Include dependencies generated by a program.
include auto-generated-dependencies.d
```

The first rule says that the *vpath.o* target must be updated whenever *lexer.c* is updated (perhaps because generating *lexer.c* has other side effects). The rule also works to ensure that a prerequisite is always updated before the target is updated. (Notice the bidirectional nature of rules. In the "forward" direction the rule says that if the *lexer.c* has been updated, perform the action to update *vpath.o*. In the "backward" direction, the rule says that if we need to make or use *vpath.o* ensure that *lexer.c* is up to date first.) This rule might be placed near the rules for managing *lexer.c* so developers are reminded of this subtle relationship. Later, the compilation rule for *vpath.o* is placed among other compilation rules. The command for this rule uses three make variables. You'll be seeing a lot of these, but for now you just need to know that a variable is either a dollar sign followed by a single character or a dollar sign followed by a word in parentheses. (I will explain more later in this chapter and a lot more in Chapter 3.) Finally, the *.o/.h* dependencies are included in the *makefile* from a separate file managed by an external program.

Wildcards

A *makefile* often contains long lists of files. To simplify this process make supports wildcards (also known as *globbing*). make's wildcards are identical to the Bourne shell's: ~, *, ?, [...], and [^...]. For instance, *.* expands to all the files containing a period. A question mark represents any single character, and [...] represents a *character class*. To select the "opposite" (negated) character class use [^...].

In addition, the tilde (~) character can be used to represent the current user's home directory. A tilde followed by a user name represents that user's home directory.

Wildcards are automatically expanded by make whenever a wildcard appears in a target, prerequisite, or command script context. In other contexts, wildcards can be expanded explicitly by calling a function. Wildcards can be very useful for creating more adaptable *makefiles*. For instance, instead of listing all the files in a program explicitly, you can use wildcards:*

```
prog: *.c
        $(CC) -o $@ $^
```

It is important to be careful with wildcards, however. It is easy to misuse them as the following example shows:

```
*.o: constants.h
```

The intent is clear: all object files depend on the header file *constants.h*, but consider how this expands on a clean directory without any object files:

```
: constants.h
```

This is a legal make expression and will not produce an error by itself, but it will also not provide the dependency the user wants. The proper way to implement this rule is to perform a wildcard on the source files (since they are always present) and transform that into a list of object files. We will cover this technique when we discuss make functions in Chapter 4.

When mp_make expands a wildcard (or indeed when mp_make looks for any file), it reads and caches the directory contents. This caching improves mp_make's performance considerably. However, once mp_make has read and cached the directory contents, mp_make will not "see" any changes made to the directory. This can be a mysterious source of errors in a mp_makefile. The issue can sometimes be resolved by using a sub-shell and globbing (e.g., shell wildcards) rather than mp_make's own wildcards, but occasionally, this is not possible and we must resort to bizarre hacks.

---

* In more controlled environments using wildcards to select the files in a program is considered bad practice because a rogue source file might be accidentally linked into a program.

Finally, it is worth noting that wildcard expansion is performed by make when the pattern appears as a target or prerequisite. However, when the pattern appears in a command, the expansion is performed by the subshell. This can occasionally be important because make will expand the wildcards immediately upon reading the *makefile*, but the shell will expand the wildcards in commands much later when the command is executed. When a lot of complex file manipulation is being done, the two wildcard expansions can be quite different.

Phony Targets

Until now all targets and prerequisites have been files to be created or updated. This is typically the case, but it is often useful for a target to be just a label representing a command script. For instance, earlier we noted that a standard first target in many *makefile*s is called all. Targets that do not represent files are known as *phony targets*. Another standard phony target is clean:

```
clean:
        rm -f *.o lexer.c
```

Normally, phony targets will always be executed because the commands associated with the rule do not create the target name.

It is important to note that make cannot distinguish between a file target and phony target. If by chance the name of a phony target exists as a file, make will associate the file with the phony target name in its dependency graph. If, for example, the file *clean* happened to be created running make clean would yield the confusing message:

```
$ make clean
make: `clean' is up to date.
```

Since most phony targets do not have prerequisites, the clean target would always be considered up to date and would never execute.

To avoid this problem, GNU make includes a special target, .PHONY, to tell make that a target is not a real file. Any target can be declared phony by including it as a prerequisite of .PHONY:

```
.PHONY: clean
clean:
        rm -f *.o lexer.c
```

Now make will always execute the commands associated with clean even if a file named *clean* exists. In addition to marking a target as always out of date, specifying that a target is phony tells make that this file does not follow the normal rules for making a target file from a source file. Therefore, make can optimize its normal rule search to improve performance.

It rarely makes sense to use a phony target as a prerequisite of a real file since the phony is always out of date and will always cause the target file to be remade. However, it is often useful to give phony targets prerequisites. For instance, the all target is usually given the list of programs to be built:

```
.PHONY: all
all: bash bashbug
```

Here the all target creates the bash shell program and the bashbug error reporting tool.

Phony targets can also be thought of as shell scripts embedded in a *makefile*. Making a phony target a prerequisite of another target will invoke the phony target script before making the actual target. Suppose we are tight on disk space and before executing a disk-intensive task we want to display available disk space. We could write:

```
.PHONY: make-documentation
make-documentation:
        df -k . | awk 'NR == 2 { printf( "%d available\n", $$4 ) }'
        javadoc ...
```

The problem here is that we may end up specifying the df and awk commands many times under different targets, which is a maintenance problem since we'll have to change every instance if we encounter a df on another system with a different format. Instead, we can place the df line in its own phony target:

```
.PHONY: make-documentation
make-documentation: df
        javadoc ...

.PHONY: df
df:
        df -k . | awk 'NR == 2 { printf( "%d available\n", $$4 ) }'
```

We can cause make to invoke our df target before generating the documentation by making df a prerequisite of make-documentation. This works well because make-documentation is also a phony target. Now I can easily reuse df in other targets.

There are a number of other good uses for phony targets. The output of make can be confusing to read and debug. There are several reasons for this: *makefiles* are written top-down but the commands are executed by make bottom-up; also, there is no indication which rule is currently being evaluated. The output of make can be made much easier to read if major targets are commented in the make output. Phony targets are a useful way to accomplish this. Here is an example taken from the bash *makefile*:

```
$(Program): build_msg $(OBJECTS) $(BUILTINS_DEP) $(LIBDEP)
        $(RM) $@
        $(CC) $(LDFLAGS) -o $(Program) $(OBJECTS) $(LIBS)
        ls -l $(Program)
        size $(Program)

.PHONY: build_msg
build_msg:
        @printf "#\n# Building $(Program)\n#\n"
```

Because the printf is in a phony target, the message is printed immediately before any prerequisites are updated. If the build message were instead placed as the first command of the $(Program) command script, then it would be executed after all compilation and dependency generation. It is important to note that because phony targets are always out of date, the phony build_msg target causes $(Program) to be regenerated even when it is not out of date. In this case, it seems a reasonable choice since most of the computation is performed while compiling the object files so only the final link will always be performed.

Phony targets can also be used to improve the "user interface" of a *makefile*. Often targets are complex strings containing directory path elements, additional filename components (such as version numbers) and standard suffixes. This can make specifying a target filename on the command line a challenge. The problem can be avoided by adding a simple phony target whose prerequisite is the actual target file.

By convention there are a set of more or less standard phony targets that many *makefiles* include. Table 2-1 lists these standard targets.

Table 2-1. Standard phony targets

Target	Function
all	Perform all tasks to build the application
install	Create an installation of the application from the compiled binaries
clean	Delete the binary files generated from sources
distclean	Delete all the generated files that were not in the original source distribution
TAGS	Create a tags table for use by editors
info	Create GNU info files from their Texinfo sources
check	Run any tests associated with this application

The target TAGS is not really a phony since the output of the ctags and etags programs is a file named *TAGS*. It is included here because it is the only standard non-phony target we know of.

Empty Targets

Empty targets are similar to phony targets in that the target itself is used as a device to leverage the capabilities of make. Phony targets are always out of date, so they always execute and they always cause their *dependent* (the target associated with the prerequisite) to be remade. But suppose we have some command, with no output file, that needs to be performed only occasionally and we don't want our dependents updated? For this, we can make a rule whose target is an empty file (sometimes referred to as a cookie):

```
prog: size prog.o
        $(CC) $(LDFLAGS) -o $@ $^

size: prog.o
        size $^
        touch size
```

Notice that the size rule uses touch to create an empty file named *size* after it completes. This empty file is used for its timestamp so that make will execute the size rule only when *prog.o* has been updated. Furthermore, the size prerequisite to *prog* will not force an update of *prog* unless its object file is also newer.

Empty files are particularly useful when combined with the automatic variable $?. We discuss automatic variables in the section "Automatic Variables," but a preview of this variable won't hurt. Within the command script part of a rule, make defines the variable $? to be the set of prerequisites that are newer than the target. Here is a rule to print all the files that have changed since the last time make print was executed:

```
print: *.[hc]
        lpr $?
        touch $@
```

Generally, empty files can be used to mark the last time a particular event has taken place.

Variables

Let's look at some of the variables we have been using in our examples. The simplest ones have the syntax:

```
$(variable-name)
```

This indicates that we want to *expand* the variable whose name is *variable-name*. Variables can contain almost any text, and variable names can contain most characters including punctuation. The variable containing the C compile command is COMPILE.c, for example. In general, a variable name must be surrounded by $( ) or ${ } to be recognized by make. As a special case, a single character variable name does not require the parentheses.

A *makefile* will typically define many variables, but there are also many special variables defined automatically by make. Some can be set by the user to control make's behavior while others are set by make to communicate with the user's *makefile*.

Automatic Variables

Automatic variables are set by make after a rule is matched. They provide access to elements from the target and prerequisite lists so you don't have to explicitly specify any filenames. They are very useful for avoiding code duplication, but are critical when defining more general pattern rules (discussed later).

There are seven "core" automatic variables:

$@ The filename representing the target.

$% The filename element of an archive member specification.

$< The filename of the first prerequisite.

$? The names of all prerequisites that are newer than the target, separated by spaces.

$^ The filenames of all the prerequisites, separated by spaces. This list has duplicate filenames removed since for most uses, such as compiling, copying, etc., duplicates are not wanted.

$+ Similar to $^, this is the names of all the prerequisites separated by spaces, except that $+ includes duplicates. This variable was created for specific situations such as arguments to linkers where duplicate values have meaning.

$* The stem of the target filename. A stem is typically a filename without its suffix. (We'll discuss how stems are computed later in the section "Pattern Rules.") Its use outside of pattern rules is discouraged.

In addition, each of the above variables has two variants for compatibility with other makes. One variant returns only the directory portion of the value. This is indicated by appending a "D" to the symbol, $(@D), $(<D), etc. The other variant returns only the file portion of the value. This is indicated by appending an F to the symbol, $(@F), $(<F), etc. Note that these variant names are more than one character long and so must be enclosed in parentheses. GNU make provides a more readable alternative with the dir and notdir functions. We will discuss functions in Chapter 4.

Automatic variables are set by make after a rule has been matched with its target and prerequisites so the variables are only available in the command script of a rule.

Here is our *makefile* with explicit filenames replaced by the appropriate automatic variable.

```
count_words: count_words.o counter.o lexer.o -lfl
        gcc $^ -o $@

count_words.o: count_words.c
        gcc -c $<

counter.o: counter.c
        gcc -c $<

lexer.o: lexer.c
        gcc -c $<

lexer.c: lexer.l
        flex -t $< > $@
```

Finding Files with VPATH and vpath

Our examples so far have been simple enough that the *makefile* and sources all lived in a single directory. Real world programs are more complex (when's the last time you worked on a single directory project?). Let's refactor our example and create a more realistic file layout. We can modify our word counting program by refactoring main into a function called counter.

```
#include <lexer.h>
#include <counter.h>
```

```
void counter( int counts[4] )
{
    while ( yylex() )
        ;

    counts[0] = fee_count;
    counts[1] = fie_count;
    counts[2] = foe_count;
    counts[3] = fum_count;
}
```

A reusable library function should have a declaration in a header file, so let's create *counter.h* containing our declaration:

```
#ifndef COUNTER_H_
#define COUNTER_H_

extern void
counter( int counts[4] );

#endif
```

We can also place the declarations for our *lexer.l* symbols in *lexer.h*:

```
#ifndef LEXER_H_
#define LEXER_H_

extern int fee_count, fie_count, foe_count, fum_count;
extern int yylex( void );

#endif
```

In a traditional source tree layout the header files are placed in an *include* directory and the source is placed in a *src* directory. We'll do this and put our *makefile* in the parent directory. Our example program now has the layout shown in Figure 2-1.

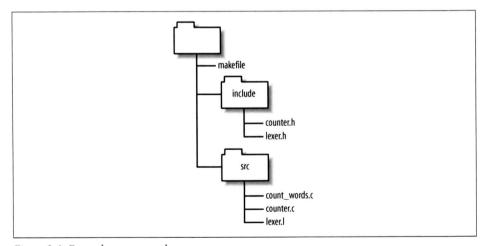

Figure 2-1. Example source tree layout

Since our source files now include header files, these new dependencies should be recorded in our *makefile* so that when a header file is modified, the corresponding object file will be updated.

```
count_words: count_words.o counter.o lexer.o -lfl
        gcc $^ -o $@

count_words.o: count_words.c include/counter.h
        gcc -c $<

counter.o: counter.c include/counter.h include/lexer.h
        gcc -c $<

lexer.o: lexer.c include/lexer.h
        gcc -c $<

lexer.c: lexer.l
        flex -t $< > $@
```

Now when we run our *makefile*, we get:

```
$ make
make: *** No rule to make target `count_words.c', needed by `count_words.o'.  Stop.
```

Oops, what happened? The *makefile* is trying to update *count_words.c*, but that's a source file! Let's "play make." Our first prerequisite is *count_words.o*. We see the file is missing and look for a rule to create it. The explicit rule for creating *count_words.o* references *count_words.c*. But why can't make find the source file? Because the source file is in the *src* directory not the current directory. Unless you direct it otherwise, make will look only in the current directory for its targets and prerequisites. How do we get make to look in the *src* directory for source files? Or, more generally, how do we tell make where our source code is?

You can tell make to look in different directories for its source files using the VPATH and vpath features. To fix our immediate problem, we can add a VPATH assignment to the *makefile*:

```
VPATH = src
```

This indicates that make should look in the directory *src* if the files it wants are not in the current directory. Now when we run our *makefile*, we get:

```
$ make
gcc -c src/count_words.c -o count_words.o
src/count_words.c:2:21: counter.h: No such file or directory
make: *** [count_words.o] Error 1
```

Notice that make now successfully tries to compile the first file, filling in correctly the relative path to the source. This is another reason to use automatic variables: make cannot use the appropriate path to the source if you hardcode the filename. Unfortunately, the compilation dies because gcc can't find the include file. We can fix this latest problem by "customizing" the implicit compilation rule with the appropriate -I option:

```
CPPFLAGS = -I include
```

and changing occurrences of gcc to gcc$(CPPFLAGS). Now the build succeeds:

```
$ make
gcc -I include -c src/count_words.c -o count_words.o
gcc -I include -c src/counter.c -o counter.o
flex -t src/lexer.l > lexer.c
gcc -I include -c lexer.c -o lexer.o
gcc count_words.o counter.o lexer.o /lib/libfl.a -o count_words
```

The VPATH variable consists of a list of directories to search when make needs a file. The list will be searched for targets as well as prerequisites, but not for files mentioned in command scripts. The list of directories can be separated by spaces or colons on Unix and separated by spaces or semicolons on Windows. I prefer to use spaces since that works on all systems and we can avoid the whole colon/semicolon imbroglio. Also, the directories are easier to read when separated by spaces.

The VPATH variable is good because it solved our searching problem above, but it is a rather large hammer. make will search each directory for *any* file it needs. If a file of the same name exists in multiple places in the VPATH list, make grabs the first one. Sometimes this can be a problem.

The vpath directive is a more precise way to achieve our goals. The syntax of this directive is:

```
vpath pattern directory-list
```

So our previous VPATH use can be rewritten as:

```
vpath %.c src
vpath %.l src
vpath %.h include
```

Now we've told make that it should search for *.c* and *.l* files in the *src* directory and we've also added a line to search for *.h* files in the *include* directory (so we can remove the *include/* from our header file prerequisites). In more complex applications, this control can save a lot of headache and debugging time.

Here we used vpath to handle the problem of finding source that is distributed among several directories. There is a related but different problem of how to build an application so that the object files are written into a "binary tree" while the source files live in a separate "source tree." Proper use of vpath can also help to solve this new problem, but the task quickly becomes complex and vpath alone is not sufficient. We'll discuss this problem in detail in later sections.

Pattern Rules

The *makefile* examples we've been looking at are a bit verbose. For a small program of a dozen files or less we may not care, but for programs with hundreds or thousands of files, specifying each target, prerequisite, and command script becomes unworkable. Furthermore, the commands themselves represent duplicate code in our *makefile*. If the commands contain a bug or ever change, we would have to update all these rules. This can be a major maintenance problem and source of bugs.

Many programs that read one file type and output another conform to standard conventions. For instance, all C compilers assume that files that have a *.c* suffix contain C source code and that the object filename can be derived by replacing the *.c* suffix with *.o* (or *.obj* for some Windows compilers). In the previous chapter, we noticed that flex input files use the *.l* suffix and that flex generates *.c* files.

These conventions allow make to simplify rule creation by recognizing common filename patterns and providing built-in rules for processing them. For example, by using these built-in rules our 17-line *makefile* can be reduced to:

```
VPATH    = src include
CPPFLAGS = -I include

count_words: counter.o lexer.o -lfl
count_words.o: counter.h
counter.o: counter.h lexer.h
lexer.o: lexer.h
```

The built-in rules are all instances of pattern rules. A *pattern rule* looks like the normal rules you have already seen except the *stem* of the file (the portion before the suffix) is represented by a % character. This *makefile* works because of three built-in rules. The first specifies how to compile a *.o* file from a *.c* file:

```
%.o: %.c
        $(COMPILE.c) $(OUTPUT_OPTION) $<
```

The second specifies how to make a *.c* file from a *.l* file:

```
%.c: %.l
        @$(RM) $@
        $(LEX.l) $< > $@
```

Finally, there is a special rule to generate a file with no suffix (always an executable) from a *.c* file:

```
%: %.o
        $(LINK.o) $^ $(LOADLIBES) $(LDLIBS) -o $@
```

We'll go into the details of this syntax in a bit, but first let's go over make's output carefully and see how make applies these built-in rules.

When we run make on our seven-line *makefile*, the output is:

```
$ make
gcc  -I include  -c -o count_words.o src/count_words.c
```

```
gcc  -I include  -c -o counter.o src/counter.c
flex  -t src/lexer.l > lexer.c
gcc  -I include  -c -o lexer.o lexer.c
gcc   count_words.o counter.o lexer.o /lib/libfl.a   -o count_words
rm lexer.c
```

First, make reads the *makefile* and sets the default goal to *count_words* since there are no command-line targets specified. Looking at the default goal, make identifies four prerequisites: *count_words.o* (this prerequisite is missing from the *makefile*, but is provided by the implicit rule), *counter.o*, *lexer.o*, and -lfl. It then tries to update each prerequisite in turn.

When make examines the first prerequisite, *count_words.o*, make finds no explicit rule for it but discovers the implicit rule. Looking in the local directory, make cannot find the source, so it begins searching the VPATH and finds a matching source file in *src*. Since *src/count_words.c* has no prerequisites, make is free to update *count_words.o* so it runs the commands for the implicit rule. *counter.o* is similar. When make considers *lexer.o*, it cannot find a corresponding source file (even in *src*) so it assumes this (nonexistent source) is an intermediate file and looks for a way to make *lexer.c* from some other source file. It discovers a rule to create a *.c* file from a *.l* file and notices that *lexer.l* exists. There is no action required to update *lexer.l*, so it moves on to the command for updating *lexer.c*, which yields the flex command line. Next make updates the object file from the C source. Using sequences of rules like this to update a target is called *rule chaining*.

Next, make examines the library specification -lfl. It searches the standard library directories for the system and discovers */lib/libfl.a*.

Now make has all the prerequisites for updating *count_words*, so it executes the final gcc command. Lastly, make realizes it created an intermediate file that is not necessary to keep so it cleans it up.

As you can see, using rules in *makefiles* allows you to omit a lot of detail. Rules can have complex interactions that yield very powerful behaviors. In particular, having a built-in database of common rules makes many types of *makefile* specifications very simple.

The built-in rules can be customized by changing the values of the variables in the command scripts. A typical rule has a host of variables, beginning with the program to execute, and including variables to set major groupings of command-line options, such as the output file, optimization, debugging, etc. You can look at make's default set of rules (and variables) by running make --print-data-base.

The Patterns

The percent character in a pattern rule is roughly equivalent to * in a Unix shell. It represents any number of any characters. The percent character can be placed

---

anywhere within the pattern but can occur only once. Here are some valid uses of percent:

```
%,v
s%.o
wrapper_%
```

Characters other than percent match literally within a filename. A pattern can contain a prefix or a suffix or both. When make searches for a pattern rule to apply, it first looks for a matching pattern rule target. The pattern rule target must start with the prefix and end with the suffix (if they exist). If a match is found, the characters between the prefix and suffix are taken as the stem of the name. Next make looks at the prerequisites of the pattern rule by substituting the stem into the prerequisite pattern. If the resulting filename exists or can be made by applying another rule, a match is made and the rule is applied. The stem word must contain at least one character.

It is also possible to have a pattern containing only a percent character. The most common use of this pattern is to build a Unix executable program. For instance, here are several pattern rules GNU make includes for building programs:

```
%: %.mod
        $(COMPILE.mod) -o $@ -e $@ $^

%: %.cpp
        $(LINK.cpp) $^ $(LOADLIBES) $(LDLIBS) -o $@

%: %.sh
        cat $< >$@
        chmod a+x $@
```

These patterns will be used to generate an executable from a Modula source file, a preprocessed C source file, and a Bourne shell script, respectively. We will see many more implicit rules in the section "The Implicit Rules Database."

Static Pattern Rules

A static pattern rule is one that applies only to a specific list of targets.

```
$(OBJECTS): %.o: %.c
        $(CC) -c $(CFLAGS) $< -o $@
```

The only difference between this rule and an ordinary pattern rule is the initial $(OBJECTS): specification. This limits the rule to the files listed in the $(OBJECTS) variable.

This is very similar to a pattern rule. Each object file in $(OBJECTS) is matched against the pattern %.o and its stem is extracted. The stem is then substituted into the pattern %.c to yield the target's prerequisite. If the target pattern does not exist, make issues a warning.

Use static pattern rules whenever it is easier to list the target files explicitly than to identify them by a suffix or other pattern.

Suffix Rules

Suffix rules are the original (and obsolete) way of defining implicit rules. Because other versions of make may not support GNU make's pattern rule syntax, you will still see suffix rules in *makefiles* intended for a wide distribution so it is important to be able to read and understand the syntax. So, although compiling GNU make for the target system is the preferred method for *makefile* portability, you may still need to write suffix rules in rare circumstances.

Suffix rules consist of one or two suffixes concatenated and used as a target:

```
.c.o:
        $(COMPILE.c) $(OUTPUT_OPTION) $<
```

This is a little confusing because the prerequisite suffix comes first and the target suffix second. This rule matches the same set of targets and prerequisites as:

```
%.o: %.c
        $(COMPILE.c) $(OUTPUT_OPTION) $<
```

The suffix rule forms the stem of the file by removing the target suffix. It forms the prerequisite by replacing the target suffix with the prerequisite suffix. The suffix rule is recognized by make only if the two suffixes are in a list of known suffixes.

The above suffix rule is known as a double-suffix rule since it contains two suffixes. There are also single-suffix rules. As you might imagine a single-suffix rule contains only one suffix, the suffix of the source file. These rules are used to create executables since Unix executables do not have a suffix:

```
.p:
        $(LINK.p) $^ $(LOADLIBES) $(LDLIBS) -o $@
```

This rule produces an executable image from a Pascal source file. This is completely analogous to the pattern rule:

```
%: %.p
        $(LINK.p) $^ $(LOADLIBES) $(LDLIBS) -o $@
```

The known suffix list is the strangest part of the syntax. A special target, .SUFFIXES, is used to set the list of known suffixes. Here is the first part of the default .SUFFIXES definition:

```
.SUFFIXES: .out .a .ln .o .c .cc .C .cpp .p .f .F .r .y .l
```

You can add your own suffixes by simply adding a .SUFFIXES rule to your *makefile*:

```
.SUFFIXES: .pdf .fo .html .xml
```

If you want to delete all the known suffixes (because they are interfering with your special suffixes) simply specify no prerequisites:

```
.SUFFIXES:
```

You can also use the command-line option `--no-builtin-rules` (or `-r`).

We will not use this old syntax in the rest of this book because GNU make's pattern rules are clearer and more general.

The Implicit Rules Database

GNU make 3.80 has about 90 built-in implicit rules. An implicit rule is either a pattern rule or a suffix rule. There are built-in pattern rules for C, C++, Pascal, FORTRAN, ratfor, Modula, Texinfo, TeX (including Tangle and Weave), Emacs Lisp, RCS, and SCCS. In addition, there are rules for supporting programs for these languages, such as cpp, as, yacc, lex, tangle, weave and dvi tools.

If you are using any of these tools, you'll probably find most of what you need in the built-in rules. If you're using some unsupported languages such as Java or XML, you will have to write rules of your own. But don't worry, you typically need only a few rules to support a language and they are quite easy to write.

To examine the rules database built into make, use the `--print-data-base` command-line option (`-p` for short). This will generate about a thousand lines of output. After version and copyright information, make prints its variable definitions each one preceded by a comment indicating the "origin" of the definition. For instance, variables can be environment variables, default values, automatic variables, etc. After the variables, come the rules. The actual format used by GNU make is:

```
%: %.C
#  commands to execute (built-in):
        $(LINK.C) $^ $(LOADLIBES) $(LDLIBS) -o $@
```

For rules defined by the *makefile*, the comment will include the file and line where the rule was defined:

```
%.html: %.xml
#  commands to execute (from `Makefile', line 168):
        $(XMLTO) $(XMLTO_FLAGS) html-nochunks $<
```

Working with Implicit Rules

The built-in implicit rules are applied whenever a target is being considered and there is no explicit rule to update it. So using an implicit rule is easy: simply do not specify a command script when adding your target to the *makefile*. This causes make to search its built-in database to satisfy the target. Usually this does just what you want, but in rare cases your development environment can cause problems. For instance, suppose you have a mixed language environment consisting of Lisp and C source code. If the file *editor.l* and *editor.c* both exist in the same directory (say one is a low-level implementation accessed by the other) make will believe that the Lisp file is really a flex file (recall flex files use the *.l* suffix) and that the C source is the output of the flex command. If *editor.o* is a target and *editor.l* is newer than *editor.c*, make will attempt to "update" the C file with the output of flex overwriting your source code. Gack.

To work around this particular problem you can delete the two rules concerning flex from the built-in rule base like this:

```
%.o: %.l
%.c: %.l
```

A pattern with no command script will remove the rule from make's database. In practice, situations such as this are very rare. However, it is important to remember the built-in rules database contains rules that will interact with your own *makefiles* in ways you may not have anticipated.

We have seen several examples of how make will "chain" rules together while trying to update a target. This can lead to some complexity, which we'll examine here. When make considers how to update a target, it searches the implicit rules for a target pattern that matches the target in hand. For each target pattern that matches the target file, make will look for an existing matching prerequisite. That is, after matching the target pattern, make immediately looks for the prerequisite "source" file. If the prerequisite is found, the rule is used. For some target patterns, there are many possible source files. For instance, a *.o* file can be made from *.c, .cc, .cpp, .p, .f, .r, .s,* and *.mod* files. But what if the source is not found after searching all possible rules? In this case, make will search the rules again, this time assuming that the matching source file should be considered as a new target for updating. By performing this search recursively, make can find a "chain" of rules that allows updating a target. We saw this in our *lexer.o* example. make was able to update the *lexer.o* target from *lexer.l* even though the intermediate *.c* file was missing by invoking the *.l* to *.c* rule, then the *.c* to *.o* rule.

One of the more impressive sequences that make can produce automatically from its database is shown here. First, we setup our experiment by creating an empty yacc source file and registering with RCS using ci (that is, we want a version-controlled yacc source file):

```
$ touch foo.y
$ ci foo.y
foo.y,v  <--  foo.y
.
initial revision: 1.1
done
```

Now, we ask make how it would create the executable *foo*. The --just-print (or -n) option tells make to report what actions it would perform without actually running them. Notice that we have no *makefile* and no "source" code, only an RCS file:

```
$ make -n foo
co  foo.y,v foo.y
foo.y,v  -->  foo.y
revision 1.1
done
bison -y  foo.y
mv -f y.tab.c foo.c
gcc    -c -o foo.o foo.c
gcc   foo.o   -o foo
rm foo.c foo.o foo.y
```

Following the chain of implicit rules and prerequisites, make determined it could create the executable, *foo*, if it had the object file *foo.o*. It could create *foo.o* if it had the C source file *foo.c*. It could create *foo.c* if it had the yacc source file *foo.y*. Finally, it realized it could create *foo.y* by checking out the file from the RCS file *foo.y,v*, which it actually has. Once make has formulated this plan, it executes it by checking out *foo.y* with co, transforming it into *foo.c* with bison, compiling it into *foo.o* with gcc, and linking it to form *foo* again with gcc. All this from the implicit rules database. Pretty cool.

The files generated by chaining rules are called *intermediate* files and are treated specially by make. First, since intermediate files do not occur in targets (otherwise they would not be intermediate), make will never simply update an intermediate file. Second, because make creates intermediate files itself as a side effect of updating a target, make will delete the intermediates before exiting. You can see this in the last line of the example.

The implicit rules database contains a lot of rules and even very large projects rarely use most of it. Because it contains such a wide variety, rules you didn't expect to fire may be used by make in unexpected ways. As a preventative measure, some large projects choose to discard the implicit rules entirely in favor of their own hand-crafted rules. You can do this easily with the --no-builtin-rules (or -r) option. (I have never had to use this option even on the largest projects.) If you use this option, you may also want to consider using --no-builtin-variables (or -R).

Rule Structure

The built-in rules have a standard structure intended to make them easily customizable. Let's go over the structure briefly then talk about customization. Here is the (by now familiar) rule for updating an object file from its C source:

```
%.o: %.c
        $(COMPILE.c) $(OUTPUT_OPTION) $<
```

The customization of this rule is controlled entirely by the set of variables it uses. We see two variables here, but COMPILE.c in particular is defined in terms of several other variables:

```
COMPILE.c = $(CC) $(CFLAGS) $(CPPFLAGS) $(TARGET_ARCH) -c
CC = gcc
OUTPUT_OPTION = -o $@
```

The C compiler itself can be changed by altering the value of the CC variable. The other variables are used for setting compilation options (CFLAGS), preprocessor options (CPPFLAGS), and architecture-specific options (TARGET_ARCH).

The variables in a built-in rule are intended to make customizing the rule as easy as possible. For that reason, it is important to be very careful when setting these variables in your *makefile*. If you set these variables in a naive way, you destroy the end user's ability to customize them. For instance, given this assignment in a *makefile*:

```
CPPFLAGS = -I project/include
```

If the user wanted to add a CPP define to the command line, they would normally invoke make like:

```
$ make CPPFLAGS=-DDEBUG
```

But in so doing they would accidentally remove the -I option that is (presumably) required for compiling. Variables set on the command line override all other assignments to the variable. (See the section "Where Variables Come From" in Chapter 3 for more details on command-line assignments). So, setting CPPFLAGS inappropriately in the *makefile* "broke" a customization feature that most users would expect to work. Instead of using simple assignment, consider redefining the compilation variable to include your own variables:

```
COMPILE.c = $(CC) $(CFLAGS) $(INCLUDES) $(CPPFLAGS) $(TARGET_ARCH) -c
INCLUDES = -I project/include
```

Or you can use append-style assignment, which is discussed in the section "Other Types of Assignment" in Chapter 3.

Implicit Rules for Source Control

make knows about two source code control systems, RCS and SCCS, and supports their use with built-in implicit rules. Unfortunately, it seems the state of the art in source code control and modern software engineering have left make behind. I've never found a use for the source control support in make, nor have I seen it used in other production software. I do not recommend the use of this feature. There are a number of reasons for this.

First, the source control tools supported by make, RCS and SCCS, although valuable and venerable tools in their day, have largely been supplanted by CVS, the Concurrent Version System, or proprietary tools. In fact, CVS uses RCS to manage individual files internally. However, using RCS directly proved to be a considerable problem when a project spanned more than one directory or more than one developer. CVS, in particular, was implemented to fill the gaps in RCS's functionality in precisely these areas. Support for CVS has never been added to make, which is probably a good thing.*

It is now well recognized that the life cycle of software becomes complex. Applications rarely move smoothly from one release to the next. More typically, one or more distinct releases of an application are being used in the field (and require bug fix support), while one or more versions are in active development. CVS provides powerful features to help manage these parallel versions of the software. But it also means that a developer must be very aware of the specific version of the code she is working on. Having the *makefile* automatically check out source during a compilation begs the

---

* CVS is, in turn, becoming supplanted by newer tools. While it is currently the most ubiquitous source control system, subversion (*http://subversion.tigris.org*) looks to be the new wave.

question of what source is being checked out and whether the newly checked out source is compatible with the source already existing in the developer's working directories. In many production environments, developers are working on three or more distinct versions of the same application in a single day. Keeping this complexity in check is hard enough without having software quietly updating your source tree for you.

Also, one of the more powerful features of CVS is that it allows access to remote repositories. In most production environments, the CVS repository (the database of controlled files) is not located on the developer's own machine, but on a server. Although network access is now quite fast (particularly on a local area network) it is not a good idea to have make probing the network server in search of source files. The performance impact would be disastrous.

So, although it is possible to use the built-in implicit rules to interface more or less cleanly with RCS and SCCS, there are no rules to access CVS for gathering source files or *makefile*. Nor do I think it makes much sense to do so. On the other hand, it is quite reasonable to use CVS in *makefiles*. For instance, to ensure that the current source is properly checked in, that the release number information is managed properly, or that test results are correct. These are uses of CVS by *makefile* authors rather than issues of CVS integration with make.

A Simple Help Command

Large *makefiles* can have many targets that are difficult for users to remember. One way to reduce this problem is to make the default target a brief help command. However, maintaining the help text by hand is always a problem. To avoid this, you can gather the available commands directly from make's rules database. The following target will present a sorted four column listing of the available make targets:

```
# help - The default goal
.PHONY: help
help:
        @$(MAKE) --print-data-base --question no-such-target | \
        $(GREP) -v -e '^no-such-target' -e '^makefile' |        \
        $(AWK) '/^[^.%][-A-Za-z0-9_]*:/                          \
                { print substr($$1, 1, length($$1)-1) }' |       \
        $(SORT) |                                                 \
        $(PR) --omit-pagination --width=80 --columns=4           \
```

The command script consists of a single pipeline. The make rule database is dumped using the `--print-data-base` command. Specifying a target of no-such-target (instead of the default target) ensures that running the makefile recursively does not trigger infinite recursion. The grep command filters out the bogus target and the *makefile* itself (which appears as a rule in the database dump). Using the `--question` option prevents make from running any actual commands. The database is then passed through a simple awk filter that grabs every line representing a target that does not begin with percent or period (pattern rules and suffix rules, respectively) and discards extra information on the line. Finally, the target list is sorted and printed in a simple four-column listing.

Another approach to the same command (my first attempt), used the awk command on the *makefile* itself. This required special handling for included *makefiles* (covered in the section "The include Directive" in Chapter 3) and could not handle generated rules at all. The version presented here handles all that automatically by allowing make to process these elements and report the resulting rule set.

Special Targets

A *special target* is a built-in phony target used to change make's default behavior. For instance, .PHONY, a special target, which we've already seen, declares that its prerequisite does not refer to an actual file and should always be considered out of date. The .PHONY target is the most common special target you will see, but there are others as well.

These special targets follow the syntax of normal targets, that is *target*: *prerequisite*, but the *target* is not a file or even a normal phony. They are really more like directives for modifying make's internal algorithms.

There are twelve special targets. They fall into three categories: as we've just said many are used to alter the behavior of make when updating a target, another set act simply as global flags to make and ignore their targets, finally the .SUFFIXES special target is used when specifying old-fashioned suffix rules (discussed in the section "Suffix Rules" earlier in this chapter).

The most useful target modifiers (aside from .PHONY) are:

.INTERMEDIATE
> Prerequisites of this special target are treated as intermediate files. If make creates the file while updating another target, the file will be deleted automatically when make exits. If the file already exists when make considers updating the file, the file will not be deleted.
>
> This can be very useful when building custom rule chains. For instance, most Java tools accept Windows-like file lists. Creating rules to build the file lists and marking their output files as intermediate allows make to clean up many temporary files.

.SECONDARY
> Prerequisites of this special target are treated as intermediate files but are never automatically deleted. The most common use of .SECONDARY is to mark object files stored in libraries. Normally these object files will be deleted as soon as they are added to an archive. Sometimes it is more convenient during development to keep these object files, but still use the make support for updating archives.

.PRECIOUS
> When make is interrupted during execution, it may delete the target file it is updating if the file was modified since make started. This is so make doesn't leave

a partially constructed (possibly corrupt) file laying around in the build tree. There are times when you don't want this behavior, particularly if the file is large and computationally expensive to create. If you mark the file as precious, make will never delete the file if interrupted.

Use of .PRECIOUS is relatively rare, but when it is needed it is often a life saver. Note that make will not perform an automatic delete if the commands of a rule generate an error. It does so only when interrupted by a signal.

.DELETE_ON_ERROR

This is sort of the opposite of .PRECIOUS. Marking a target as .DELETE_ON_ERROR says that make *should* delete the target if any of the commands associated with the rule generates an error. make normally only deletes the target if it is interrupted by a signal.

The other special targets will be covered later when their use is more relevant. We'll discuss .EXPORT_ALL_VARIABLES in Chapter 3 and the targets relating to parallel execution in Chapter 10.

Automatic Dependency Generation

When we refactored our word counting program to use header files, a thorny little problem snuck up on us. We added the dependency between the object files and the C header files to the *makefile* by hand. It was easy to do in this case, but in normal programs (not toy examples) this can be tedious and error-prone. In fact, in most programs it is virtually impossible because most header files include other header files forming a complex tree. For instance, on my system, the single header file *stdio.h* (the most commonly referenced header file in C) expands to include 15 other header files. Resolving these relationships by hand is a hopeless task. But failing to recompile files can lead to hours of debugging headaches or worse, bugs in the resulting program. So what do we do?

Well, computers are pretty good at searching and pattern matching. Let's use a program to identify the relationships between files and maybe even have this program write out these dependencies in *makefile* syntax. As you have probably guessed, such a program already exists—at least for C/C++. There is a option to gcc and many other C/C++ compilers that will read the source and write *makefile* dependencies. For instance, here is how I found the dependencies for *stdio.h*:

```
$ echo "#include <stdio.h>" > stdio.c
$ gcc -M stdio.c
stdio.o: stdio.c /usr/include/stdio.h /usr/include/_ansi.h \
  /usr/include/newlib.h /usr/include/sys/config.h \
  /usr/include/machine/ieeefp.h /usr/include/cygwin/config.h \
  /usr/lib/gcc-lib/i686-pc-cygwin/3.2/include/stddef.h \
  /usr/lib/gcc-lib/i686-pc-cygwin/3.2/include/stdarg.h \
  /usr/include/sys/reent.h /usr/include/sys/_types.h \
  /usr/include/sys/types.h /usr/include/machine/types.h \
```

```
/usr/include/sys/features.h /usr/include/cygwin/types.h \
/usr/include/sys/sysmacros.h /usr/include/stdint.h \
/usr/include/sys/stdio.h
```

"Fine." I hear you cry, "Now I need to run gcc and use an editor to paste the results of -M into my *makefiles*. What a pain." And you'd be right if this was the whole answer. There are two traditional methods for including automatically generated dependencies into *makefiles*. The first and oldest is to add a line such as:

```
# Automatically generated dependencies follow - Do Not Edit
```

to the end of the *makefile* and then write a shell script to update these generated lines. This is certainly better than updating them by hand, but it's also very ugly. The second method is to add an include directive to the make program. By now most versions of make have the include directive and GNU make most certainly does.

So, the trick is to write a *makefile* target whose action runs gcc over all your source with the -M option, saves the results in a dependency file, and then re-runs make including the generated dependency file in the *makefile* so it can trigger the updates we need. Before GNU make, this is exactly what was done and the rule looked like:

```
depend: count_words.c lexer.c counter.c
        $(CC) -M $(CPPFLAGS) $^ > $@
```

```
include depend
```

Before running make to build the program, you would first execute make depend to generate the dependencies. This was good as far as it went, but often people would add or remove dependencies from their source without regenerating the *depend* file. Then source wouldn't get recompiled and the whole mess started again.

GNU make solved this last niggling problem with a cool feature and a simple algorithm. First, the algorithm. If we generated each source file's dependencies into its own dependency file with, say, a *.d* suffix and added the *.d* file itself as a target to this dependency rule, then make could know that the *.d* needed to be updated (along with the object file) when the source file changed:

```
counter.o counter.d: src/counter.c include/counter.h include/lexer.h
```

Generating this rule can be accomplished with a pattern rule and a (fairly ugly) command script (this is taken directly from the GNU make manual):[*]

---

[*] This is an impressive little command script, but I think it requires some explanation. First, we use the C compiler with the -M option to create a temporary file containing the dependencies for this target. The temporary filename is created from the target, $@, with a unique numeric suffix added, $$$$. In the shell, the variable $$ returns the process number of the currently running shell. Since process numbers are unique, this produces a unique filename. We then use sed to add the .d file as a target to the rule. The sed expression consists of a search part, \($*\)\.o[:]*, and a replacement part, \1.o $@ :, separated by commas. The search expression begins with the target stem, $*, enclosed in a regular expression (RE) group, \(\), followed by the file suffix, \.o. After the target filename, there come zero or more spaces or colons, [:]*. The replacement portion restores the original target by referencing the first RE group and appending the suffix, \1.o, then adding the dependency file target, $@.

```
%.d: %.c
        $(CC) -M $(CPPFLAGS) $< > $@.$$$$;                        \
        sed 's,\($*\)\.o[ :]*,\1.o $@ : ,g' < $@.$$$$ > $@; \
        rm -f $@.$$$$
```

Now, for the cool feature. make will treat any file named in an include directive as a target to be updated. So, when we mention the *.d* files we want to include, make will automatically try to create these files as it reads the *makefile*. Here is our *makefile* with the addition of automatic dependency generation:

```
VPATH    = src include
CPPFLAGS = -I include

SOURCES  = count_words.c \
           lexer.c        \
           counter.c

count_words: counter.o lexer.o -lfl
count_words.o: counter.h
counter.o: counter.h lexer.h
lexer.o: lexer.h

include $(subst .c,.d,$(SOURCES))

%.d: %.c
        $(CC) -M $(CPPFLAGS) $< > $@.$$$$;                        \
        sed 's,\($*\)\.o[ :]*,\1.o $@ : ,g' < $@.$$$$ > $@;       \
        rm -f $@.$$$$
```

The include directive should always be placed after the hand-written dependencies so that the default goal is not hijacked by some dependency file. The include directive takes a list of files (whose names can include wildcards). Here we use a make function, subst, to transform the list of source files into a list of dependency filenames. (We'll discuss subst in detail in the section "String Functions" in Chapter 4.) For now, just note that this use replaces the string *.c* with *.d* in each of the words in $(SOURCES).

When we run this *makefile* with the --just-print option, we get:

```
$ make --just-print
Makefile:13: count_words.d: No such file or directory
Makefile:13: lexer.d: No such file or directory
Makefile:13: counter.d: No such file or directory
gcc -M -I include src/counter.c > counter.d.$$;                  \
sed 's,\(counter\)\.o[ :]*,\1.o counter.d : ,g' < counter.d.$$ > \
counter.d; \
rm -f counter.d.$$
flex  -t src/lexer.l > lexer.c
gcc -M -I include lexer.c > lexer.d.$$;                          \
sed 's,\(lexer\)\.o[ :]*,\1.o lexer.d : ,g' < lexer.d.$$ > lexer.d;
\
rm -f lexer.d.$$
gcc -M -I include src/count_words.c > count_words.d.$$;
```

```
                      \
sed 's,\(count_words\)\.o[ :]*,\1.o count_words.d : ,g' < count_words.d.
$$
count_words.d;        \
rm -f count_words.d.$$
rm lexer.c
gcc   -I include  -c -o count_words.o src/count_words.c
gcc   -I include  -c -o counter.o src/counter.c
gcc   -I include  -c -o lexer.o lexer.c
gcc   count_words.o counter.o lexer.o /lib/libfl.a   -o count_words
```

At first the response by make is a little alarming—it looks like a make error message. But not to worry, this is just a warning. make looks for the include files and doesn't find them, so it issues the No such file or directory warning before searching for a rule to create these files. This warning can be suppressed by preceding the include directive with a hyphen (-). The lines following the warnings show make invoking gcc with the -M option, then running the sed command. Notice that make must invoke flex to create *lexer.c*, then it deletes the temporary *lexer.c* before beginning to satisfy the default goal.

This gives you a taste of automatic dependency generation. There's lots more to say, such as how do you generate dependencies for other languages or build tree layouts. We'll return to this topic in more depth in Part II of this book.

Managing Libraries

An *archive* library, usually called simply a library or archive, is a special type of file containing other files called *members*. Archives are used to group related object files into more manageable units. For example, the C standard library *libc.a* contains low-level C functions. Libraries are very common so make has special support for creating, maintaining, and referencing them. Archives are created and modified with the ar program.

Let's look at an example. We can modify our word counting program by refactoring the reusable parts into a reusable library. Our library will consist of the two files *counter.o* and *lexer.o*. The ar command to create this library is:

```
$ ar rv libcounter.a counter.o lexer.o
a - counter.o
a - lexer.o
```

The options rv indicate that we want to *r*eplace members of the archive with the object files listed and that ar should *v*erbosely echo its actions. We can use the replace option even though the archive doesn't exist. The first argument after the options is the archive name followed by a list of object files. (Some versions of ar also require the "c" option, for *c*reate, if the archive does not exist but GNU ar does not.)

The two lines following the ar command are its verbose output indicating the object files were added.

Using the replace option to ar allows us to create or update an archive incrementally:

```
$ ar rv libcounter.a counter.o
r - counter.o
$ ar rv libcounter.a lexer.o
r - lexer.o
```

Here ar echoed each action with "r" to indicate the file was replaced in the archive.

A library can be linked into an executable in several ways. The most straightforward way is to simply list the library file on the command line. The compiler or linker will use the file suffix to determine the type of a particular file on the command line and do the Right Thing™:

```
cc count_words.o libcounter.a /lib/libfl.a -o count_words
```

Here cc will recognize the two files *libcounter.a* and */lib/libfl.a* as libraries and search them for undefined symbols. The other way to reference libraries on the command line is with the -l option:

```
cc count_words.o -lcounter -lfl -o count_words
```

As you can see, with this option you omit the prefix and suffix of the library filename. The -l option makes the command line more compact and easier to read, but it has a far more useful function. When cc sees the -l option it *searches* for the library in the system's standard library directories. This relieves the programmer from having to know the precise location of a library and makes the command line more portable. Also, on systems that support shared libraries (libraries with the extension *.so* on Unix systems), the linker will search for a shared library first, before searching for an archive library. This allows programs to benefit from shared libraries without specifically requiring them. This is the default behavior of GNU's linker/compiler. Older linker/compilers may not perform this optimization.

The search path used by the compiler can be changed by adding -L options indicating the directories to search and in what order. These directories are added before the system libraries and are used for all -l options on the command line. In fact, the last example fails to link because the current directory is not in cc's library search path. We can fix this error by adding the current directory like this:

```
cc count_words.o -L. -lcounter -lfl -o count_words
```

Libraries add a bit of complication to the process of building a program. How can make help to simplify the situation? GNU make includes special features to support both the creation of libraries and their use in linking programs. Let's see how they work.

Creating and Updating Libraries

Within a *makefile*, a library file is specified with its name just like any other file. A simple rule to create our library is:

```
libcounter.a: counter.o lexer.o
        $(AR) $(ARFLAGS) $@ $^
```

This uses the built-in definition for the ar program in AR and the standard options rv in ARFLAGS. The archive output file is automatically set in $@ and the prerequisites are set in $^.

Now, if you make *libcounter.a* a prerequisite of *count_words* make will update our library before linking the executable. Notice one small irritation, however. All members of the archive are replaced even if they have not been modified. This is a waste of time and we can do better:

```
libcounter.a: counter.o lexer.o
        $(AR) $(ARFLAGS) $@ $?
```

If you use $? instead of $^, make will pass only those objects files that are newer than the target to ar.

Can we do better still? Maybe, but maybe not. make has support for updating individual files within an archive, executing one ar command for each object file member, but before we go delving into those details there are several points worth noting about this style of building libraries. One of the primary goals of make is to use the processor efficiently by updating only those files that are out of date. Unfortunately, the style of invoking ar once for each out-of-date member quickly bogs down. If the archive contains more than a few dozen files, the expense of invoking ar for each update begins to outweigh the "elegance" factor of using the syntax we are about to introduce. By using the simple method above and invoking ar in an explicit rule, we can execute ar once for all files and save ourselves many fork/exec calls. In addition, on many systems using the r to ar is very inefficient. On my 1.9 GHz Pentium 4, building a large archive from scratch (with 14,216 members totaling 55 MB) takes 4 minutes 24 seconds. However, updating a single object file with ar r on the resulting archive takes 28 seconds. So building the archive from scratch is faster if I need to replace more than 10 files (out of 14,216!). In such situations it is probably more prudent to perform a single update of the archive with all modified object files using the $? automatic variable. For smaller libraries and faster processors there is no performance reason to prefer the simple approach above to the more elegant one below. In those situations, using the special library support that follows is a fine approach.

In GNU make, a member of an archive can be referenced using the notation:

```
libgraphics.a(bitblt.o): bitblt.o
        $(AR) $(ARFLAGS) $@ $<
```

Here the library name is *libgraphics.a* and the member name is *bitblt.o* (for *bit block transfer*). The syntax *libname.a(module.o)* refers to the module contained within the library. The prerequisite for this target is simply the object file itself and the command adds the object file to the archive. The automatic variable $< is used in the command to get only the first prerequisite. In fact, there is a built-in pattern rule that does exactly this.

When we put this all together, our *makefile* looks like this:

```
VPATH    = src include
CPPFLAGS = -I include

count_words: libcounter.a /lib/libfl.a

libcounter.a: libcounter.a(lexer.o) libcounter.a(counter.o)

libcounter.a(lexer.o): lexer.o
        $(AR) $(ARFLAGS) $@ $<

libcounter.a(counter.o): counter.o
        $(AR) $(ARFLAGS) $@ $<

count_words.o: counter.h
counter.o: counter.h lexer.h
lexer.o: lexer.h
```

When executed, make produces this output:

```
$ make
gcc  -I include  -c -o count_words.o src/count_words.c
flex  -t src/lexer.l> lexer.c
gcc  -I include  -c -o lexer.o lexer.c
ar rv libcounter.a lexer.o
ar: creating libcounter.a
a - lexer.o
gcc  -I include  -c -o counter.o src/counter.c
ar rv libcounter.a counter.o
a - counter.o
gcc    count_words.o libcounter.a /lib/libfl.a   -o count_words
rm lexer.c
```

Notice the archive updating rule. The automatic variable $@ is expanded to the library name even though the target in the *makefile* is *libcounter.a(lexer.o)*..

Finally, it should be mentioned that an archive library contains an index of the symbols it contains. Newer archive programs such as GNU ar manage this index automatically when a new module is added to the archive. However, many older versions of ar do not. To create or update the index of an archive another program ranlib is used. On these systems, the built-in implicit rule for updating archives is insufficient. For these systems, a rule such as:

```
libcounter.a: libcounter.a(lexer.o) libcounter.a(counter.o)
        $(RANLIB) $@
```

must be used. Or if you choose to use the alternate approach for large archives:

```
libcounter.a: counter.o lexer.o
        $(RM) $@
        $(AR) $(ARFLGS) $@ $^
        $(RANLIB) $@
```

Of course, this syntax for managing the members of an archive can be used with the built-in implicit rules as well. GNU make comes with a built-in rule for updating an archive. When we use this rule, our *makefile* becomes:

```
VPATH    = src include
CPPFLAGS = -I include

count_words: libcounter.a -lfl
libcounter.a: libcounter.a(lexer.o) libcounter.a(counter.o)
count_words.o: counter.h
counter.o: counter.h lexer.h
lexer.o: lexer.h
```

Using Libraries as Prerequisites

When libraries appear as prerequisites, they can be referenced using either a standard filename or with the -l syntax. When filename syntax is used:

```
xpong: $(OBJECTS) /lib/X11/libX11.a /lib/X11/libXaw.a
        $(LINK) $^ -o $@
```

the linker will simply read the library files listed on the command line and process them normally. When the -l syntax is used, the prerequisites aren't proper files at all:

```
xpong: $(OBJECTS) -lX11 -lXaw
        $(LINK) $^ -o $@
```

When the -l form is used in a prerequisite, make will search for the library (preferring a shared library) and substitute its value, as an absolute path, into the $^ and $? variables. One great advantage of the second form is that it allows you to use the search and shared library preference feature even when the system's linker cannot perform these duties. Another advantage is that you can customize make's search path so it can find your application's libraries as well as system libraries. In this case, the first form would ignore the shared library and use the archive library since that is what was specified on the link line. In the second form, make knows that shared libraries are preferred and will search first for a shared version of *X11* before settling for the archive version. The pattern for recognizing libraries from the -l format is stored in .LIBPATTERNS and can be customized for other library filename formats.

Unfortunately, there is a small wrinkle. If a *makefile* specifies a library file target, it cannot use the -1 option for that file in a prerequisite. For instance, the following *makefile*:

```
count_words: count_words.o -lcounter -lfl
        $(CC) $^ -o $@

libcounter.a: libcounter.a(lexer.o) libcounter.a(counter.o)
```

fails with the error:

```
No rule to make target `-lcounter', needed by `count_words'
```

It appears that this error occurs because make does not expand -lcounter to *libcounter.a* and search for a target, but instead does a straight library search. So for libraries built within the *makefile*, the filename form must be used.

Getting complex programs to link without error can be somewhat of a black art. The linker will search libraries in the order in which they are listed on the command line. So if library *A* includes an undefined symbol, say open, that is defined in library *B*, the link command line must list *A* before *B* (that is, *A* requires *B*). Otherwise, when the linker reads *A* and sees the undefined symbol open, it's too late to go back to *B*. The linker doesn't ever go back. As you can see, the order of libraries on the command line is of fundamental importance.

When the prerequisites of a target are saved in the $^ and $? variables, their order is preserved. So using $^ as in the previous example expands to the same files in the same order as the prerequisites list. This is true even when the prerequisites are split across multiple rules. In that case, the prerequisites of each rule are appended to the target prerequisite list in the order they are seen.

A closely related problem is mutual reference between libraries, often referred to as *circular references* or *circularities*. Suppose a change is made and library *B* now references a symbol defined in library *A*. We know *A* must come before *B*, but now *B* must come before *A*. Hmm, a problem. The solution is to reference *A* both before and *after* *B*: -1*A* -1*B* -1*A*. In large, complex programs, libraries often need to be repeated in this way, sometimes more than twice.

This situation poses a minor problem for make because the automatic variables normally discard duplicates. For example, suppose we need to repeat a library prerequisite to satisfy a library circularity:

```
xpong: xpong.o libui.a libdynamics.a libui.a -lX11
        $(CC) $^ -o $@
```

This prerequisite list will be processed into the following link command:

```
gcc xpong.o libui.a libdynamics.a /usr/lib/X11R6/libX11.a -o xpong
```

Oops. To overcome this behavior of $^ an additional variable is available in make, $+. This variable is identical to $^ with the exception that duplicate prerequisites are preserved. Using $+:

```
xpong: xpong.o libui.a libdynamics.a libui.a -lX11
        $(CC) $+ -o $@
```

This prerequisite list will be processed into the following link command:

```
gcc xpong.o libui.a libdynamics.a libui.a /usr/lib/X11R6/libX11.a -o xpong
```

Double-Colon Rules

Double-colon rules are an obscure feature that allows the same target to be updated with different commands depending on which set of prerequisites are newer than the target. Normally, when a target appears more than once all the prerequisites are appended in a long list with only one command script to perform the update. With double-colon rules, however, each occurrence of the target is considered a completely separate entity and is handled individually. This means that for a particular target, all the rules must be of the same type, either they are all double-colon rules or all single-colon rules.

Realistic, useful examples of this feature are difficult to come by (which is why it is an obscure feature), but here is an artificial example:

```
file-list:: generate-list-script
        chmod +x $<
        generate-list-script $(files) > file-list

file-list:: $(files)
        generate-list-script $(files) > file-list
```

We can regenerate the *file-list* target two ways. If the generating script has been updated, we make the script executable, then run it. If the source files have changed, we simply run the script. Although a bit far-fetched, this gives you a feel for how the feature might be used.

We've covered most of the features of make rules and, along with variables and commands, this is the essence of make. We've focused largely on the specific syntax and behavior of the features without going much into how to apply them in more complex situations. That is the subject of Part II. For now, we will continue our discussion with variables and then commands.

## CHAPTER 3

Variables and Macros

We've been looking at *makefile* variables for a while now and we've seen many examples of how they're used in both the built-in and user-defined rules. But the examples we've seen have only scratched the surface. Variables and macros get much more complicated and give GNU make much of its incredible power.

Before we go any further, it is important to understand that make is sort of two languages in one. The first language describes dependency graphs consisting of targets and prerequisites. (This language was covered in Chapter 2.) The second language is a macro language for performing textual substitution. Other macro languages you may be familiar with are the C preprocessor, m4, T$_E$X, and macro assemblers. Like these other macro languages, make allows you to define a shorthand term for a longer sequence of characters and use the shorthand in your program. The macro processor will recognize your shorthand terms and replace them with their expanded form. Although it is easy to think of *makefile* variables as traditional programming language variables, there is a distinction between a macro "variable" and a "traditional" variable. A macro variable is expanded "in place" to yield a text string that may then be expanded further. This distinction will become more clear as we proceed.

A variable name can contain almost any characters including most punctuation. Even spaces are allowed, but if you value your sanity you should avoid them. The only characters actually disallowed in a variable name are :, #, and =.

Variables are case-sensitive, so cc and CC refer to different variables. To get the value of a variable, enclose the variable name in $( ). As a special case, single-letter variable names can omit the parentheses and simply use $*letter*. This is why the automatic variables can be written without the parentheses. As a general rule you should use the parenthetical form and avoid single letter variable names.

Variables can also be expanded using curly braces as in ${CC} and you will often see this form, particularly in older *makefiles*. There is seldom an advantage to using one over the other, so just pick one and stick with it. Some people use curly braces for variable reference and parentheses for function call, similar to the way the shell uses them. Most modern *makefiles* use parentheses and that's what we'll use throughout this book.

Variables representing constants a user might want to customize on the command line or in the environment are written in all uppercase, by convention. Words are separated by underscores. Variables that appear only in the *makefile* are all lowercase with words separated by underscores. Finally, in this book, user-defined functions in variables and macros use lowercase words separated by dashes. Other naming conventions will be explained where they occur. (The following example uses features we haven't discussed yet. I'm using them to illustrate the variable naming conventions, don't be too concerned about the righthand side for now.)

```
# Some simple constants.
CC     := gcc
MKDIR := mkdir -p

# Internal variables.
sources = *.c
objects = $(subst .c,.o,$(sources))

# A function or two.
maybe-make-dir  = $(if $(wildcard $1),,$(MKDIR) $1)
assert-not-null = $(if $1,,$(error Illegal null value.))
```

The value of a variable consists of all the words to the right of the assignment symbol with leading space trimmed. Trailing spaces are not trimmed. This can occasionally cause trouble, for instance, if the trailing whitespace is included in the variable and subsequently used in a command script:

```
LIBRARY = libio.a # LIBRARY has a trailing space.
missing_file:
        touch $(LIBRARY)
        ls -l | grep '$(LIBRARY)'
```

The variable assignment contains a trailing space that is made more apparent by the comment (but a trailing space can also be present without a trailing comment). When this *makefile* is run, we get:

```
$ make
touch libio.a
ls -l | grep 'libio.a '
make: *** [missing_file] Error 1
```

Oops, the grep search string also included the trailing space and failed to find the file in ls's output. We'll discuss whitespace issues in more detail later. For now, let's look more closely at variables.

What Variables Are Used For

In general it is a good idea to use variables to represent external programs. This allows users of the *makefile* to more easily adapt the *makefile* to their specific environment.

For instance, there are often several versions of awk on a system: awk, nawk, gawk. By creating a variable, AWK, to hold the name of the awk program you make it easier for other users of your *makefile*. Also, if security is an issue in your environment, a good practice is to access external programs with absolute paths to avoid problems with user's paths. Absolute paths also reduce the likelihood of issues if trojan horse versions of system programs have been installed somewhere in a user's path. Of course, absolute paths also make *makefiles* less portable to other systems. Your own requirements should guide your choice.

Though your first use of variables should be to hold simple constants, they can also store user-defined command sequences such as:[*]

```
DF  = df
AWK = awk
free-space := $(DF) . | $(AWK) 'NR == 2 { print $$4 }'
```

for reporting on free disk space. Variables are used for both these purposes and more, as we will see.

Variable Types

There are two types of variables in make: simply expanded variables and recursively expanded variables. A *simply expanded* variable (or a simple variable) is defined using the := assignment operator:

```
MAKE_DEPEND := $(CC) -M
```

It is called "simply expanded" because its righthand side is expanded immediately upon reading the line from the *makefile*. Any make variable references in the righthand side are expanded and the resulting text saved as the value of the variable. This behavior is identical to most programming and scripting languages. For instance, the normal expansion of this variable would yield:

```
gcc -M
```

However, if CC above had not yet been set, then the value of the above assignment would be:

```
<space>-M
```

$(CC) is expanded to its value (which contains no characters), and collapses to nothing. It is not an error for a variable to have no definition. In fact, this is extremely useful. Most of the implicit commands include undefined variables that serve as place holders for user customizations. If the user does not customize a variable it

---

[*] The df command returns a list of each mounted filesystem and statistics on the filesystem's capacity and usage. With an argument, it prints statistics for the specified filesystem. The first line of the output is a list of column titles. This output is read by awk which examines the second line and ignores all others. Column four of df's output is the remaining free space in blocks.

collapses to nothing. Now notice the leading space. The righthand side is first parsed by make to yield the string $(CC) -M. When the variable reference is collapsed to nothing, make does not rescan the value and trim blanks. The blanks are left intact.

The second type of variable is called a recursively expanded variable. A *recursively expanded* variable (or a recursive variable) is defined using the = assignment operator:

```
MAKE_DEPEND = $(CC) -M
```

It is called "recursively expanded" because its righthand side is simply slurped up by make and stored as the value of the variable without evaluating or expanding it in any way. Instead, the expansion is performed when the variable is *used*. A better term for this variable might be *lazily expanded* variable, since the evaluation is deferred until it is actually used. One surprising effect of this style of expansion is that assignments can be performed "out of order":

```
MAKE_DEPEND = $(CC) -M
...
# Some time later
CC = gcc
```

Here the value of MAKE_DEPEND within a command script is gcc -M even though CC was undefined when MAKE_DEPEND was assigned.

In fact, recursive variables aren't really just a lazy assignment (at least not a normal lazy assignment). Each time the recursive variable is used, its righthand side is re-evaluated. For variables that are defined in terms of simple constants such as MAKE_DEPEND above, this distinction is pointless since all the variables on the righthand side are also simple constants. But imagine if a variable in the righthand side represented the execution of a program, say date. Each time the recursive variable was expanded the date program would be executed and each variable expansion would have a different value (assuming they were executed at least one second apart). At times this is very useful. At other times it is very annoying!

Other Types of Assignment

From previous examples we've seen two types of assignment: = for creating recursive variables and := for creating simple variables. There are two other assignment operators provided by make.

The ?= operator is called the *conditional variable assignment operator*. That's quite a mouth-full so we'll just call it conditional assignment. This operator will perform the requested variable assignment only if the variable does not yet have a value.

```
# Put all generated files in the directory $(PROJECT_DIR)/out.
OUTPUT_DIR ?= $(PROJECT_DIR)/out
```

Here we set the output directory variable, OUTPUT_DIR, only if it hasn't been set earlier. This feature interacts nicely with environment variables. We'll discuss this in the section "Where Variables Come From" later in this chapter.

The other assignment operator, +=, is usually referred to as *append*. As its name suggests, this operator appends text to a variable. This may seem unremarkable, but it is an important feature when recursive variables are used. Specifically, values on the righthand side of the assignment are appended to the variable *without changing the original values in the variable*. "Big deal, isn't that what append always does?" I hear you say. Yes, but hold on, this is a little tricky.

Appending to a simple variable is pretty obvious. The += operator might be implemented like this:

```
simple := $(simple) new stuff
```

Since the value in the simple variable has already undergone expansion, make can expand $(simple), append the text, and finish the assignment. But recursive variables pose a problem. An implementation like the following isn't allowed.

```
recursive = $(recursive) new stuff
```

This is an error because there's no good way for make to handle it. If make stores the current definition of recursive plus new stuff, make can't expand it again at runtime. Furthermore, attempting to expand a recursive variable containing a reference to itself yields an infinite loop.

```
$ make
makefile:2: *** Recursive variable `recursive' references itself (eventually).  Stop.
```

So, += was implemented specifically to allow adding text to a recursive variable and does the Right Thing™. This operator is particularly useful for collecting values into a variable incrementally.

Macros

Variables are fine for storing values as a single line of text, but what if we have a multiline value such as a command script we would like to execute in several places? For instance, the following sequence of commands might be used to create a Java archive (or *jar*) from Java class files:

```
echo Creating $@...
$(RM) $(TMP_JAR_DIR)
$(MKDIR) $(TMP_JAR_DIR)
$(CP) -r $^ $(TMP_JAR_DIR)
cd $(TMP_JAR_DIR) && $(JAR) $(JARFLAGS) $@ .
$(JAR) -ufm $@ $(MANIFEST)
$(RM) $(TMP_JAR_DIR)
```

At the beginning of long sequences such as this, I like to print a brief message. It can make reading make's output much easier. After the message, we collect our class files into a clean temporary directory. So we delete the temporary *jar* directory in case an old one is left lying about,* then we create a fresh temporary directory. Next we copy our prerequisite files (and all their subdirectories) into the temporary directory. Then we switch to our temporary directory and create the jar with the target filename. We add the manifest file to the jar and finally clean up. Clearly, we do not want to duplicate this sequence of commands in our *makefile* since that would be a maintenance problem in the future. We might consider packing all these commands into a recursive variable, but that is ugly to maintain and difficult to read when make echoes the command line (the whole sequence is echoed as one enormous line of text).

Instead, we can use a GNU make "canned sequence" as created by the define directive. The term "canned sequence" is a bit awkward, so we'll call this a *macro*. A macro is just another way of defining a variable in make, and one that can contain embedded newlines! The GNU make manual seems to use the words *variable* and *macro* interchangeably. In this book, we'll use the word *macro* specifically to mean variables defined using the define directive and *variable* only when assignment is used.

```
define create-jar
  @echo Creating $@...
  $(RM) $(TMP_JAR_DIR)
  $(MKDIR) $(TMP_JAR_DIR)
  $(CP) -r $^ $(TMP_JAR_DIR)
  cd $(TMP_JAR_DIR) && $(JAR) $(JARFLAGS) $@ .
  $(JAR) -ufm $@ $(MANIFEST)
  $(RM) $(TMP_JAR_DIR)
endef
```

The define directive is followed by the macro name and a newline. The body of the macro includes all the text up to the endef keyword, which must appear on a line by itself. A macro created with define is expanded pretty much like any other variable, except that when it is used in the context of a command script, each line of the macro has a tab prepended to the line. An example use is:

```
$(UI_JAR): $(UI_CLASSES)
        $(create-jar)
```

Notice we've added an @ character in front of our echo command. Command lines prefixed with an @ character are not echoed by make when the command is executed. When we run make, therefore, it doesn't print the echo command, just the output of that command. If the @ prefix is used within a macro, the prefix character applies to the individual lines on which it is used. However, if the prefix character is used on the macro reference, the entire macro body is hidden:

```
$(UI_JAR): $(UI_CLASSES)
        @$(create-jar)
```

---

* For best effect here, the RM variable should be defined to hold rm -rf. In fact, its default value is rm -f, safer but not quite as useful. Further, MKDIR should be defined as mkdir -p, and so on.

This displays only:

```
$ make
Creating ui.jar...
```

The use of @ is covered in more detail in the section "Command Modifiers" in Chapter 5.

When Variables Are Expanded

In the previous sections, we began to get a taste of some of the subtleties of variable expansion. Results depend a lot on what was previously defined, and where. You could easily get results you don't want, even if make fails to find any error. So what are the rules for expanding variables? How does this really work?

When make runs, it performs its job in two phases. In the first phase, make reads the *makefile* and any included *makefiles*. At this time, variables and rules are loaded into make's internal database and the dependency graph is created. In the second phase, make analyzes the dependency graph and determines the targets that need to be updated, then executes command scripts to perform the required updates.

When a recursive variable or define directive is processed by make, the lines in the variable or body of the macro are stored, including the newlines without being expanded. The very last newline of a macro definition is not stored as part of the macro. Otherwise, when the macro was expanded an extra newline would be read by make.

When a macro is expanded, the expanded text is then immediately scanned for further macro or variable references and those are expanded and so on, recursively. If the macro is expanded in the context of an action, each line of the macro is inserted with a leading tab character.

To summarize, here are the rules for when elements of a *makefile* are expanded:

- For variable assignments, the lefthand side of the assignment is always expanded immediately when make reads the line during its first phase.
- The righthand side of = and ?= are deferred until they are used in the second phase.
- The righthand side of := is expanded immediately.
- The righthand side of += is expanded immediately if the lefthand side was originally defined as a simple variable. Otherwise, its evaluation is deferred.
- For macro definitions (those using define), the macro variable name is immediately expanded and the body of the macro is deferred until used.
- For rules, the targets and prerequisites are always immediately expanded while the commands are always deferred.

Table 3-1 summarizes what occurs when variables are expanded.

Table 3-1. Rules for immediate and deferred expansion

Definition	Expansion of a	Expansion of b
a = b	Immediate	Deferred
a ?= b	Immediate	Deferred
a := b	Immediate	Immediate
a += b	Immediate	Deferred or immediate
define a b... b... b... endef	Immediate	Deferred

As a general rule, always define variables and macros before they are used. In particular, it is required that a variable used in a target or prerequisite be defined before its use.

An example will make all this clearer. Suppose we reimplement our free-space macro. We'll go over the example a piece at a time, then put them all together at the end.

```
BIN    := /usr/bin
PRINTF := $(BIN)/printf
DF     := $(BIN)/df
AWK    := $(BIN)/awk
```

We define three variables to hold the names of the programs we use in our macro. To avoid code duplication we factor out the *bin* directory into a fourth variable. The four variable definitions are read and their righthand sides are immediately expanded because they are simple variables. Because BIN is defined before the others, its value can be plugged into their values.

Next, we define the free-space macro.

```
define free-space
  $(PRINTF) "Free disk space "
  $(DF) . | $(AWK) 'NR == 2 { print $$4 }'
endef
```

The define directive is followed by a variable name that is immediately expanded. In this case, no expansion is necessary. The body of the macro is read and stored unexpanded.

Finally, we use our macro in a rule.

```
OUTPUT_DIR := /tmp

$(OUTPUT_DIR)/very_big_file:
        $(free-space)
```

When *$(OUTPUT_DIR)/very_big_file* is read, any variables used in the targets and prerequisites are immediately expanded. Here, $(OUTPUT_DIR) is expanded to */tmp* to form the */tmp/very_big_file* target. Next, the command script for this target is read. Command lines are recognized by the leading tab character and are read and stored, but not expanded.

Here is the entire example *makefile*. The order of elements in the file has been scrambled intentionally to illustrate make's evaluation algorithm.

```
OUTPUT_DIR := /tmp

$(OUTPUT_DIR)/very_big_file:
        $(free-space)

define free-space
  $(PRINTF) "Free disk space "
  $(DF) . | $(AWK) 'NR == 2 { print $$4 }'
endef

BIN    := /usr/bin
PRINTF := $(BIN)/printf
DF     := $(BIN)/df
AWK    := $(BIN)/awk
```

Notice that although the order of lines in the *makefile* seems backward, it executes just fine. This is one of the surprising effects of recursive variables. It can be immensely useful and confusing at the same time. The reason this *makefile* works is that expansion of the command script and the body of the macro are deferred until they are actually used. Therefore, the relative order in which they occur is immaterial to the execution of the *makefile*.

In the second phase of processing, after the *makefile* is read, make identifies the targets, performs dependency analysis, and executes the actions for each rule. Here the only target, `$(OUTPUT_DIR)/very_big_file`, has no prerequisites, so make will simply execute the actions (assuming the file doesn't exist). The command is `$(free-space)`. So make expands this as if the programmer had written:

```
/tmp/very_big_file:
        /usr/bin/printf "Free disk space "
        /usr/bin/df . | /usr/bin/awk 'NR == 2 { print $$4 }'
```

Once all variables are expanded, it begins executing commands one at a time.

Let's look at the two parts of the makefile where the order is important. As explained earlier, the target *$(OUTPUT_DIR)/very_big_file* is expanded immediately. If the definition of the variable OUTPUT_DIR had followed the rule, the expansion of the target would have yielded */very_big_file*. Probably not what the user wanted. Similarly, if the definition of BIN had been moved after AWK, those three variables would have expanded to */printf*, */df*, and */awk* because the use of `:=` causes immediate evaluation of the righthand side of the assignment. However, in this case, we could avoid the problem for PRINTF, DF, and AWK by changing `:=` to `=`, making them recursive variables.

One last detail. Notice that changing the definitions of OUTPUT_DIR and BIN to recursive variables would not change the effect of the previous ordering problems. The important issue is that when *$(OUTPUT_DIR)/very_big_file* and the righthand sides of PRINTF, DF, and AWK are expanded, their expansion happens immediately, so the variables they refer to must be already defined.

Target- and Pattern-Specific Variables

Variables usually have only one value during the execution of a *makefile*. This is ensured by the two-phase nature of *makefile* processing. In phase one, the *makefile* is read, variables are assigned and expanded, and the dependency graph is built. In phase two, the dependency graph is analyzed and traversed. So when command scripts are being executed, all variable processing has already completed. But suppose we wanted to redefine a variable for just a single rule or pattern.

In this example, the particular file we are compiling needs an extra command-line option, -DUSE_NEW_MALLOC=1, that should not be provided to other compiles:

```
gui.o: gui.h
        $(COMPILE.c) -DUSE_NEW_MALLOC=1 $(OUTPUT_OPTION) $<
```

Here, we've solved the problem by duplicating the compilation command script and adding the new required option. This approach is unsatisfactory in several respects. First, we are duplicating code. If the rule ever changes or if we choose to replace the built-in rule with a custom pattern rule, this code would need to be updated and we might forget. Second, if many files require special treatment, the task of pasting in this code will quickly become very tedious and error-prone (imagine a hundred files like this).

To address this issue and others, make provides *target-specific variables*. These are variable definitions attached to a target that are valid only during the processing of that target and any of its prerequisites. We can rewrite our previous example using this feature like this:

```
gui.o: CPPFLAGS += -DUSE_NEW_MALLOC=1
gui.o: gui.h
        $(COMPILE.c) $(OUTPUT_OPTION) $<
```

The variable CPPFLAGS is built in to the default C compilation rule and is meant to contain options for the C preprocessor. By using the += form of assignment, we append our new option to any existing value already present. Now the compile command script can be removed entirely:

```
gui.o: CPPFLAGS += -DUSE_NEW_MALLOC=1
gui.o: gui.h
```

While the *gui.o* target is being processed, the value of CPPFLAGS will contain -DUSE_NEW_MALLOC=1 in addition to its original contents. When the *gui.o* target is finished, CPPFLAGS will revert to its original value. Pattern-specific variables are similar, only they are specified in a pattern rule (see page 21).

The general syntax for target-specific variables is:

```
target...: variable = value
target...: variable := value
target...: variable += value
target...: variable ?= value
```

As you can see, all the various forms of assignment are valid for a target-specific variable. The variable does not need to exist before the assignment.

Furthermore, the variable assignment is not actually performed until the processing of the target begins. So the righthand side of the assignment can itself be a value set in another target-specific variable. The variable is valid during the processing of all prerequisites as well.

Where Variables Come From

So far, most variables have been defined explicitly in our own *makefiles*, but variables can have a more complex ancestry. For instance, we have seen that variables can be defined on the make command line. In fact, make variables can come from these sources:

File

Of course, variables can be defined in the *makefile* or a file included by the *makefile* (we'll cover the include directive shortly).

Command line

Variables can be defined or redefined directly from the make command line:

```
$ make CFLAGS=-g CPPFLAGS='-DBSD -DDEBUG'
```

A command-line argument containing an = is a variable assignment. Each variable assignment on the command line must be a single shell argument. If the value of the variable (or heaven forbid, the variable itself) contains spaces, the argument must be surrounded by quotes or the spaces must be escaped.

An assignment of a variable on the command line overrides any value from the environment and any assignment in the *makefile*. Command-line assignments can set either simple or recursive variables by using := or =, respectively. It is possible using the override directive to allow a *makefile* assignment to be used instead of a command-line assignment.

```
# Use big-endian objects or the program crashes!
override LDFLAGS = -EB
```

Of course, you should ignore a user's explicit assignment request only under the most urgent circumstances (unless you just want to irritate your users).

Environment

All the variables from your environment are automatically defined as make variables when make starts. These variables have very low precedence, so assignments within the *makefile* or command-line arguments will override the value of an environment variable. You can cause environment variables to override *makefile* variables using the --environment-overrides (or -e) command-line option.

When make is invoked recursively, some variables from the parent make are passed through the environment to the child make. By default, only those variables that originally came from the environment are exported to the child's environment, but any variable can be exported to the environment by using the export directive:

```
export CLASSPATH := $(HOME)/classes:$(PROJECT)/classes
SHELLOPTS = -x
export SHELLOPTS
```

You can cause all variables to be exported with:

```
export
```

Note that make will export even those variables whose names contain invalid shell variable characters. For example:

```
export valid-variable-in-make = Neat!
show-vars:
        env | grep '^valid-'
        valid_variable_in_shell=Great
        invalid-variable-in-shell=Sorry


$ make
env | grep '^valid-'
valid-variable-in-make=Neat!
valid_variable_in_shell=Great
invalid-variable-in-shell=Sorry
/bin/sh: line 1: invalid-variable-in-shell=Sorry: command not found
make: *** [show-vars] Error 127
```

An "invalid" shell variable was created by exporting valid-variable-in-make. This variable is not accessible through normal shell syntax, only through trickery such as running grep over the environment. Nevertheless, this variable is inherited by any sub-make where it is valid and accessible. We will cover use of "recursive" make in Part II.

You can also prevent an environment variable from being exported to the subprocess:

```
unexport DISPLAY
```

The mp_export and mp_unexport directives work the same way the mp_sh commands mp_export and mp_unset work.

The conditional assignment operator interacts very nicely with environment variables. Suppose you have a default output directory set in your *makefile*, but you want users to be able to override the default easily. Conditional assignment is perfect for this situation:

```
# Assume the output directory $(PROJECT_DIR)/out.
OUTPUT_DIR ?= $(PROJECT_DIR)/out
```

Here the assignment is performed only if OUTPUT_DIR has never been set. We can get nearly the same effect more verbosely with:

```
ifndef OUTPUT_DIR
  # Assume the output directory $(PROJECT_DIR)/out.
  OUTPUT_DIR = $(PROJECT_DIR)/out
endif
```

The difference is that the conditional assignment operator will skip the assignment if the variable has been set in any way, even to the empty value, while the ifdef and ifndef operators test for a nonempty value. Thus, OUTPUT_DIR= is considered set by the conditional operator but not defined by ifdef.

It is important to note that excessive use of environment variables makes your *makefiles* much less portable, since other users are not likely to have the same set of environment variables. In fact, I rarely use this feature for precisely that reason.

Automatic

Finally, make creates automatic variables immediately before executing the command script of a rule.

Traditionally, environment variables are used to help manage the differences between developer machines. For instance, it is common to create a development environment (source code, compiled output tree, and tools) based on environment variables referenced in the *makefile*. The *makefile* would refer to one environment variable for the root of each tree. If the source file tree is referenced from a variable PROJECT_SRC, binary output files from PROJECT_BIN, and libraries from PROJECT_LIB, then developers are free to place these trees wherever is appropriate.

A potential problem with this approach (and with the use of environment variables in general) occurs when these "root" variables are not set. One solution is to provide default values in the *makefile* using the ?= form of assignment:

```
PROJECT_SRC ?= /dev/$(USER)/src
PROJECT_BIN ?= $(patsubst %/src,%/bin,$(PROJECT_SRC))
PROJECT_LIB ?= /net/server/project/lib
```

By using these variables to access project components, you can create a development environment that is adaptable to varying machine layouts. (We will see more comprehensive examples of this in Part II.) Beware of overreliance on environment variables, however. Generally, a *makefile* should be able to run with a minimum of support from the developer's environment so be sure to provide reasonable defaults and check for the existence of critical components.

Conditional and include Processing

Parts of a *makefile* can be omitted or selected while the *makefile* is being read using *conditional processing* directives. The condition that controls the selection can have several forms such as "is defined" or "is equal to." For example:

```
# COMSPEC is defined only on Windows.
ifdef COMSPEC
  PATH_SEP := ;
  EXE_EXT  := .exe
else
  PATH_SEP := :
  EXE_EXT  :=
endif
```

This selects the first branch of the conditional if the variable COMSPEC is defined.

The basic syntax of the conditional directive is:

```
if-condition
  text if the condition is true
endif
```

or:

```
if-condition
  text if the condition is true
else
  text if the condition is false
endif
```

The *if-condition* can be one of:

```
ifdef   variable-name
ifndef  variable-name
ifeq    test
ifneq   test
```

The *variable-name* should not be surrounded by $( ) for the ifdef/ifndef test. Finally, the *test* can be expressed as either of:

```
"a" "b"
(a,b)
```

in which single or double quotes can be used interchangeably (but the quotes you use must match).

The conditional processing directives can be used within macro definitions and command scripts as well as at the top level of *makefile*s:

```
libGui.a: $(gui_objects)
        $(AR) $(ARFLAGS) $@ $<
    ifdef RANLIB
        $(RANLIB) $@
    endif
```

I like to indent my conditionals, but careless indentation can lead to errors. In the preceding lines, the conditional directives are indented four spaces while the enclosed commands have a leading tab. If the enclosed commands didn't begin with a tab, they would not be recognized as commands by make. If the conditional directives had a leading tab, they would be misidentified as commands and passed to the subshell.

The ifeq and ifneq conditionals test if their arguments are equal or not equal. Whitespace in conditional processing can be tricky to handle. For instance, when using the parenthesis form of the test, whitespace after the comma is ignored, but all other whitespace is significant:

```
ifeq (a, a)
  # These are equal
endif

ifeq ( b, b )
  # These are not equal - ' b' != 'b '
endif
```

Personally, I stick with the quoted forms of equality:

```
ifeq "a" "a"
  # These are equal
endif

ifeq 'b' 'b'
  # So are these
endif
```

Even so, it often occurs that a variable expansion contains unexpected whitespace. This can cause problems since the comparison includes all characters. To create more robust *makefiles*, use the strip function:

```
ifeq "$(strip $(OPTIONS))" "-d"
  COMPILATION_FLAGS += -DDEBUG
endif
```

The include Directive

We first saw the include directive in Chapter 2, in the section "Automatic Dependency Generation." Now let's go over it in more detail.

A *makefile* can include other files. This is most commonly done to place common make definitions in a make header file or to include automatically generated dependency information. The include directive is used like this:

```
include definitions.mk
```

The directive can be given any number of files and shell wildcards and make variables are also allowed.

include and Dependencies

When make encounters an include directive, it expands the wildcards and variable references, then tries to read the include file. If the file exists, we continue normally. If the file does not exist, however, make reports the problem and continues reading the rest of the *makefile*. When all reading is complete, make looks in the rules database for any rule to update the include files. If a match is found, make follows the normal process for updating a target. If any of the include files is updated by a rule, make then clears its internal database and rereads the entire *makefile*. If, after completing the process of reading, updating, and rereading, there are still include directives that have failed due to missing files, make terminates with an error status.

We can see this process in action with the following two-file example. We use the warning built-in function to print a simple message from make. (This and other functions are covered in detail in Chapter 4.) Here is the *makefile*:

```
# Simple makefile including a generated file.
include foo.mk
$(warning Finished include)

foo.mk: bar.mk
        m4 --define=FILENAME=$@ bar.mk > $@
```

and here is *bar.mk*, the source for the included file:

```
# bar.mk - Report when I am being read.
$(warning Reading FILENAME)
```

When run, we see:

```
$ make
Makefile:2: foo.mk: No such file or directory
Makefile:3: Finished include
m4 --define=FILENAME=foo.mk bar.mk > foo.mk
foo.mk:2: Reading foo.mk
Makefile:3: Finished include
make: `foo.mk' is up to date.
```

The first line shows that make cannot find the include file, but the second line shows that make keeps reading and executing the *makefile*. After completing the read, make discovers a rule to create the include file, *foo.mk*, and it does so. Then make starts the whole process again, this time without encountering any difficulty reading the include file.

Now is a good time to mention that make will also treat the *makefile* itself as a possible target. After the entire *makefile* has been read, make will look for a rule to remake the currently executing *makefile*. If it finds one, make will process the rule, then check if the *makefile* has been updated. If so, make will clear its internal state and reread the *makefile*, performing the whole analysis over again. Here is a silly example of an infinite loop based on this behavior:

```
.PHONY: dummy
makefile: dummy
        touch $@
```

When make executes this *makefile*, it sees that the *makefile* is out of date (because the .PHONY target, *dummy*, is out of date) so it executes the touch command, which updates the timestamp of the *makefile*. Then make rereads the file and discovers that the *makefile* is out of date.... Well, you get the idea.

Where does make look for included files? Clearly, if the argument to include is an absolute file reference, make reads that file. If the file reference is relative, make first looks in its current working directory. If make cannot find the file, it then proceeds to search through any directories you have specified on the command line using the --include-dir (or -I) option. After that, make searches a compiled search path similar to: */usr/local/include*, */usr/gnu/include*, */usr/include*. There may be slight variations of this path due to the way make was compiled.

If make cannot find the include file and it cannot create it using a rule, make exits with an error. If you want make to ignore include files it cannot load, add a leading dash to the include directive:

```
-include i-may-not-exist.mk
```

For compatibility with other makes, the word sinclude is an alias for -include.

It is worth noting that using an include directive before the first target in a makefile might change the default goal. That is, if the include file contains any targets at all the first of those targets will become the default goal for the makefile. This can be avoided by simply placing the desired default goal before the include (even without prerequisites or targets):

```
# Ensure all is the default goal.
all:
include support.mk
# Now that we have our variables defined, complete the all target.
all: $(programs)
```

Standard make Variables

In addition to automatic variables, make maintains variables revealing bits and pieces of its own state as well as variables for customizing built-in rules:

MAKE_VERSION

This is the version number of GNU make. At the time of this writing, its value is 3.80, and the value in the CVS repository is 3.81rc1.

The previous version of make, 3.79.1, did not support the eval and value functions (among other changes) and it is still very common. So when I write *makefiles* that require these features, I use this variable to test the version of make I'm running. We'll see an example of that in the section "Flow Control" in Chapter 4.

CURDIR

This variable contains the current working directory (cwd) of the executing make process. This will be the same directory the make program was executed from (and it will be the same as the shell variable PWD), unless the --directory (-C) option is used. The --directory option instructs make to change to a different directory before searching for any *makefile*. The complete form of the option is --directory=*directory-name* or -C *directory-name*. If --directory is used, CURDIR will contain the directory argument to --include-dir.

I typically invoke make from emacs while coding. For instance, my current project is in Java and uses a single *makefile* in a top-level directory (not necessarily the directory containing the code). In this case, using the --directory option allows me to invoke make from any directory in the source tree and still access the *makefile*. Within the *makefile*, all paths are relative to the *makefile* directory. Absolute paths are occasionally required and these are accessed using CURDIR.

MAKEFILE_LIST
> This variable contains a list of each file make has read including the default *makefile* and *makefiles* specified on the command line or through include directives. Just before each file is read, the name is appended to the MAKEFILE_LIST variable. So a *makefile* can always determine its own name by examining the last word of the list.

MAKECMDGOALS
> The MAKECMDGOALS variable contains a list of all the targets specified on the command line for the current execution of make. It does not include command-line options or variable assignments. For instance:
> ```
> $ make -f- FOO=bar -k goal <<< 'goal:;# $(MAKECMDGOALS)'
> # goal
> ```
> The example uses the "trick" of telling make to read the *makefile* from the *stdin* with the -f- (or --file) option. The *stdin* is redirected from a command-line string using bash's *here string*, "<<<", syntax.* The *makefile* itself consists of the default goal goal, while the command script is given on the same line by separating the target from the command with a semicolon. The command script contains the single line:
> ```
> # $(MAKECMDGOALS)
> ```
> MAKECMDGOALS is typically used when a target requires special handling. The primary example is the "clean" target. When invoking "clean," make should not perform the usual dependency file generation triggered by include (discussed in the section "Automatic Dependency Generation" in Chapter 2). To prevent this use ifneq and MAKECMDGOALS:
> ```
> ifneq "$(MAKECMDGOALS)" "clean"
>   -include $(subst .xml,.d,$(xml_src))
> endif
> ```

---

* For those of you who want to run this type of example in another shell, use:
```
$ echo 'goal:;# $(MAKECMDGOALS)' | make -f- FOO=bar -k goal
```

```
.VARIABLES
```
This contains a list of the names of all the variables defined in *makefiles* read so far, with the exception of target-specific variables. The variable is read-only and any assignment to it is ignored.

```
list:
        @echo "$(.VARIABLES)" | tr ' ' '\015' | grep MAKEF
$ make
MAKEFLAGS
MAKEFILE_LIST
MAKEFILES
```

As you've seen, variables are also used to customize the implicit rules built in to make. The rules for C/C++ are typical of the form these variables take for all programming languages. Figure 3-1 shows the variables controlling translation from one file type to another.

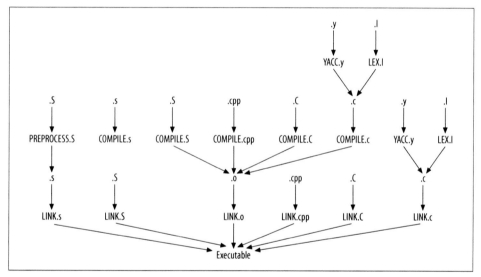

Figure 3-1. Variables for C/C++ compilation

The variables have the basic form: *ACTION.suffix*. The *ACTION* is COMPILE for creating an object file, LINK for creating an executable, or the "special" operations PREPROCESS, YACC, LEX for running the C preprocessor, yacc, or lex, respectively. The *suffix* indicates the source file type.

The standard "path" through these variables for, say, C++, uses two rules. First, compile C++ source files to object files. Then link the object files into an executable.

```
%.o: %.C
        $(COMPILE.C) $(OUTPUT_OPTION) $<

%: %.o
        $(LINK.o) $^ $(LOADLIBES) $(LDLIBS) -o $@
```

The first rule uses these variable definitions:

```
COMPILE.C    = $(COMPILE.cc)
COMPILE.cc   = $(CXX) $(CXXFLAGS) $(CPPFLAGS) $(TARGET_ARCH) -c
CXX          = g++
OUTPUT_OPTION = -o $@
```

GNU make supports either of the suffixes *.C* or *.cc* for denoting C++ source files. The CXX variable indicates the C++ compiler to use and defaults to g++. The variables CXXFLAGS, CPPFLAGS, and TARGET_ARCH have no default value. They are intended for use by end-users to customize the build process. The three variables hold the C++ compiler flags, C preprocessor flags, and architecture-specific compilation options, respectively. The OUTPUT_OPTION contains the output file option.

The linking rule is a bit simpler:

```
LINK.o = $(CC) $(LDFLAGS) $(TARGET_ARCH)
CC     = gcc
```

This rule uses the C compiler to combine object files into an executable. The default for the C compiler is gcc. LDFLAGS and TARGET_ARCH have no default value. The LDFLAGS variable holds options for linking such as -L flags. The LOADLIBES and LDLIBS variables contain lists of libraries to link against. Two variables are included mostly for portability.

This was a quick tour through the make variables. There are more, but this gives you the flavor of how variables are integrated with rules. Another group of variables deals with T$_E$X and has its own set of rules. Recursive make is another feature supported by variables. We'll discuss this topic in Chapter 6.

## CHAPTER 4

Functions

GNU make supports both built-in and user-defined functions. A function invocation looks much like a variable reference, but includes one or more parameters separated by commas. Most built-in functions expand to some value that is then assigned to a variable or passed to a subshell. A user-defined function is stored in a variable or macro and expects one or more parameters to be passed by the caller.

User-Defined Functions

Storing command sequences in variables opens the door to a wide range of applications. For instance, here's a nice little macro to kill a process:[*]

```
AWK   := awk
KILL := kill

# $(kill-acroread)
define kill-acroread
  @ ps -W |                                      \
  $(AWK) 'BEGIN       { FIELDWIDTHS = "9 47 100" }  \
          /AcroRd32/ {                             \
                       print "Killing " $$3;       \
                       system( "$(KILL) -f " $$1 )  \
                     }'
endef
```

---

[*] "Why would you want to do this in a *makefile?*" you ask. Well, on Windows, opening a file locks it against writing by other processes. While I was writing this book, the *PDF* file would often be locked by the Acrobat Reader and prevent my *makefile* from updating the *PDF*. So I added this command to several targets to terminate Acrobat Reader before attempting to update the locked file.

(This macro was written explicitly to use the Cygwin tools,* so the program name we search for and the options to ps and kill are not standard Unix.) To kill a process we pipe the output of ps to awk. The awk script looks for the Acrobat Reader by its Windows program name and kills the process if it is running. We use the FIELDWIDTHS feature to treat the program name and all its arguments as a single field. This correctly prints the complete program name and arguments even when it contains embedded blanks. Field references in awk are written as $1, $2, etc. These would be treated as make variables if we did not quote them in some way. We can tell make to pass the $n reference to awk instead of expanding it itself by escaping the dollar sign in $n with an additional dollar sign, $$n. make will see the double dollar sign, collapse it to a single dollar sign and pass it to the subshell.

Nice macro. And the define directive saves us from duplicating the code if we want to use it often. But it isn't perfect. What if we want to kill processes other than the Acrobat Reader? Do we have to define another macro and duplicate the script? No!

Variables and macros can be passed arguments so that each expansion can be different. The parameters of the macro are referenced within the body of the macro definition with $1, $2, etc. To parameterize our kill-acroread function, we only need to add a search parameter:

```
AWK        := awk
KILL       := kill
KILL_FLAGS := -f
PS         := ps
PS_FLAGS   := -W
PS_FIELDS  := "9 47 100"

# $(call kill-program,awk-pattern)
define kill-program
  @ $(PS) $(PS_FLAGS) |                              \
    $(AWK) 'BEGIN { FIELDWIDTHS = $(PS_FIELDS) }     \
        /$1/  {                                      \
                print "Killing " $$3;                \
                system( "$(KILL) $(KILL_FLAGS) " $$1 ) \
              }'
endef
```

We've replaced the awk search pattern, /AcroRd32/, with a parameter reference, $1. Note the subtle distinction between the macro parameter, $1, and the awk field reference, $$1. It is very important to remember which program is the intended recipient for a variable reference. As long as we're improving the function, we have also

---

* The *Cygwin* tools are a port of many of the standard GNU and Linux programs to Windows. It includes the compiler suite, X11R6, ssh, and even inetd. The port relies on a compatibility library that implements Unix system calls in terms of Win32 API functions. It is an incredible feat of engineering and I highly recommend it. Download it from *http://www.cygwin.com*.

renamed it appropriately and replaced the Cygwin-specific, hardcoded values with variables. Now we have a reasonably portable macro for terminating processes.

So let's see it in action:

```
FOP         := org.apache.fop.apps.Fop
FOP_FLAGS   := -q
FOP_OUTPUT := > /dev/null
%.pdf: %.fo
        $(call kill-program,AcroRd32)
        $(JAVA) $(FOP) $(FOP_FLAGS) $< $@ $(FOP_OUTPUT)
```

This pattern rule kills the *Acrobat* process, if one is running, and then converts an *fo* (Formatting Objects) file into a *pdf* file by invoking the Fop processor (*http://xml. apache.org/fop*). The syntax for expanding a variable or macro is:

```
$(call macro-name[, param1...])
```

call is a built-in make function that expands its first argument and replaces occurrences of $1, $2, etc., with the remaining arguments it is given. (In fact, it doesn't really "call" its macro argument at all in the sense of transfer of control, rather it performs a special kind of macro expansion.) The macro-name is the name of any macro or variable (remember that macros are just variables where embedded newlines are allowed). The macro or variable value doesn't even have to contain a $n reference, but then there isn't much point in using call at all. Arguments to the macro following macro-name are separated by commas.

Notice that the first argument to call is an unexpanded variable name (that is, it does not begin with a dollar sign). That is fairly unusual. Only one other built-in function, origin, accepts unexpanded variables. If you enclose the first argument to call in a dollar sign and parentheses, that argument is expanded as a variable and its value is passed to call.

There is very little in the way of argument checking with call. Any number of arguments can be given to call. If a macro references a parameter $n and there is no corresponding argument in the call instance, the variable collapses to nothing. If there are more arguments in the call instance than there are $n references, the extra arguments are never expanded in the macro.

If you invoke one macro from another, you should be aware of a somewhat strange behavior in make 3.80. The call function defines the arguments as normal make variables for the duration of the expansion. So if one macro invokes another, it is possible that the parent's arguments will be visible in the child macro's expansion:

```
define parent
  echo "parent has two parameters: $1, $2"
  $(call child,$1)
endef

define child
  echo "child has one parameter: $1"
```

```
      echo "but child can also see parent's second parameter: $2!"
    endef

    scoping_issue:
            @$(call parent,one,two)
```

When run, we see that the macro implementation has a scoping issue.

```
$ make
parent has two parameters: one, two
child has one parameter: one
but child can also see parent's second parameter: two!
```

This has been resolved in 3.81 so that $2 in child collapses to nothing.

We'll spend a lot more time with user-defined functions throughout the rest of the book, but we need more background before we can get into the really fun stuff!

Built-in Functions

Once you start down the road of using make variables for more than just simple constants you'll find that you want to manipulate the variables and their contents in more and more complex ways. Well, you can. GNU make has a couple dozen built-in functions for working with variables and their contents. The functions fall into several broad categories: string manipulation, filename manipulation, flow control, user-defined functions, and some (important) miscellaneous functions.

But first, a little more about function syntax. All functions have the form:

```
$(function-name arg1[, argn])
```

The $(is followed by built-in function name and then followed by the arguments to the function. Leading whitespace is trimmed from the first argument, but all subsequent arguments include any leading (and, of course, embedded and following) whitespace.

Function arguments are separated by commas, so a function with one argument uses no commas, a function with two arguments uses one comma, etc. Many functions accept a single argument, treating it as a list of space-separated words. For these functions, the whitespace between words is treated as a single-word separator and is otherwise ignored.

I like whitespace. It makes the code more readable and easier to maintain. So I'll be using whitespace wherever I can "get away" with it. Sometimes, however, the whitespace in an argument list or variable definition can interfere with the proper functioning of the code. When this happens, you have little choice but to remove the problematic whitespace. We already saw one example earlier in the chapter where trailing whitespace was accidentally inserted into the search pattern of a grep command. As we proceed with more examples, we'll point out where whitespace issues arise.

Many make functions accept a *pattern* as an argument. This pattern uses the same syntax as the patterns used in pattern rules (see the section "Pattern Rules" in Chapter 2). A pattern contains a single % with leading or trailing characters (or both). The % character represents zero or more characters of any kind. To match a target string, the pattern must match the entire string, not just a subset of characters within the string. We'll illustrate this with an example shortly. The % character is optional in a pattern and is commonly omitted when appropriate.

String Functions

Most of make's built-in functions manipulate text in one form or another, but certain functions are particularly strong at string manipulation, and these will be discussed here.

A common string operation in make is to select a set of files from a list. This is what grep is typically used for in shell scripts. In make we have the filter, filter-out, and findstring functions.

$(filter pattern...,text)

> The filter function treats text as a sequence of space separated words and returns a list of those words matching pattern. For instance, to build an archive of user-interface code, we might want to select only the object files in the *ui* subdirectory. In the following example, we extract the filenames starting with *ui/* and ending in *.o* from a list of filenames. The % character matches any number of characters in between:

```
$(ui_library): $(filter ui/%.o,$(objects))
        $(AR) $(ARFLAGS) $@ $^
```

> It is also possible for filter to accept multiple patterns, separated by spaces. As noted above, the pattern must match an entire word for the word to be included in the output list. So, for instance:

```
words := he the hen other the%
get-the:
        @echo he matches: $(filter he, $(words))
        @echo %he matches: $(filter %he, $(words))
        @echo he% matches: $(filter he%, $(words))
        @echo %he% matches: $(filter %he%, $(words))
```

> When executed the *makefile* generates the output:

```
$ make
he matches: he
%he matches: he the
he% matches: he hen
%he% matches: the%
```

> As you can see, the first pattern matches only the word he, because the pattern must match the entire word, not just a part of it. The other patterns match he plus words that contain he in the right position.

A pattern can contain only one %. If additional % characters are included in the pattern, all but the first are treated as literal characters.

It may seem odd that `filter` cannot match substrings within words or accept more than one wildcard character. You will find times when this functionality is sorely missed. However, you can implement something similar using looping and conditional testing. We'll show you how later.

$(filter-out pattern...,text)

The `filter-out` function does the opposite of `filter`, selecting every word that does not match the pattern. Here we select all files that are not C headers.

```
all_source := count_words.c counter.c lexer.l counter.h lexer.h
to_compile := $(filter-out %.h, $(all_source))
```

$(findstring string,text)

This function looks for `string` in text. If the string is found, the function returns `string`; otherwise, it returns nothing.

At first, this function might seem like the substring searching grep function we thought `filter` might be, but not so. First, and most important, this function returns just the search string, not the word it finds that contains the search string. Second, the search string cannot contain wildcard characters (putting it another way, % characters in the search string are matched literally).

This function is mostly useful in conjunction with the `if` function discussed later. There is, however, one situation where I've found `findstring` to be useful in its own right.

Suppose you have several trees with parallel structure such as reference source, sandbox source, debugging binary, and optimized binary. You'd like to be able to find out which tree you are in from your current directory (without the current relative path from the root). Here is some skeleton code to determine this:

```
find-tree:
        # PWD = $(PWD)
        # $(findstring /test/book/admin,$(PWD))
        # $(findstring /test/book/bin,$(PWD))
        # $(findstring /test/book/dblite_0.5,$(PWD))
        # $(findstring /test/book/examples,$(PWD))
        # $(findstring /test/book/out,$(PWD))
        # $(findstring /test/book/text,$(PWD))
```

(Each line begins with a tab and a shell comment character so each is "executed" in its own subshell just like other commands. The Bourne Again Shell, bash, and many other Bourne-like shells simply ignore these lines. This is a more convenient way to print out the expansion of simple make constructs than typing @echo. You can achieve almost the same effect using the more portable : shell operator, but the : operator performs redirections. Thus, a command line containing > word creates the file *word* as a side effect.) When run, it produces:

```
$ make
# PWD = /test/book/out/ch03-findstring-1
```

```
#
#
#
# /test/book/out
#
```

As you can see, each test against $(PWD) returns null until we test our parent directory. Then the parent directory itself is returned. As shown, the code is merely as a demonstration of findstring. This can be used to write a function returning the current tree's root directory.

There are two search and replace functions:

$(subst search-string,replace-string,text)

This is a simple, nonwildcard, search and replace. One of its most common uses is to replace one suffix with another in a list of filenames:

```
sources := count_words.c counter.c lexer.c
objects := $(subst .c,.o,$(sources))
```

This replaces all occurrences of ".c" with ".o" anywhere in $(sources), or, more generally, all occurrences of the search string with the replacement string.

This example is a commonly found illustration of where spaces are significant in function call arguments. Note that there are no spaces after the commas. If we had instead written:

```
sources := count_words.c counter.c lexer.c
objects := $(subst .c, .o, $(sources))
```

(notice the space after each comma), the value of $(objects) would have been:

```
count_words .o counter .o lexer .o
```

Not at all what we want. The problem is that the space before the .o argument is part of the replacement text and was inserted into the output string. The space before the .c is fine because all whitespace before the first argument is stripped off by make. In fact, the space before $(sources) is probably benign as well since $(objects) will most likely be used as a simple command-line argument where leading spaces aren't a problem. However, I would never mix different spacing after commas in a function call even if it yields the correct results:

```
# Yech, the spacing in this call is too subtle.
objects := $(subst .c,.o, $(source))
```

Note that subst doesn't understand filenames or file suffixes, just strings of characters. If one of my source files contains a .c internally, that too will be substituted. For instance, the filename *car.cdr.c* would be transformed into *car.odr.o*. Probably not what we want.

In the section "Automatic Dependency Generation" in Chapter 2, we talked about dependency generation. The last example *makefile* of that section used subst like this:

```
VPATH    = src include
CPPFLAGS = -I include
```

```
SOURCES  = count_words.c \
          lexer.c       \
          counter.c
count_words: counter.o lexer.o -lfl
count_words.o: counter.h
counter.o: counter.h lexer.h
lexer.o: lexer.h
include $(subst .c,.d,$(SOURCES))
%.d: %.c
        $(CC) -M $(CPPFLAGS) $< > $@.$$$$;                    \
        sed 's,\($*\)\.o[ :]*,\1.o $@ : ,g' < $@.$$$$ > $@;   \
        rm -f $@.$$$$
```

The subst function is used to transform the source file list into a dependency file list. Since the dependency files appear as an argument to include, they are considered prerequisites and are updated using the %.d rule.

$(patsubst search-pattern,replace-pattern,text)

This is the wildcard version of search and replace. As usual, the pattern can contain a single %. A percent in the replace-pattern is expanded with the matching text. It is important to remember that the search-pattern must match the entire value of text. For instance, the following will delete a trailing slash in text, not every slash in text:

```
strip-trailing-slash = $(patsubst %/,%,$(directory-path))
```

Substitution references are a portable way of performing the same substitution. The syntax of a substitution reference is:

```
$(variable:search=replace)
```

The *search* text can be a simple string; in which case, the string is replaced with *replace* whenever it occurs at the end of a word. That is, whenever it is followed by whitespace or the end of the variable value. In addition, *search* can contain a % representing a wildcard character; in which case, the search and replace follow the rules of patsubst. I find this syntax to be obscure and difficult to read in comparison to patsubst.

As we've seen, variables often contain lists of words. Here are functions to select words from a list, count the length of a list, etc. As with all make functions, words are separated by whitespace.

$(words text)

This returns the number of words in text.

```
CURRENT_PATH := $(subst /, ,$(HOME))
words:
        @echo My HOME path has $(words $(CURRENT_PATH)) directories.
```

This function has many uses, as we'll see shortly, but we need to cover a few more functions to use it effectively.

`$(word n,text)`

> This returns the nth word in text. The first word is numbered 1. If n is larger than the number of words in text, the value of the function is empty.
>
> ```
> version_list  := $(subst ., ,$(MAKE_VERSION))
> minor_version := $(word 2, $(version_list))
> ```
>
> The variable MAKE_VERSION is a built-in variable. (See the section "Standard make Variables" in Chapter 3.)
>
> You can always get the last word in a list with:
>
> ```
> current := $(word $(words $(MAKEFILE_LIST)), $(MAKEFILE_LIST))
> ```
>
> This returns the name of the most recently read *makefile*.

`$(firstword text)`

> This returns the first word in text. This is equivalent to `$(word 1,text)`.
>
> ```
> version_list := $(subst ., ,$(MAKE_VERSION))
> major_version := $(firstword $(version_list))
> ```

`$(wordlist start,end,text)`

> This returns the words in text from start to end, inclusive. As with the word function, the first word is numbered 1. If start is greater than the number of words, the value is empty. If start is greater than end, the value is empty. If end is greater than the number of words, all words from start on are returned.
>
> ```
> # $(call uid_gid, user-name)
> uid_gid = $(wordlist 3, 4, \
>               $(subst :, , \
>                 $(shell grep "^$1:" /etc/passwd)))
> ```

Important Miscellaneous Functions

Before we push on to functions for managing filenames, let's introduce two very useful functions: sort and shell.

`$(sort list)`

> The sort function sorts its list argument and removes duplicates. The resulting list contains all the unique words in lexicographic order, each separated by a single space. In addition, sort strips leading and trailing blanks.
>
> ```
> $ make -f- <<< 'x:;@echo =$(sort    d  b s  d     t  )='
> =b d s t=
> ```
>
> The sort function is, of course, implemented directly by make, so it does not support any of the options of the sort program. The function operates on its argument, typically a variable or the return value of another make function.

`$(shell command)`

> The shell function accepts a single argument that is expanded (like all arguments) and passed to a subshell for execution. The standard output of the command is then read and returned as the value of the function. Sequences of

newlines in the output are collapsed to a single space. Any trailing newline is deleted. The standard error is not returned, nor is any program exit status.

```
stdout := $(shell echo normal message)
stderr := $(shell echo error message 1>&2)
shell-value:
        # $(stdout)
        # $(stderr)
```

As you can see, messages to *stderr* are sent to the terminal as usual and so are not included in the output of the shell function:

```
$ make
error message
# normal message
#
```

Here is a loop to create a set of directories:

```
REQUIRED_DIRS = ...
_MKDIRS := $(shell for d in $(REQUIRED_DIRS); \
             do                                \
               [[ -d $$d ]] || mkdir -p $$d;   \
             done)
```

Often, a *makefile* is easier to implement if essential output directories can be guaranteed to exist before any command scripts are executed. This variable creates the necessary directories by using a bash shell "for" loop to ensure that a set of directories exists. The double square brackets are bash test syntax similar to the test program except that word splitting and pathname expansion are not performed. Therefore if the variable contains a filename with embedded spaces, the test still works correctly (and without quoting). By placing this make variable assignment early in the *makefile*, we ensure it is executed before command scripts or other variables use the output directories. The actual value of _MKDIRS is irrelevant and _MKDIRS itself would never be used.

Since the shell function can be used to invoke any external program, you should be careful how you use it. In particular, you should consider the distinction between simple variables and recursive variables.

```
START_TIME   := $(shell date)
CURRENT_TIME  = $(shell date)
```

The START_TIME variable causes the date command to execute once when the variable is defined. The CURRENT_TIME variable will reexecute date each time the variable is used in the *makefile*.

Our toolbox is now full enough to write some fairly interesting functions. Here is a function for testing whether a value contains duplicates:

```
# $(call has-duplicates, word-list)
has-duplicates = $(filter              \
                   $(words $1)         \
                   $(words $(sort $1)))
```

We count the words in the list and the unique list, then "compare" the two numbers. There are no make functions that understand numbers, only strings. To compare two numbers, we must compare them as strings. The easiest way to do that is with filter. We search for one number in the other number. The has-duplicates function will be non-null if there are duplicates.

Here is a simple way to generate a filename with a timestamp:

```
RELEASE_TAR := mpwm-$(shell date +%F).tar.gz
```

This produces:

```
mpwm-2003-11-11.tar.gz
```

We could produce the same filename and have date do more of the work with:

```
RELEASE_TAR := $(shell date +mpwm-%F.tar.gz)
```

The next function can be used to convert relative paths (possibly from a *com* directory) into a fully qualified Java class name:

```
# $(call file-to-class-name, file-name)
file-to-class-name := $(subst /,.,$(patsubst %.java,%,$1))
```

This particular pattern can be accomplished with two substs as well:

```
# $(call file-to-class-name, file-name)
file-to-class-name := $(subst /,.,$(subst .java,,$1))
```

We can then use this function to invoke the Java class like this:

```
CALIBRATE_ELEVATOR := com/wonka/CalibrateElevator.java
calibrate:
        $(JAVA) $(call file-to-class-name,$(CALIBRATE_ELEVATOR))
```

If there are more parent directory components in $(sources) above com, they can be removed with the following function by passing the root of the directory tree as the first argument:[*]

```
# $(call file-to-class-name, root-dir, file-name)
file-to-class-name := $(subst /,.,          \
                    $(subst .java,,     \
                      $(subst $1/,,$2)))
```

When reading functions such as this, it is typically easiest to try to understand them inside out. Beginning at the inner-most subst, the function removes the string $1/, then removes the string *.java*, and finally converts all slashes to periods.

---

[*] In Java, it is suggested that all classes be declared within a package containing the developer's complete Internet domain name, reversed. Also, the directory structure typically mirrors the package structure. Therefore, many source trees look like *root-dir*/com/*company-name*/*dir*.

Filename Functions

Makefile writers spend a lot of time handling files. So it isn't surprising there are a lot of make functions to help with this task.

$(wildcard pattern...)

Wildcards were covered in Chapter 2, in the context of targets, prerequisites, and command scripts. But what if we want this functionality in another context, say a variable definition? With the shell function, we could simply use the sub-shell to expand the pattern, but that would be terribly slow if we needed to do this very often. Instead, we can use the wildcard function:

```
sources := $(wildcard *.c *.h)
```

The wildcard function accepts a list of patterns and performs expansion on each one.* If a pattern does not match any files, the empty string is returned. As with wildcard expansion in targets and prerequisites, the normal shell globbing characters are supported: ~, *, ?, [...], and [^...].

Another use of wildcard is to test for the existence of a file in conditionals. When used in conjunction with the if function (described shortly) you often see wildcard function calls whose argument contains no wildcard characters at all. For instance,

```
dot-emacs-exists := $(wildcard ~/.emacs)
```

will return the empty string if the user's home directory does not contain a *.emacs* file.

$(dir list...)

The dir function returns the directory portion of each word in list. Here is an expression to return every subdirectory that contains C files:

```
source-dirs := $(sort                        \
                 $(dir                        \
                   $(shell find . -name '*.c')))
```

The find returns all the source files, then the dir function strips off the file portion leaving the directory, and the sort removes duplicate directories. Notice that this variable definition uses a simple variable to avoid reexecuting the find each time the variable is used (since we assume source files will not spontaneously appear and disappear during the execution of the *makefile*). Here's a function implementation that requires a recursive variable:

```
# $(call source-dirs, dir-list)
source-dirs = $(sort                          \
                $(dir                         \
                  $(shell find $1 -name '*.c')))
```

---

* The make 3.80 manual fails to mention that more than one pattern is allowed.

This version accepts a space-separated directory list to search as its first parameter. The first arguments to find are one or more directories to search. The end of the directory list is recognized by the first dash argument. (A find feature I didn't know about for several decades!)

$(notdir name...)

The notdir function returns the filename portion of a file path. Here is an expression to return the Java class name from a Java source file:

```
# $(call get-java-class-name, file-name)
get-java-class-name = $(notdir $(subst .java,,$1))
```

There are many instances where dir and notdir can be used together to produce the desired output. For instance, suppose a custom shell script must be executed in the same directory as the output file it generates.

```
$(OUT)/myfile.out: $(SRC)/source1.in $(SRC)/source2.in
        cd $(dir $@); \
        generate-myfile $^ > $(notdir $@)
```

The automatic variable, $@, representing the target, can be decomposed to yield the target directory and file as separate values. In fact, if OUT is an absolute path, it isn't necessary to use the notdir function here, but doing so will make the output more readable.

In command scripts, another way to decompose a filename is through the use of $(@D) and $(@F) as mentioned in the section "Automatic Variables" in Chapter 2.

Here are functions for adding and removing file suffixes, etc.

$(suffix name...)

The suffix function returns the suffix of each word in its argument. Here is a function to test whether all the words in a list have the same suffix:

```
# $(call same-suffix, file-list)
same-suffix = $(filter 1, $(words $(sort $(suffix $1))))
```

A more common use of the suffix function is within conditionals in conjunction with findstring.

$(basename name...)

The basename function is the complement of suffix. It returns the filename without its suffix. Any leading path components remain intact after the basename call. Here are the earlier file-to-class-name and get-java-class-name functions rewritten with basename:

```
# $(call file-to-class-name, root-directory, file-name)
file-to-class-name  := $(subst /,.,        \
                          $(basename        \
                             $(subst $1/,,$2)))
# $(call get-java-class-name, file-name)
get-java-class-name =  $(notdir $(basename $1))
```

$(addsuffix suffix,name...)

The addsuffix function appends the given suffix text to each word in name. The suffix text can be anything. Here is a function to find all the files in the PATH that match an expression:

```
# $(call find-program, filter-pattern)
find-program = $(filter $1,                          \
                  $(wildcard                          \
                    $(addsuffix /*,                   \
                      $(sort                          \
                        $(subst :, ,                  \
                          $(subst ::,:.:,             \
                            $(patsubst :%,.:%,         \
                              $(patsubst %:,%:.,$(PATH)))))))))
find:
        @echo $(words $(call find-program, %))
```

The inner-most three substitutions account for a special case in shell syntax. An empty path component is taken to mean the current directory. To normalize this special syntax we search for an empty trailing path component, an empty leading path component, and an empty interior path component, in that order. Any matching components are replaced with ".". Next, the path separator is replaced with a space to create separate words. The sort function is used to remove repeated path components. Then the globbing suffix /* is appended to each word and wildcard is invoked to expand the globbing expressions. Finally, the desired patterns are extracted by filter.

Although this may seem like an extremely slow function to run (and it may well be on many systems), on my 1.9 GHz P4 with 512 MB this function executes in 0.20 seconds and finds 4,335 programs. This performance can be improved by moving the $1 argument inside the call to wildcard. The following version eliminates the call to filter and changes addsuffix to use the caller's argument.

```
# $(call find-program,wildcard-pattern)
find-program = $(wildcard                            \
                  $(addsuffix /$1,                    \
                    $(sort                            \
                      $(subst :, ,                    \
                        $(subst ::,:.:,               \
                          $(patsubst :%,.:%,          \
                            $(patsubst %:,%:.,$(PATH))))))))
find:
        @echo $(words $(call find-program,*))
```

This version runs in 0.17 seconds. It runs faster because wildcard no longer returns every file only to make the function discard them later with filter. A similar example occurs in the GNU make manual. Notice also that the first version uses filter-style globbing patterns (using % only) while the second version uses wildcard-style globbing patterns (~, *, ?, [...], and [^...]).

`$(addprefix prefix,name...)`

The `addprefix` function is the complement of `addsuffix`. Here is an expression to test whether a set of files exists and is nonempty:

```
# $(call valid-files, file-list)
valid-files = test -s . $(addprefix -a -s ,$1)
```

This function is different from most of the previous examples in that it is intended to be executed in a command script. It uses the shell's test program with the `-s` option ("true if the file exists and is not empty") to perform the test. Since the test command requires a `-a` (and) option between multiple filenames, `addprefix` prepends the `-a` before each filename. The first file used to start the "and" chain is dot, which always yields true.

`$(join prefix-list,suffix-list)`

The `join` function is the complement of `dir` and `notdir`. It accepts two lists and concatenates the first element from `prefix-list` with the first element from `suffix-list`, then the second element from `prefix-list` with the second element from `suffix-list` and so on. It can be used to reconstruct lists decomposed with `dir` and `notdir`.

Flow Control

Because many of the functions we have seen so far are implemented to perform their operations on lists, they work well even without a looping construct. But without a true looping operator and conditional processing of some kind the make macro language would be very limited, indeed. Fortunately, make provides both of these language features. I have also thrown into this section the fatal error function, clearly a very extreme form of flow control!

`$(if condition,then-part,else-part)`

The `if` function (not to be confused with the conditional directives `ifeq`, `ifneq`, `ifdef`, and `ifndef` discussed in Chapter 3) selects one of two macro expansions depending on the "value" of the conditional expression. The condition is true if its expansion contains any characters (even space). In this case, the then-part is expanded. Otherwise, if the expansion of condition is empty, it is false and the else-part is expanded.[*]

Here is an easy way to test whether the *makefile* is running on Windows. Look for the COMSPEC environment variable defined only on Windows:

```
PATH_SEP := $(if $(COMSPEC),;,:)
```

---

[*] In Chapter 3, I made a distinction between macro languages and other programming languages. Macro languages work by transforming source text into output text through defining and expanding macros. This distinction becomes clearer as we see how the `if` function works.

make evaluates the condition by first removing leading and trailing whitespace, then expanding the expression. If the expansion yields any characters (including whitespace), the expression is true. Now PATH_SEP contains the proper character to use in paths, whether the *makefile* is running on Windows or Unix.

In the last chapter, we mentioned checking the version of make if you use some of the newest features (like eval). The if and filter functions are often used together to test the value of a string:

```
$(if $(filter $(MAKE_VERSION),3.80),,\
    $(error This makefile requires GNU make version 3.80.))
```

Now, as subsequent versions of make are released, the expression can be extended with more acceptable versions:

```
$(if $(filter $(MAKE_VERSION),3.80 3.81 3.90 3.92),,\
    $(error This makefile requires one of GNU make version ….))
```

This technique has the disadvantage that the code must be updated when a new version of make is installed. But that doesn't happen very often. (For instance, 3.80 has been the release version since October 2002.) The above test can be added to a *makefile* as a top-level expression since the if collapses to nothing if true and error terminates the make otherwise.

$(error text)

The error function is used for printing fatal error messages. After the function prints its message, make terminates with an exit status of 2. The output is prefixed with the name of the current *makefile*, the current line number, and the message text. Here is an implementation of the common assert programming construct for make:

```
# $(call assert,condition,message)
define assert
  $(if $1,,$(error Assertion failed: $2))
endef
# $(call assert-file-exists,wildcard-pattern)
define assert-file-exists
  $(call assert,$(wildcard $1),$1 does not exist)
endef
# $(call assert-not-null,make-variable)
define assert-not-null
  $(call assert,$($1),The variable "$1" is null)
endef
error-exit:
        $(call assert-not-null,NON_EXISTENT)
```

The first function, assert, just tests its first argument and prints the user's error message if it is empty. The second function builds on the first and tests that a wildcard pattern yields an existing file. Note that the argument can include any number of globbing patterns.

The third function is a very useful assert that relies on *computed variables*. A make variable can contain anything, including the name of another make variable. But

if a variable contains the name of another variable how can you access the value
of that other variable? Well, very simply by expanding the variable twice:

```
NO_SPACE_MSG := No space left on device.
NO_FILE_MSG  := File not found.
...;
STATUS_MSG   := NO_SPACE_MSG
$(error $($(STATUS_MSG)))
```

This example is slightly contrived to keep it simple, but here STATUS_MSG is set to
one of several error messages by storing the error message variable name. When
it comes time to print the message, STATUS_MSG is first expanded to access the
error message variable name, $(STATUS_MSG), then expanded again to access the
message text, $($(STATUS_MSG)). In our assert-not-null function we assume
the argument to the function is the *name* of a make variable. We first expand the
argument, $1, to access the variable name, then expand again, $($1), to deter-
mine if it has a value. If it is null, then we have the variable name right in $1 to
use in the error message.

```
$ make
Makefile:14: *** Assertion failed: The variable "NON_EXISTENT" is null.  Stop.
```

There is also a warning function (see the section "Less Important Miscellaneous
Functions" later in this chapter) that prints a message in the same format as
error, but does not terminate make.

$(foreach variable,list,body)

The foreach function provides a way to expand text repeatedly while substituting different values into each expansion. Notice that this is different from executing a function repeatedly with different arguments (although it can do that,
too). For example:

```
letters := $(foreach letter,a b c d,$(letter))
show-words:
        # letters has $(words $(letters)) words: '$(letters)'
$ make
# letters has 4 words: 'a b c d'
```

When this foreach is executed, it sets the loop control variable, letter, to each
value in a b c d and expands the body of the loop, $(letter), once for each
value. The expanded text is accumulated with a space separating each expansion.

Here is a function to test if a set of variables is set:

```
VARIABLE_LIST := SOURCES OBJECTS HOME
$(foreach i,$(VARIABLE_LIST), \
  $(if $($i),,                  \
    $(shell echo $i has no value > /dev/stderr)))
```

(The pseudo file */dev/stderr* in the shell function requires setting SHELL to bash.)
This loop sets i to each word of VARIABLE_LIST. The test expression inside the if
first evaluates $i to get the variable name, then evaluates this again in a com-
puted expression $($i) to see if it is non-null. If the expression has a value, the
then part does nothing; otherwise, the *else* part prints a warning. Note that if we

omit the redirection from the echo, the output of the shell command will be substituted into the *makefile*, yielding a syntax error. As shown, the entire foreach loop expands to nothing.

As promised earlier, here is a function that gathers all the words that contain a substring from a list:

```
# $(call grep-string, search-string, word-list)
define grep-string
$(strip                                        \
  $(foreach w, $2,                             \
    $(if $(findstring $1, $w),                 \
      $w)))
endef
words := count_words.c counter.c lexer.l lexer.h counter.h
find-words:
        @echo $(call grep-string,un,$(words))
```

Unfortunately, this function does not accept patterns, but it does find simple substrings:

```
$ make
count_words.c counter.c counter.h
```

Style note concerning variables and parentheses

As noted earlier, parentheses are not required for make variables of one character. For instance, all of the basic automatic variables are one character. Automatic variables are universally written without parentheses even in the GNU make manual. However, the make manual uses parentheses for virtually all other variables, even single character variables, and strongly urges users to follow suit. This highlights the special nature of make variables since almost all other programs that have "dollar variables" (such as shells, perl, awk, yacc, etc.) don't require parentheses. One of the more common make programming errors is forgetting parentheses. Here is a common use of foreach containing the error:

```
INCLUDE_DIRS := …
INCLUDES := $(foreach i,$INCLUDE_DIRS,-I $i)
# INCLUDES now has the value "-I NCLUDE_DIRS"
```

However, I find that reading macros can be much easier through the judicious use of single-character variables and omitting unnecessary parentheses. For instance, I think the has-duplicates function is easier to read without full parentheses:

```
# $(call has-duplicates, word-list)
has-duplicates = $(filter                \
                   $(words $1)           \
                   $(words $(sort $1))))
```

versus:

```
# $(call has-duplicates, word-list)
has-duplicates = $(filter                \
                   $(words $(1))         \
                   $(words $(sort $(1)))))
```

However, the `kill-program` function might be more readable with full parentheses since it would help distinguish make variables from shell variables or variables used in other programs:

```
define kill-program
  @ $(PS) $(PS_FLAGS) |                                    \
  $(AWK) 'BEGIN { FIELDWIDTHS = $(PS_FIELDS) }             \
          /$(1)/{                                          \
                 print "Killing " $$3;                     \
                 system( "$(KILL) $(KILLFLAGS) " $$1 )     \
               }'
endef
```

The search string contains the first parameter to the macro, $(1). $$3 and $$1 refer to awk variables.

I use single-character variables and omit the parentheses only when it seems to make the code more readable. I typically do this for the parameters to macros and the control variable in `foreach` loops. You should follow a style that suits your situation. If you have any doubts about the maintainability of your *makefiles*, follow the make manual's suggestion and use full parentheses. Remember, the make program is all about easing the problems associated with maintaining software. If you keep that in mind as you write your *makefiles*, you will most likely stay clear of trouble.

Less Important Miscellaneous Functions

Finally, we have some miscellaneous (but important) string functions. Although minor in comparison with `foreach` or `call`, you'll find yourself using these very often.

$(strip text)

> The `strip` function removes all leading and trailing whitespace from text and replaces all internal whitespace with a single space. A common use for this function is to clean up variables used in conditional expressions.
>
> I most often use this function to remove unwanted whitespace from variable and macro definitions I've formatted across multiple lines. But it can also be a good idea to wrap the function parameters $1, $2, etc., with `strip` if the function is sensitive to leading blanks. Often programmers unaware of the subtleties of make will add a space after commas in a `call` argument list.

$(origin variable)

> The `origin` function returns a string describing the origin of a variable. This can be very useful in deciding how to use the value of a variable. For instance, you might want to ignore the value of a variable if it came from the environment, but not if it was set from the command line. For a more concrete example, here is a new assert function that tests if a variable is defined:

```
# $(call assert-defined,variable-name)
define assert-defined
  $(call assert,                          \
```

```
    $(filter-out undefined,$(origin $1)), \
      '$1' is undefined)
  endef
```

The possible return values of origin are:

undefined
> The variable has never been defined.

default
> The variable's definition came from make's built-in database. If you alter the value of a built-in variable, origin returns the origin of the most recent definition.

environment
> The variable's definition came from the environment (and the --environment-overrides option is *not* turned on).

environment override
> The variable's definition came from the environment (and the --environment-overrides option *is* turned on).

file
> The variable's definition came from the *makefile*.

command line
> The variable's definition came from the command line.

override
> The variable's definition came from an override directive.

automatic
> The variable is an automatic variable defined by make.

$(warning text)
> The warning function is similar to the error function except that it does not cause make to exit. Like the error function, the output is prefixed with the name of the current *makefile* and the current line number followed by the message text. The warning function expands to the empty string so it can be used almost anywhere.

```
  $(if $(wildcard $(JAVAC)),,                              \
    $(warning The java compiler variable, JAVAC ($(JAVAC)), \
          is not properly set.))
```

Advanced User-Defined Functions

We'll spend a lot of time writing macro functions. Unfortunately, there aren't many features in make for helping to debug them. Let's begin by trying to write a simple debugging trace function to help us out.

As we've mentioned, call will bind each of its parameters to the numbered variables $1, $2, etc. Any number of arguments can be given to call. As a special case, the name of the currently executing function (i.e., the variable name) is accessible through $0. Using this information, we can write a pair of debugging functions for tracing through macro expansion:

```
# $(debug-enter)
debug-enter = $(if $(debug_trace),\
               $(warning Entering $0($(echo-args))))

# $(debug-leave)
debug-leave = $(if $(debug_trace),$(warning Leaving $0))

comma := ,
echo-args   = $(subst ' ','$(comma) ',\
               $(foreach a,1 2 3 4 5 6 7 8 9,'$($a)'))
```

If we want to watch how functions a and b are invoked, we can use these trace functions like this:

```
debug_trace = 1

define a
  $(debug-enter)
  @echo $1 $2 $3
  $(debug-leave)
endef

define b
  $(debug-enter)
  $(call a,$1,$2,hi)
  $(debug-leave)
endef

trace-macro:
        $(call b,5,$(MAKE))
```

By placing debug-enter and debug-leave variables at the start and end of your functions, you can trace the expansions of your own functions. These functions are far from perfect. The echo-args function will echo only the first nine arguments and, worse, it cannot determine the number of actual arguments in the call (of course, neither can make!). Nevertheless, I've used these macros "as is" in my own debugging. When executed, the *makefile* generates this trace output:

```
$ make
makefile:14: Entering b( '5', 'make', '', '', '', '', '', '', '')
makefile:14: Entering a( '5', 'make', 'hi', '', '', '', '', '', '')
makefile:14: Leaving a
makefile:14: Leaving b
5 make hi
```

As a friend said to me recently, "I never thought of *make* as a programming language before." GNU make isn't your grandmother's make!

eval and value

The eval function is completely different from the rest of the built-in functions. Its purpose is to feed text directly to the make parser. For instance,

```
$(eval sources := foo.c bar.c)
```

The argument to eval is first scanned for variables and expanded (as all arguments to all functions are), then the text is parsed and evaluated as if it had come from an input file. This example is so simple you might be wondering why you would bother with this function. Let's try a more interesting example. Suppose you have a *makefile* to compile a dozen programs and you want to define several variables for each program, say sources, headers, and objects. Instead of repeating these variable assignments over and over with each set of variables:

```
ls_sources := ls.c glob.c
ls_headers := ls.h glob.h
ls_objects := ls.o glob.o
...
```

We might try to define a macro to do the job:

```
# $(call program-variables, variable-prefix, file-list)
define program-variables
  $1_sources = $(filter %.c,$2)
  $1_headers = $(filter %.h,$2)
  $1_objects = $(subst .c,.o,$(filter %.c,$2))
endef

$(call program-variables, ls, ls.c ls.h glob.c glob.h)

show-variables:
        # $(ls_sources)
        # $(ls_headers)
        # $(ls_objects)
```

The program-variables macro accepts two arguments: a prefix for the three variables and a file list from which the macro selects files to set in each variable. But, when we try to use this macro, we get the error:

```
$ make
Makefile:7: *** missing separator.  Stop.
```

This doesn't work as expected because of the way the make parser works. A macro (at the top parsing level) that expands to multiple lines is illegal and results in syntax errors. In this case, the parser believes this line is a rule or part of a command script but is missing a separator token. Quite a confusing error message. The eval function was introduced to handle this issue. If we change our call line to:

```
$(eval $(call program-variables, ls, ls.c ls.h glob.c glob.h))
```

we get what we expect:

```
$ make
# ls.c glob.c
```

```
# ls.h glob.h
# ls.o glob.o
```

Using eval resolves the parsing issue because eval handles the multiline macro expansion and itself expands to zero lines.

Now we have a macro that defines three variables very concisely. Notice how the assignments in the macro compose variable names from a prefix passed in to the function and a fixed suffix, $1_sources. These aren't precisely computed variables as described previously, but they have much the same flavor.

Continuing this example, we realize we can also include our rules in the macro:

```
# $(call program-variables,variable-prefix,file-list)
define program-variables
  $1_sources = $(filter %.c,$2)
  $1_headers = $(filter %.h,$2)
  $1_objects = $(subst .c,.o,$(filter %.c,$2))

  $($1_objects): $($1_headers)
endef

ls: $(ls_objects)

$(eval $(call program-variables,ls,ls.c ls.h glob.c glob.h))
```

Notice how these two versions of program-variables illustrate a problem with spaces in function arguments. In the previous version, the simple uses of the two function parameters were immune to leading spaces on the arguments. That is, the code behaved the same regardless of any leading spaces in $1 or $2. The new version, however, introduced the computed variables $($1_objects) and $($1_headers). Now adding a leading space to the first argument to our function (ls) causes the computed variable to begin with a leading space, which expands to nothing because no variable we've defined begins with a leading space. This can be quite an insidious problem to diagnose.

When we run this *makefile*, we discover that somehow the *.h* prerequisites are being ignored by make. To diagnose this problem, we examine make's internal database by running make with its --print-data-base option and we see something strange:

```
$ make --print-database | grep ^ls
ls_headers = ls.h glob.h
ls_sources = ls.c glob.c
ls_objects = ls.o glob.o
ls.c:
ls.o: ls.c
ls: ls.o
```

The *.h* prerequisites for *ls.o* are missing! There is something wrong with the rule using computed variables.

When make parses the eval function call, it first expands the user-defined function, program-variables. The first line of the macro expands to:

```
ls_sources = ls.c glob.c
```

Notice that each line of the macro is expanded immediately as expected. The other variable assignments are handled similarly. Then we get to the rule:

```
$($1_objects): $($1_headers)
```

The computed variables first have their variable name expanded:

```
$(ls_objects): $(ls_headers)
```

Then the outer variable expansion is performed, yielding:

```
:
```

Wait! Where did our variables go? The answer is that the previous three assignment statements were expanded *but not evaluated* by make. Let's keep going to see how this works. Once the call to program-variables has been expanded, make sees something like:

```
$(eval   ls_sources = ls.c glob.c
ls_headers = ls.h glob.h
ls_objects = ls.o glob.o

:)
```

The eval function then executes and defines the three variables. So, the answer is that the variables in the rule are being expanded before they have actually been defined.

We can resolve this problem by explicitly deferring the expansion of the computed variables until the three variables are defined. We can do this by quoting the dollar signs in front of the computed variables:

```
$$($1_objects): $$($1_headers)
```

This time the make database shows the prerequisites we expect:

```
$ make -p | grep ^ls
ls_headers = ls.h glob.h
ls_sources = ls.c glob.c
ls_objects = ls.o glob.o
ls.c:
ls.o: ls.c ls.h glob.h
ls: ls.o
```

To summarize, the argument to eval is expanded *twice*: once when when make prepares the argument list for eval, and once again by eval.

We resolved the last problem by deferring evaluation of the computed variables. Another way of handling the problem is to force early evaluation of the variable assignments by wrapping each one with eval:

```
# $(call program-variables,variable-prefix,file-list)
define program-variables
```

```
  $(eval $1_sources = $(filter %.c,$2))
  $(eval $1_headers = $(filter %.h,$2))
  $(eval $1_objects = $(subst .c,.o,$(filter %.c,$2)))

  $($1_objects): $($1_headers)
endef

ls: $(ls_objects)

$(eval $(call program-variables,ls,ls.c ls.h glob.c glob.h))
```

By wrapping the variable assignments in their own eval calls, we cause them to be internalized by make while the program-variables macro is being expanded. They are then available for use within the macro immediately.

As we enhance our *makefile*, we realize we have another rule we can add to our macro. The program itself depends on its objects. So, to finish our parameterized *makefile*, we add a top-level *all* target and need a variable to hold all the programs our *makefile* can manage:

```
#$(call program-variables,variable-prefix,file-list)
define program-variables
  $(eval $1_sources = $(filter %.c,$2))
  $(eval $1_headers = $(filter %.h,$2))
  $(eval $1_objects = $(subst .c,.o,$(filter %.c,$2)))

  programs += $1

  $1: $($1_objects)

  $($1_objects): $($1_headers)
endef

# Place all target here, so it is the default goal.
all:

$(eval $(call program-variables,ls,ls.c ls.h glob.c glob.h))
$(eval $(call program-variables,cp,...))
$(eval $(call program-variables,mv,...))
$(eval $(call program-variables,ln,...))
$(eval $(call program-variables,rm,...))

# Place the programs prerequisite here where it is defined.
all: $(programs)
```

Notice the placement of the all target and its prerequisite. The programs variable is not properly defined until after the five eval calls, but we would like to place the all target first in the *makefile* so all is the default goal. We can satisfy all our constrains by putting all first and adding the prerequisites later.

The program-variables function had problems because some variables were evaluated too early. make actually offers a value function to help address this situation. The value function returns the value of its variable argument *unexpanded*. This unexpanded value can then be passed to eval for processing. By returning an unexpanded value, we can avoid the problem of having to quote some of the variable references in our macros.

Unfortunately, this function cannot be used with the program-variables macro. That's because value is an all-or-nothing function. If used, value will not expand *any* of the variables in the macro. Furthermore, value doesn't accept parameters (and wouldn't do anything with them if it did) so our program name and file list parameters wouldn't be expanded.

Because of these limitations, you won't see value used very often in this book.

Hooking Functions

User-defined functions are just variables holding text. The call function will expand $1, $2, etc. references in the variable text if they exist. If the function doesn't contain any of these variable references, call doesn't care. In fact, if the variable doesn't contain any text, call doesn't care. No error or warning occurs. This can be very frustrating if you happen to misspell a function name. But it can also be very useful.

Functions are all about reusable code. The more often you reuse a function, the more worthwhile it is to write it well. Functions can be made more reusable by adding *hooks* to them. A *hook* is a function reference that can be redefined by a user to perform their own custom tasks during a standard operation.

Suppose you are building many libraries in your *makefile*. On some systems, you'd like to run ranlib and on others you might want to run chmod. Rather than writing explicit commands for these operations, you might choose to write a function and add a hook:

```
# $(call build-library, object-files)
define build-library
  $(AR) $(ARFLAGS) $@ $1
  $(call build-library-hook,$@)
endef
```

To use the hook, define the function build-library-hook:

```
$(foo_lib): build-library-hook = $(RANLIB) $1
$(foo_lib): $(foo_objects)
        $(call build-library,$^)

$(bar_lib): build-library-hook = $(CHMOD) 444 $1
$(bar_lib): $(bar_objects)
        $(call build-library,$^)
```

Passing Parameters

A function can get its data from four "sources": parameters passed in using call, global variables, automatic variables, and target-specific variables. Of these, relying on parameters is the most modular choice, since their use insulates the function from any changes to global data, but sometimes that isn't the most important criteria.

Suppose we have several projects using a common set of make functions. Each project might be identified by a variable prefix, say PROJECT1_, and critical variables for the project all use the prefix with cross-project suffixes. The earlier example, PROJECT_SRC, might look like PROJECT1_SRC, PROJECT1_BIN, and PROJECT1_LIB. Rather than write a function that requires these three variables we could instead use computed variables and pass a single argument, the prefix:

```
# $(call process-xml,project-prefix,file-name)
define process-xml
  $($1_LIB)/xmlto -o $($1_BIN)/xml/$2 $($1_SRC)/xml/$2
endef
```

Another approach to passing arguments uses target-specific variables. This is particularly useful when most invocations use a standard value but a few require special processing. Target-specific variables also provide flexibility when the rule is defined in an include file, but invoked from a *makefile* where the variable is defined.

```
release: MAKING_RELEASE = 1
release: libraries executables

...
$(foo_lib):
        $(call build-library,$^)

...
# $(call build-library, file-list)
define build-library
  $(AR) $(ARFLAGS) $@           \
    $(if $(MAKING_RELEASE),     \
      $(filter-out debug/%,$1), \
      $1)
endef
```

This code sets a target-specific variable to indicate when a release build is being executed. In that case, the library-building function will filter out any debugging modules from the libraries.

CHAPTER 5

Commands

We've already covered many of the basic elements of make commands, but just to make sure we're all on the same page, let's review a little.

Commands are essentially one-line shell scripts. In effect, make grabs each line and passes it to a subshell for execution. In fact, make can optimize this (relatively) expensive fork/exec algorithm if it can guarantee that omitting the shell will not change the behavior of the program. It checks this by scanning each command line for shell special characters, such as wildcard characters and i/o redirection. If none are found, make directly executes the command without passing it to a subshell.

By default, */bin/sh* is used for the shell. This shell is controlled by the make variable SHELL but it is not inherited from the environment. When make starts, it imports all the variables from the user's environment as make variables, except SHELL. This is because the user's choice of shell should not cause a *makefile* (possibly included in some downloaded software package) to fail. If a user really wants to change the default shell used by make, he can set the SHELL variable explicitly in the *makefile*. We will discuss this issue in the section "Which Shell to Use" later in this chapter.

Parsing Commands

Following a make target, lines whose first character is a tab are assumed to be commands (unless the previous line was continued with a backslash). GNU make tries to be as smart as possible when handling tabs in other contexts. For instance, when there is no possible ambiguity, comments, variable assignments, and include directives may all use a tab as their first character. If make reads a command line that does not immediately follow a target, an error message is displayed:

```
makefile:20: *** commands commence before first target.  Stop.
```

The wording of this message is a bit odd because it often occurs in the middle of a *makefile* long after the "first" target was specified, but we can now understand it without too much trouble. A better wording for this message might be, "encountered a command outside the context of a target."

When the parser sees a command in a legal context, it switches to "command parsing" mode, building the script one line at a time. It stops appending to the script when it encounters a line that cannot possibly be part of the command script. There the script ends. The following may appear in a command script:

- Lines beginning with a tab character are commands that will be executed by a subshell. Even lines that would normally be interpreted as make constructs (e.g., ifdef, comments, include directives) are treated as commands while in "command parsing" mode.

- Blank lines are ignored. They are not "executed" by a subshell.

- Lines beginning with a #, possibly with leading spaces (not tabs!), are *makefile* comments and are ignored.

- Conditional processing directives, such as ifdef and ifeq, are recognized and processed normally within command scripts.

Built-in make functions terminate command parsing mode unless preceded by a tab character. This means they must expand to valid shell commands or to nothing. The functions warning and eval expand to no characters.

The fact that blank lines and make comments are allowed in command scripts can be surprising at first. The following lines show how it is carried out:

```
long-command:
        @echo Line 2: A blank line follows

        @echo Line 4: A shell comment follows
        # A shell comment (leading tab)
        @echo Line 6: A make comment follows
# A make comment, at the beginning of a line
        @echo Line 8: Indented make comments follow
  # A make comment, indented with leading spaces
        # Another make comment, indented with leading spaces
        @echo Line 11: A conditional follows
    ifdef COMSPEC
        @echo Running Windows
    endif
        @echo Line 15: A warning "command" follows
        $(warning A warning)
        @echo Line 17: An eval "command" follows
        $(eval $(shell echo Shell echo 1>&2))
```

Notice that lines 5 and 10 appear identical, but are quite different. Line 5 is a shell comment, indicated by a leading tab, while line 10 is a make comment indented eight spaces. Obviously, we do not recommend formatting make comments this way (unless you intend entering an obfuscated *makefile* contest). As you can see in the following output, make comments are not executed and are not echoed to the output even though they occur within the context of a command script:

```
$ make
makefile:2: A warning
Shell echo
Line 2: A blank line follows
Line 4: A shell comment follows
# A shell comment (leading tab)
Line 6: A make comment follows
Line 8: Indented make comments follow
Line 11: A conditional follows
Running Windows
Line 15: A warning command follows
Line 17: An eval command follows
```

The output of the warning and eval functions appears to be out of order, but don't worry, it isn't. (We'll discuss the order of evaluation later this chapter in the section "Evaluating Commands.") The fact that command scripts can contain any number of blank lines and comments can be a frustrating source of errors. Suppose you accidentally introduce a line with a leading tab. If a previous target (with or without commands) exists and you have only comments or blank lines intervening, make will treat your accidental tabbed line as a command associated with the preceding target. As you've seen, this is perfectly legal and will not generate a warning or error unless the same target has a rule somewhere else in the *makefile* (or one of its include files).

If you're lucky, your *makefile* will include a nonblank, noncomment between your accidental tabbed line and the previous command script. In that case, you'll get the "commands commence before first target" message.

Now is a good time to briefly mention software tools. I think everyone agrees, now, that using a leading tab to indicate a command line was an unfortunate decision, but it's a little late to change. Using a modern, syntax-aware editor can help head off potential problems by visibly marking dubious constructs. GNU emacs has a very nice mode for editing *makefiles*. This mode performs syntax highlighting and looks for simple syntactic errors, such as spaces after continuation lines and mixing leading spaces and tabs. I'll talk more about using emacs and make later on.

Continuing Long Commands

Since each command is executed in its own shell (or at least *appears* to be), sequences of shell commands that need to be run together must be handled specially. For instance, suppose I need to generate a file containing a list of files. The Java compiler accepts such a file for compiling many source files. I might write a command script like this:

```
.INTERMEDIATE: file_list
file_list:
        for d in logic ui
```

```
        do
          echo $d/*.java
        done > $@
```

By now it should be clear that this won't work. It generates the error:

```
$ make
for d in logic ui
/bin/sh: -c: line 2: syntax error: unexpected end of file
make: *** [file_list] Error 2
```

Our first fix is to add continuation characters to each line:

```
.INTERMEDIATE: file_list
file_list:
        for d in logic ui      \
        do                     \
          echo $d/*.java       \
        done > $@
```

which generates the error:

```
$ make
for d in logic ui      \
do                     \
  echo /*.java \
done > file_list
/bin/sh: -c: line 1: syntax error near unexpected token `>'
/bin/sh: -c: line 1: `for d in logic ui  do                       echo /*.java
make: *** [file_list] Error 2
```

What happened? Two problems. First, the reference to the loop control variable, d, needs to be escaped. Second, since the for loop is passed to the subshell as a single line, we must add semicolon separators after the file list and for-loop statement:

```
.INTERMEDIATE: file_list
file_list:
        for d in logic ui;     \
        do                     \
          echo $$d/*.java;     \
        done > $@
```

Now we get the file we expect. The target is declared .INTERMEDIATE so that make will delete this temporary target after the compile is complete.

In a more realistic example, the list of directories would be stored in a make variable. If we are sure that the number of files is relatively small, we can perform this same operation without a for loop by using make functions:

```
.INTERMEDIATE: file_list
file_list:
        echo $(addsuffix /*.java,$(COMPILATION_DIRS)) > $@
```

But the for-loop version is less likely to run up against command-line length issues if we expect the list of directories to grow with time.

Another common problem in make command scripts is how to switch directories. Again, it should be clear that a simple command script like:

```
TAGS:
        cd src
        ctags --recurse
```

will not execute the ctags program in the *src* subdirectory. To get the effect we want, we must either place both commands on a single line or escape the newline with a backslash (and separate the commands with a semicolon):

```
TAGS:
        cd src;         \
        ctags --recurse
```

An even better version would check the status of the cd before executing the ctags program:

```
TAGS:
        cd src &&        \
        ctags --recurse
```

Notice that in some circumstances omitting the semicolon might not produce a make or shell error:

```
disk-free = echo "Checking free disk space..." \
            df . | awk '{ print $$4 }'
```

This example prints a simple message followed by the number of free blocks on the current device. Or does it? We have accidentally omitted the semicolon after the echo command, so we never actually run the df program. Instead, we echo:

```
Checking free disk space... df .
```

into awk which dutifully prints the fourth field, space....

It might have occurred to you to use the define directive, which is intended for creating multiline command sequences, rather than continuation lines. Unfortunately, this isn't quite the same problem. When a multiline macro is expanded, each line is inserted into the command script with a leading tab and make treats each line independently. The lines of the macro are not executed in a single subshell. So you will need to pay attention to command-line continuation in macros as well.

Command Modifiers

A command can be modified by several prefixes. We've already seen the "silent" prefix, @, used many times before. The complete list of prefixes, along with some gory details, are:

@   Do not echo the command. For historical compatibility, you can make your target a prerequisite of the special target .SILENT if you want all of its commands to be hidden. Using @ is preferred, however, because it can be applied to individual commands within a command script. If you want to apply this modifier to all targets (although it is hard to imagine why), you can use the --silent (or -s) option.

Hiding commands can make the output of make easier on the eyes, but it can also make debugging the commands more difficult. If you find yourself removing the @ modifiers and restoring them frequently, you might create a variable, say QUIET, containing the @ modifier and use that on commands:

```
QUIET = @
hairy_script:
        $(QUIET) complex script …
```

Then, if you need to see the complex script as make runs it, just reset the QUIET variable from the command line:

```
$ make QUIET= hairy_script
complex script …
```

- The dash prefix indicates that errors in the command should be ignored by make. By default, when make executes a command, it examines the exit status of the program or pipeline, and if a nonzero (failure) exit status is returned, make terminates execution of the remainder of the command script and exits. This modifier directs make to ignore the exit status of the modified line and continue as if no error occurred. We'll discuss this topic in more depth in the next section.

  For historical compatibility, you can ignore errors in any part of a command script by making the target a prerequisite of the .IGNORE special target. If you want to ignore all errors in the entire *makefile,* you can use the --ignore-errors (or -i) option. Again, this doesn't seem too useful.

+ The plus modifier tells make to execute the command even if the --just-print (or -n) command-line option is given to make. It is used when writing recursive *makefiles.* We'll discuss this topic in more detail in the section "Recursive make" in Chapter 6.

Any or all of these modifiers are allowed on a single line. Obviously, the modifiers are stripped before the commands are executed.

Errors and Interrupts

Every command that make executes returns a status code. A status of zero indicates that the command succeeded. A status of nonzero indicates some kind of failure. Some programs use the return status code to indicate something more meaningful than simply "error." For instance, grep returns 0 (success) if a match is found, 1 if no match is found, and 2 if some kind of error occurred.

Normally, when a program fails (i.e., returns a nonzero exit status), make stops executing commands and exits with an error status. Sometimes you want make to continue, trying to complete as many targets as possible. For instance, you might want to compile as many files as possible to see all the compilation errors in a single run. You can do this with the --keep-going (or -k) option.

Although the - modifier causes make to ignore errors in individual commands, I try to avoid its use whenever possible. This is because it complicates automated error processing and is visually jarring.

When make ignores an error it prints a warning along with the name of the target in square brackets. For example, here is the output when rm tries to delete a nonexistent file:

```
rm non-existent-file
rm: cannot remove `non-existent-file': No such file or directory
make: [clean] Error 1 (ignored)
```

Some commands, like rm, have options that suppress their error exit status. The -f option will force rm to return success while also suppressing error messages. Using such options is better than depending on a preceding dash.

Occasionally, you want a command to fail and would like to get an error if the program succeeds. For these situations, you should be able to simply negate the exit status of the program:

```
# Verify there are no debug statements left in the code.
.PHONY: no_debug_printf
no_debug_printf: $(sources)
        ! grep --line-number '"debug:' $^
```

Unfortunately, there is a bug in make 3.80 that prevents this straightforward use. make does not recognize the ! character as requiring shell processing and executes the command line itself, resulting in an error. In this case, a simple work around is to add a shell special character as a clue to make:

```
# Verify there are no debug statement left in the code
.PHONY: no_debug_printf
no_debug_printf: $(sources)
        ! grep --line-number '"debug:' $^ < /dev/null
```

Another common source of unexpected command errors is using the shell's if construct without an else.

```
$(config): $(config_template)
        if [ ! -d $(dir $@) ];    \
        then                      \
          $(MKDIR) $(dir $@);     \
        fi
        $(M4) $^ > $@
```

The first command tests if the output directory exists and calls mkdir to create it if it does not. Unfortunately, if the directory does exist, the if command returns a failure exit status (the exit status of the test), which terminates the script. One solution is to add an else clause:

```
$(config): $(config_template)
        if [ ! -d $(dir $@) ];    \
        then                      \
          $(MKDIR) $(dir $@);     \
```

```
        else                    \
          true;                 \
        fi
        $(M4) $^ > $@
```

In the shell, the colon (:) is a no-op command that always returns true, and can be used instead of true. An alternative implementation that works well here is:

```
$(config): $(config_template)
        [[ -d $(dir $@) ]] || $(MKDIR) $(dir $@)
        $(M4) $^ > $@
```

Now the first statement is true when the directory exists or when the mkdir succeeds. Another alternative is to use mkdir -p. This allows mkdir to succeed even when the directory already exists. All these implementations execute something in a subshell even when the directory exists. By using wildcard, we can omit the execution entirely if the directory is present.

```
# $(call make-dir, directory)
make-dir = $(if $(wildcard $1),,$(MKDIR) -p $1)

$(config): $(config_template)
        $(call make-dir, $(dir $@))
        $(M4) $^ > $@
```

Because each command is executed in its own shell, it is common to have multiline commands with each component separated by semicolons. Be aware that errors within these scripts may not terminate the script:

```
target:
        rm rm-fails; echo But the next command executes anyway
```

It is best to minimize the length of command scripts and give make a chance to manage exit status and termination for you. For instance:

```
path-fixup = -e "s;[a-zA-Z:/]*/src/;$(SOURCE_DIR)/;g" \
             -e "s;[a-zA-Z:/]*/bin/;$(OUTPUT_DIR)/;g"

# A good version.
define fix-project-paths
  sed $(path-fixup) $1 > $2.fixed && \
  mv $2.fixed $2
endef

# A better version.
define fix-project-paths
  sed $(path-fixup) $1 > $2.fixed
  mv $2.fixed $2
endef
```

This macro transforms DOS-style paths (with forward slashes) into destination paths for a particular source and output tree. The macro accepts two filenames, the input and output files. It is careful to overwrite the output file only if the sed command completes correctly. The "good" version does this by connecting the sed and mv with

&& so they execute in a single shell. The "better" version executes them as two separate commands, letting make terminate the script if the sed fails. The "better" version is no more expensive (the mv doesn't need a shell and is executed directly), is easier to read, and provides more information when errors occur (because make will indicate which command failed).

Note that this is a different issue than the common problem with cd:

```
TAGS:
        cd src && \
        ctags --recurse
```

In this case, the two statements must be executed within the same subshell. Therefore, the commands must be separated by some kind of statement connector, such as ; or &&.

Deleting and preserving target files

If an error occurs, make assumes that the target cannot be remade. Any other targets that have the current target as a prerequisite also cannot be remade, so make will not attempt them nor execute any part of their command scripts. If the --keep-going (or -k) option is used, the next goal will be attempted; otherwise, make exits. If the current target is a file, it may be corrupt if the command exits before finishing its work. Unfortunately, for reasons of historical compatibility, make will leave this potentially corrupt file on disk. Because the file's timestamp has been updated, subsequent executions of make may not update the file with correct data. You can avoid this problem and cause make to delete these questionable files when an error occurs by making the target file a prerequisite of .DELETE_ON_ERROR. If .DELETE_ON_ERROR is used with no prerequisites, errors in any target file build will cause make to delete the target.

A complementary problem occurs when make is interrupted by a signal, such as a Ctrl-C. In this case, make deletes the current target file if the file has been modified. Sometimes deleting the file is the wrong thing to do. Perhaps the file is very expensive to create and partial contents are better than none, or perhaps the file must exist for other parts of the build to proceed. In these cases, you can protect the file by making it a prerequisite of the special target .PRECIOUS.

Which Shell to Use

When make needs to pass a command line to a subshell, it uses /bin/sh. You can change the shell by setting the make variable SHELL. Think carefully before doing this. Usually, the purpose of using make is to provide a tool for a community of developers to build a system from its source components. It is quite easy to create a *makefile* that fails in this goal by using tools that are not available or assumptions that are not true for other developers in the community. It is considered very bad form to use any shell other than */bin/sh* in any widely distributed application (one distributed via anonymous ftp or open cvs). We'll discuss portability in more detail in Chapter 7.

There is another context for using make, however. Often, in closed development environments, the developers are working on a limited set of machines and operating systems with an approved group of developers. In fact, this is the environment I've most often found myself in. In this situation, it can make perfect sense to customize the environment make is expected to run under. Developers are instructed in how to set up their environment to work properly with the build and life goes on.

In environments such as this, I prefer to make some portability sacrifices "up front." I believe this can make the entire development process go much more smoothly. One such sacrifice is to explicitly set the SHELL variable to */usr/bin/bash*. The bash shell is a portable, POSIX-compliant shell (and, therefore, a superset of sh) and is the standard shell on GNU/Linux. Many portability problems in *makefiles* are due to using nonportable constructs in command scripts. This can be solved by explicitly using one standard shell rather than writing to the portable subset of sh. Paul Smith, the maintainer of GNU make, has a web page "Paul's Rules of Makefiles" (*http://make. paulandlesley.org/rules.html*) on which he states, "Don't hassle with writing portable makefiles, use a portable *make* instead!" I would also say, "Where possible, don't hassle with writing portable command scripts, use a portable shell (bash) instead." The bash shell runs on most operating systems including virtually all variants of Unix, Windows, BeOS, Amiga, and OS/2.

For the remainder of this book, I will note when a command script uses bash-specific features.

Empty Commands

An *empty command* is one that does nothing.

```
header.h: ;
```

Recall that the prerequisites list for a target can be followed by a semicolon and the command. Here a semicolon with nothing after it indicates that there are no commands. You could instead follow the target with a line containing only a tab, but that would be impossible to read. Empty commands are most often used to prevent a pattern rule from matching the target and executing commands you don't want.

Note that in other versions of make, empty targets are sometimes used as phony targets. In GNU make, use the .PHONY special target instead; it's safer and clearer.

Command Environment

Commands executed by make inherit their processing environment from make itself. This environment includes the current working directory, file descriptors, and the environment variables passed by make.

When a subshell is created, make adds a few variables to the environment:

```
MAKEFLAGS
MFLAGS
MAKELEVEL
```

The MAKEFLAGS variable includes the command-line options passed to make. The MFLAGS variable mirrors MAKEFLAGS and exists for historical reasons. The MAKELEVEL variable indicates the number of nested make invocations. That is, when make recursively invokes make, the MAKELEVEL variable increases by one. Subprocesses of a single parent make will have a MAKELEVEL of one. These variables are typically used for managing recursive make. We'll discuss them in the section "Recursive make" in Chapter 6.

Of course, the user can add whatever variables they like to the subprocess environment with the use of the export directive.

The current working directory for an executed command is the working directory of the parent make. This is typically the same as the directory the make program was executed from, but can be changed with the the --directory=*directory* (or -C) command-line option. Note that simply specifying a different *makefile* using --file does not change the current directory, only the *makefile* read.

Each subprocess make spawns inherits the three standard file descriptors: *stdin*, *stdout*, and *stderr*. This is not particularly noteworthy except to observe that it is possible for a command script to read its *stdin*. This is "reasonable" and works. Once the script completes its read, the remaining commands are executed as expected. But *makefiles* are generally expected to run without this kind of interaction. Users often expect to be able to start a make and "walk away" from the process, returning later to examine the results. Of course, reading the *stdin* will also tend to interact poorly with cron-based automated builds.

A common error in *makefiles* is to read the *stdin* accidentally:

```
$(DATA_FILE): $(RAW_DATA)
        grep pattern $(RAW_DATA_FILES) > $@
```

Here the input file to grep is specified with a variable (misspelled in this example). If the variable expands to nothing, the grep is left to read the *stdin* with no prompt or indication of why the make is "hanging." A simple way around this issue is to always include */dev/null* on the command line as an additional "file":

```
$(DATA_FILE): $(RAW_DATA)
        grep pattern $(RAW_DATA_FILES) /dev/null > $@
```

This grep command will never attempt to read *stdin*. Of course, debugging the *makefile* is also appropriate!

Evaluating Commands

Command script processing occurs in four steps: read the code, expand variables, evaluate make expressions, and execute commands. Let's see how these steps apply to a complex command script. Consider this (somewhat contrived) *makefile*. An application is linked, then optionally stripped of symbols and compressed using the upx executable packer:

```
# $(call strip-program, file)
define strip-program
  strip $1
endef

complex_script:
        $(CC) $^ -o $@
    ifdef STRIP
        $(call strip-program, $@)
    endif
        $(if $(PACK), upx --best $@)
        $(warning Final size: $(shell ls -s $@))
```

The evaluation of command scripts is deferred until they are executed, but ifdef directives are processed immediately wherever they occur. Therefore, make reads the command script, ignoring the content and storing each line until it gets to the line ifdef STRIP. It evaluates the test and, if STRIP is not defined, make reads and discards all the text up to and including the closing endif. make then continues reading and storing the rest of the script.

When a command script is to be executed, make first scans the script for make constructs that need to be expanded or evaluated. When macros are expanded, a leading tab is prepended to each line. Expanding and evaluating before any commands are executed can lead to an unexpected execution order if you aren't prepared for it. In our example, the last line of the script is wrong. The shell and warning commands are executed *before* linking the application. Therefore, the ls command will be executed before the file it is examining has been updated. This explains the "out of order" output seen earlier in the section "Parsing Commands."

Also, notice that the ifdef STRIP line is evaluated while reading the file, but the $(if...) line is evaluated immediately before the commands for complex_script are executed. Using the if function is more flexible since there are more opportunities to control when the variable is defined, but it is not very well suited for managing large blocks of text.

As this example shows, it is important to always attend to what program is evaluating an expression (e.g., make or the shell) and when the evaluation is performed:

```
$(LINK.c) $(shell find $(if $(ALL),$(wildcard core ext*),core) -name '*.o')
```

This convoluted command script attempts to link a set of object files. The sequence of evaluation and the program performing the operation (in parentheses) is:

1. Expand $ALL (make).
2. Evaluate if (make).
3. Evaluate the wildcard, assuming ALL is not empty (make).
4. Evaluate the shell (make).
5. Execute the find (sh).
6. After completing the expansion and evaluation of the make constructs, execute the link command (sh).

Command-Line Limits

When working with large projects, you occasionally bump up against limitations in the length of commands make tries to execute. Command-line limits vary widely with the operating system. Red Hat 9 GNU/Linux appears to have a limit of about 128K characters, while Windows XP has a limit of 32K. The error message generated also varies. On Windows using the Cygwin port, the message is:

```
C:\usr\cygwin\bin\bash: /usr/bin/ls: Invalid argument
```

when ls is given too long an argument list. On Red Hat 9 the message is:

```
/bin/ls: argument list too long
```

Even 32K sounds like a lot of data for a command line, but when your project contains 3,000 files in 100 subdirectories and you want to manipulate them all, this limit can be constraining.

There are two basic ways to get yourself into this mess: expand some basic value using shell tools, or use make itself to set a variable to a very long value. For example, suppose we want to compile all our source files in a single command line:

```
compile_all:
        $(JAVAC) $(wildcard $(addsuffix /*.java,$(source_dirs)))
```

The make variable source_dirs may contain only a couple hundred words, but after appending the wildcard for Java files and expanding it using wildcard, this list can easily exceed the command-line limit of the system. By the way, make has no built-in limits to constrain us. So long as there is virtual memory available, make will allow any amount of data you care to create.

When you find yourself in this situation, it can feel like the old Adventure game, "You are in a twisty maze of passages all alike." For instance, you might try to solve the above using xargs, since xargs will manage long command lines by parceling out arguments up to the system-specific length:

```
compile_all:
        echo $(wildcard $(addsuffix /*.java,$(source_dirs))) | \
        xargs $(JAVAC)
```

Unfortunately, we've just moved the command-line limit problem from the `javac` command line to the `echo` command line. Similarly, we cannot use `echo` or `printf` to write the data to a file (assuming the compiler can read the file list from a file).

No, the way to handle this situation is to avoid creating the file list all at once in the first place. Instead, use the shell to glob one directory at a time:

```
compile_all:
        for d in $(source_dirs); \
        do                       \
            $(JAVAC) $$d/*.java;  \
        done
```

We could also pipe the file list to `xargs` to perform the task with fewer executions:

```
compile_all:
        for d in $(source_dirs); \
        do                       \
            echo $$d/*.java;     \
        done |                   \
        xargs $(JAVAC)
```

Sadly, neither of these command scripts handle errors during compilation properly. A better approach would be to save the full file list and feed it to the compiler, if the compiler supports reading its arguments from a file. Java compilers support this feature:

```
compile_all: $(FILE_LIST)
        $(JAVA) @$<

.INTERMEDIATE: $(FILE_LIST)
$(FILE_LIST):
        for d in $(source_dirs); \
        do                       \
            echo $$d/*.java;     \
        done > $@
```

Notice the subtle error in the `for` loop. If any of the directories does not contain a Java file, the string `*.java` will be included in the file list and the Java compiler will generate a "File not found" error. We can make `bash` collapse empty globbing patterns by setting the `nullglob` option.

```
compile_all: $(FILE_LIST)
        $(JAVA) @$<

.INTERMEDIATE: $(FILE_LIST)
$(FILE_LIST):
        shopt -s nullglob;       \
        for d in $(source_dirs); \
        do                       \
            echo $$d/*.java;     \
        done > $@
```

Many projects have to make lists of files. Here is a macro containing a `bash` script producing file lists. The first argument is the root directory to change to. All the files

in the list will be relative to this root directory. The second argument is a list of directories to search for matching files. The third and fourth arguments are optional and
represent file suffixes.

```
# $(call collect-names, root-dir, dir-list, suffix1-opt, suffix2-opt)
define collect-names
  echo Making $@ from directory list...
  cd $1;                                                      \
  shopt -s nullglob;                                          \
  for f in $(foreach file,$2,'$(file)'); do                  \
    files=( $$f$(if $3,/*.{$3$(if $4,$(comma)$4)}) );         \
    if (( $${#files[@]} > 0 ));                               \
    then                                                      \
      printf '"%s"\n' $${files[@]};                           \
    else :; fi;                                               \
  done
endef
```

Here is a pattern rule for creating a list of image files:

```
%.images:
        @$(call collect-names,$(SOURCE_DIR),$^,gif,jpeg) > $@
```

The macro execution is hidden because the script is long and there is seldom a reason to cut and paste this code. The directory list is provided in the prerequisites.
After changing to the root directory, the script enables null globbing. The rest is a for
loop to process each directory we want to search. The file search expression is a list
of words passed in parameter $2. The script protects words in the file list with single
quotes because they may contain shell-special characters. In particular, filenames in
languages like Java can contain dollar signs:

```
for f in $(foreach file,$2,'$(file)'); do
```

We search a directory by filling the files array with the result of globbing. If the
files array contains any elements, we use printf to write each word followed by a
newline. Using the array allows the macro to properly handle paths with embedded
spaces. This is also the reason printf surrounds the filename with double quotes.

The file list is produced with the line:

```
files=( $$f$(if $3,/*.{$3$(if $4,$(comma)$4)}) );
```

The $$f is the directory or file argument to the macro. The following expression is a
make if testing whether the third argument is nonempty. This is how you can imple-
ment optional arguments. If the third argument is empty, it is assumed the fourth is
as well. In this case, the file passed by the user should be included in the file list as is.
This allows the macro to build lists of arbitrary files for which wildcard patterns are
inappropriate. If the third argument is provided, the if appends /*.{$3} to the root
file. If the fourth argument is provided, it appends ,$4 after the $3. Notice the subter-
fuge we must use to insert a comma into the wildcard pattern. By placing a comma
in a make variable we can sneak it past the parser, otherwise, the comma would be

interpreted as separating the *then* part from the *else* part of the if. The definition of comma is straightforward:

```
comma := ,
```

All the preceding for loops also suffer from the command-line length limit, since they use wildcard expansion. The difference is that the wildcard is expanded with the contents of a single directory, which is far less likely to exceed the limits.

What do we do if a make variable contains our long file list? Well, then we are in real trouble. There are only two ways I've found to pass a very long make variable to a subshell. The first approach is to pass only a subset of the variable contents to any one subshell invocation by filtering the contents.

```
compile_all:
        $(JAVAC) $(wordlist 1, 499, $(all-source-files))
        $(JAVAC) $(wordlist 500, 999, $(all-source-files))
        $(JAVAC) $(wordlist 1000, 1499, $(all-source-files))
```

The filter function can be used as well, but that can be more uncertain since the number of files selected will depend on the distribution within the pattern space chosen. Here we choose a pattern based on the alphabet:

```
compile_all:
        $(JAVAC) $(filter a%, $(all-source-files))
        $(JAVAC) $(filter b%, $(all-source-files))
```

Other patterns might use special characteristics of the filenames themselves.

Notice that it is difficult to automate this further. We could try to wrap the alphabet approach in a foreach loop:

```
compile_all:
        $(foreach l,a b c d e ...,                        \
          $(if $(filter $l%, $(all-source-files)),        \
            $(JAVAC) $(filter $l%, $(all-source-files));))
```

but this doesn't work. make expands this into a single line of text, thus compounding the line-length problem. We can instead use eval:

```
compile_all:
        $(foreach l,a b c d e ...,                   \
          $(if $(filter $l%, $(all-source-files)), \
            $(eval                                   \
              $(shell                                \
                $(JAVAC) $(filter $l%, $(all-source-files));))))
```

This works because eval will execute the shell command immediately, expanding to nothing. So the foreach loop expands to nothing. The problem is that error reporting is meaningless in this context, so compilation errors will not be transmitted to make correctly.

The wordlist approach is worse. Due to make's limited numerical capabilities, there is no way to enclose the wordlist technique in a loop. In general, there are very few satisfying ways to deal with immense file lists.

## PART II

Advanced and Specialized Topics

In Part II, we take a problem-oriented view of make. It is often not obvious how to apply make to real-world problems such as multidirectory builds, new programming languages, portability and performance issues, or debugging. Each of these problems is discussed, along with a chapter covering several complex examples.

## CHAPTER 6

Managing Large Projects

What do you call a large project? For our purposes, it is one that requires a team of developers, may run on multiple architectures, and may have several field releases that require maintenance. Of course, not all of these are required to call a project large. A million lines of prerelease C++ on a single platform is still large. But software rarely stays prerelease forever. And if it is successful, someone will eventually ask for it on another platform. So most large software systems wind up looking very similar after awhile.

Large software projects are usually simplified by dividing them into major components, often collected into distinct programs, libraries, or both. These components are often stored under their own directories and managed by their own *makefiles*. One way to build an entire system of components employs a top-level *makefile* that invokes the *makefile* for each component in the proper order. This approach is called *recursive make* because the top-level *makefile* invokes make recursively on each component's *makefile*. Recursive make is a common technique for handling component-wise builds. An alternative suggested by Peter Miller in 1998 avoids many issues with recursive make by using a single *makefile* that includes information from each component directory.[*]

Once a project gets beyond building its components, it eventually finds that there are larger organizational issues in managing builds. These include handling development on multiple versions of a project, supporting several platforms, providing efficient access to source and binaries, and performing automated builds. We will discuss these problems in the second half of this chapter.

---

[*] Miller, P.A., *Recursive Make Considered Harmful*, AUUGN Journal of AUUG Inc., 19(1), pp. 14–25 (1998). Also available from *http://aegis.sourceforge.net/auug97.pdf*.

Recursive make

The motivation behind recursive make is simple: make works very well within a sin-gle directory (or small set of directories) but becomes more complex when the num-ber of directories grows. So, we can use make to build a large project by writing a simple, self-contained *makefile* for each directory, then executing them all individu-ally. We could use a scripting tool to perform this execution, but it is more effective to use make itself since there are also dependencies involved at the higher level.

For example, suppose I have an mp3 player application. It can logically be divided into several components: the user interface, codecs, and database management. These might be represented by three libraries: *libui.a*, *libcodec.a*, and *libdb.a*. The application itself consists of glue holding these pieces together. A straightforward mapping of these components onto a file structure might look like Figure 6-1.

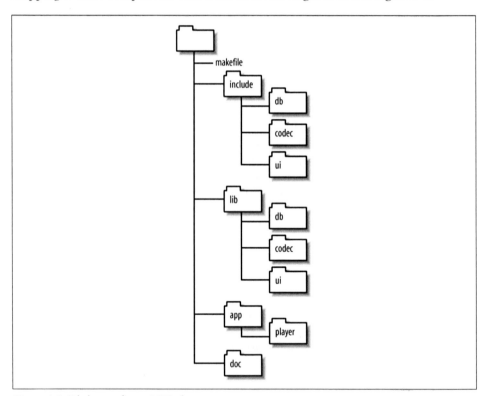

Figure 6-1. File layout for an MP3 player

A more traditional layout would place the application's main function and glue in the top directory rather than in the subdirectory *app/player*. I prefer to put applica-tion code in its own directory to create a cleaner layout at the top level and allow for growth of the system with additional modules. For instance, if we choose to add a separate cataloging application later it can neatly fit under *app/catalog*.

If each of the directories *lib/db*, *lib/codec*, *lib/ui*, and *app/player* contains a *makefile*, then it is the job of the top-level *makefile* to invoke them.

```
lib_codec := lib/codec
lib_db    := lib/db
lib_ui    := lib/ui
libraries := $(lib_ui) $(lib_db) $(lib_codec)
player    := app/player

.PHONY: all $(player) $(libraries)
all: $(player)

$(player) $(libraries):
        $(MAKE) --directory=$@

$(player): $(libraries)
$(lib_ui): $(lib_db) $(lib_codec)
```

The top-level *makefile* invokes make on each subdirectory through a rule that lists the subdirectories as targets and whose action is to invoke make:

```
$(player) $(libraries):
        $(MAKE) --directory=$@
```

The variable MAKE should always be used to invoke make within a *makefile*. The MAKE variable is recognized by make and is set to the actual path of make so recursive invocations all use the same executable. Also, lines containing the variable MAKE are handled specially when the command-line options --touch (-t), --just-print (-n), and --question (-q) are used. We'll discuss this in detail in the section "Command-Line Options" later in this chapter.

The target directories are marked with .PHONY so the rule fires even though the target may be up to date. The --directory (-C) option is used to cause make to change to the target directory before reading a *makefile*.

This rule, although a bit subtle, overcomes several problems associated with a more straightforward command script:

```
all:
        for d in $(player) $(libraries); \
        do                               \
          $(MAKE) --directory=$$d;       \
        done
```

This command script fails to properly transmit errors to the parent make. It also does not allow make to execute any subdirectory builds in parallel. We'll discuss this feature of make in Chapter 10.

As make is planning the execution of the dependency graph, the prerequisites of a target are independent of one another. In addition, separate targets with no dependency relationships to one another are also independent. For example, the libraries have no *inherent* relationship to the app/player target or to each other. This means make is free to execute the *app/player makefile* before building any of the libraries. Clearly, this would cause the build to fail since linking the application requires the libraries. To solve this problem, we provide additional dependency information.

```
$(player): $(libraries)
$(lib_ui): $(lib_db) $(lib_codec)
```

Here we state that the *makefiles* in the library subdirectories must be executed before the *makefile* in the player directory. Similarly, the *lib/ui* code requires the *lib/db* and *lib/codec* libraries to be compiled. This ensures that any generated code (such as yacc/lex files) have been generated before the *ui* code is compiled.

There is a further subtle ordering issue when updating prerequisites. As with all dependencies, the order of updating is determined by the analysis of the dependency graph, but when the prerequisites of a target are listed on a single line, GNU make happens to update them from left to right. For example:

```
all: a b c
all: d e f
```

If there are no other dependency relationships to be considered, the six prerequisites can be updated in any order (e.g., "d b a c e f"), but GNU make uses left to right within a single target line, yielding the update order: "a b c d e f" *or* "d e f a b c." Although this ordering is an accident of the implementation, the order of execution appears correct. It is easy to forget that the correct order is a happy accident and fail to provide full dependency information. Eventually, the dependency analysis will yield a different order and cause problems. So, if a set of targets must be updated in a specific order, enforce the proper order with appropriate prerequisites.

When the top-level *makefile* is run, we see:

```
$ make
make --directory=lib/db
make[1]: Entering directory `/test/book/out/ch06-simple/lib/db'
Update db library...
make[1]: Leaving directory `/test/book/out/ch06-simple/lib/db'
make --directory=lib/codec
make[1]: Entering directory `/test/book/out/ch06-simple/lib/codec'
Update codec library...
make[1]: Leaving directory `/test/book/out/ch06-simple/lib/codec'
make --directory=lib/ui
make[1]: Entering directory `/test/book/out/ch06-simple/lib/ui'
Update ui library...
make[1]: Leaving directory `/test/book/out/ch06-simple/lib/ui'
make --directory=app/player
make[1]: Entering directory `/test/book/out/ch06-simple/app/player'
Update player application...
make[1]: Leaving directory `/test/book/out/ch06-simple/app/player'
```

When make detects that it is invoking another make recursively, it enables the --print-directory (-w) option, which causes make to print the Entering directory and Leaving directory messages. This option is also enabled when the --directory (-C) option is used. The value of the make variable MAKELEVEL is printed in square brackets in each line as well. In this simple example, each component *makefile* prints a simple message about updating the component.

Command-Line Options

Recursive make is a simple idea that quickly becomes complicated. The perfect recursive make implementation would behave as if the many *makefiles* in the system are a single *makefile*. Achieving this level of coordination is virtually impossible, so compromises must be made. The subtle issues become more clear when we look at how command-line options must be handled.

Suppose we have added comments to a header file in our mp3 player. Rather than recompiling all the source that depends on the modified header, we realize we can instead perform a make --touch to bring the timestamps of the files up to date. By executing the make --touch with the top-level *makefile,* we would like make to touch all the appropriate files managed by sub-makes. Let's see how this works.

Usually, when --touch is provided on the command line, the normal processing of rules is suspended. Instead, the dependency graph is traversed and the selected targets and those prerequisites that are not marked .PHONY are brought up to date by executing touch on the target. Since our subdirectories are marked .PHONY, they would normally be ignored (touching them like normal files would be pointless). But we don't want those targets ignored, we want their command script executed. To do the right thing, make automatically labels any line containing MAKE with the + modifier, meaning make runs the sub-make regardless of the --touch option.

When make runs the sub-make it must also arrange for the --touch flag to be passed to the sub-process. It does this through the MAKEFLAGS variable. When make starts, it automatically appends most command-line options to MAKEFLAGS. The only exceptions are the options --directory (-C), --file (-f), --old-file (-o), and --new-file (-W). The MAKEFLAGS variable is then exported to the environment and read by the sub-make as it starts.

With this special support, sub-makes behave mostly the way you want. The recursive execution of $(MAKE) and the special handling of MAKEFLAGS that is applied to --touch (-t) is also applied to the options --just-print (-n) and --question (-q).

Passing Variables

As we have already mentioned, variables are passed to sub-makes through the environment and controlled using the export and unexport directives. Variables passed through the environment are taken as default values, but are overridden by any assignment to the variable. Use the `--environment-overrides` (`-e`) option to allow environment variables to override the local assignment. You can explicitly override the environment for a specific assignment (even when the `--environment-overrides` option is used) with the override directive:

```
override TMPDIR = ~/tmp
```

Variables defined on the command line are automatically exported to the environment if they use legal shell syntax. A variable is considered legal if it uses only letters, numbers, and underscores. Variable assignments from the command line are stored in the MAKEFLAGS variable along with command-line options.

Error Handling

What happens when a recursive make gets an error? Nothing very unusual, actually. The make receiving the error status terminates its processing with an exit status of 2. The parent make then exits, propagating the error status up the recursive make process tree. If the `--keep-going` (`-k`) option is used on the top-level make, it is passed to sub-makes as usual. The sub-make does what it normally does, skips the current target and proceeds to the next goal that does not use the erroneous target as a prerequisite.

For example, if our mp3 player program encountered a compilation error in the lib/db component, the lib/db make would exit, returning a status of 2 to the top-level *makefile*. If we used the `--keep-going` (`-k`) option, the top-level *makefile* would proceed to the next unrelated target, lib/codec. When it had completed that target, regardless of its exit status, the make would exit with a status of 2 since there are no further targets that can be processed due to the failure of lib/db.

The `--question` (`-q`) option behaves very similarly. This option causes make to return an exit status of 1 if some target is not up to date, 0 otherwise. When applied to a tree of *makefiles*, make begins recursively executing *makefiles* until it can determine if the project is up to date. As soon as an out-of-date file is found, make terminates the currently active make and unwinds the recursion.

Building Other Targets

The basic build target is essential for any build system, but we also need the other support targets we've come to depend upon, such as clean, install, print, etc. Because these are .PHONY targets, the technique described earlier doesn't work very well.

For instance, there are several broken approaches, such as:

```
clean: $(player) $(libraries)
        $(MAKE) --directory=$@ clean
```

or:

```
$(player) $(libraries):
        $(MAKE) --directory=$@ clean
```

The first is broken because the prerequisites would trigger a build of the default target in the $(player) and $(libraries) *makefiles*, not a build of the clean target. The second is illegal because these targets already exist with a different command script.

One approach that works relies on a shell for loop:

```
clean:
        for d in $(player) $(libraries); \
        do                               \
          $(MAKE) --directory=$$d clean; \
        done
```

A for loop is not very satisfying for all the reasons described earlier, but it (and the preceding illegal example) points us to this solution:

```
$(player) $(libraries):
        $(MAKE) --directory=$@ $(TARGET)
```

By adding the variable $(TARGET) to the recursive make line and setting the TARGET variable on the make command line, we can add arbitrary goals to the sub-make:

> **$ make TARGET=clean**

Unfortunately, this does not invoke the $(TARGET) on the top-level *makefile*. Often this is not necessary because the top-level *makefile* has nothing to do, but, if necessary, we can add another invocation of make protected by an if:

```
$(player) $(libraries):
        $(MAKE) --directory=$@ $(TARGET)
        $(if $(TARGET), $(MAKE) $(TARGET))
```

Now we can invoke the clean target (or any other target) by simply setting TARGET on the command line.

Cross-Makefile Dependencies

The special support in make for command-line options and communication through environment variables suggests that recursive make has been tuned to work well. So what are the serious complications alluded to earlier?

Separate *makefiles* linked by recursive $(MAKE) commands record only the most superficial top-level links. Unfortunately, there are often subtle dependencies buried in some directories.

For example, suppose a *db* module includes a yacc-based parser for importing and exporting music data. If the *ui* module, *ui.c*, includes the generated yacc header, we have a dependency between these two modules. If the dependencies are properly modeled, make should know to recompile our *ui* module whenever the grammar header is updated. This is not difficult to arrange using the automatic dependency generation technique described earlier. But what if the yacc file itself is modified? In this case, when the *ui makefile* is run, a correct *makefile* would recognize that yacc must first be run to generate the parser and header before compiling *ui.c*. In our recursive make decomposition, this does not occur, because the rule and dependencies for running yacc are in the *db makefile*, not the *ui makefile*.

In this case, the best we can do is to ensure that the *db makefile* is always executed before executing the *ui makefile*. This higher-level dependency must be encoded by hand. We were astute enough in the first version of our *makefile* to recognize this, but, in general, this is a very difficult maintenance problem. As code is written and modified, the top-level *makefile* will fail to properly record the intermodule dependencies.

To continue the example, if the yacc grammar in *db* is updated and the *ui makefile* is run before the *db makefile* (by executing it directly instead of through the top-level *makefile*), the *ui makefile* does not know there is an unsatisfied dependency in the *db makefile* and that yacc must be run to update the header file. Instead, the *ui makefile* compiles its program with the old yacc header. If new symbols have been defined and are now being referenced, then a compilation error is reported. Thus, the recursive make approach is inherently more fragile than a single *makefile*.

The problem worsens when code generators are used more extensively. Suppose that the use of an RPC stub generator is added to *ui* and the headers are referenced in *db*. Now we have mutual reference to contend with. To resolve this, it may be required to visit *db* to generate the yacc header, then visit *ui* to generate the RPC stubs, then visit *db* to compile the files, and finally visit *ui* to complete the compilation process. The number of passes required to create and compile the source for a project is dependent on the structure of the code and the tools used to create it. This kind of mutual reference is common in complex systems.

The standard solution in real-world *makefile*s is usually a hack. To ensure that all files are up to date, every *makefile* is executed when a command is given to the top-level *makefile*. Notice that this is precisely what our mp3 player *makefile* does. When the top-level *makefile* is run, each of the four sub-*makefile*s is unconditionally run. In complex cases, *makefile*s are run repeatedly to ensure that all code is first generated then compiled. Often this iterative execution is a complete waste of time, but occasionally it is required.

Avoiding Duplicate Code

The directory layout of our application includes three libraries. The *makefile*s for these libraries are very similar. This makes sense because the three libraries serve different purposes in the final application but are all built with similar commands. This kind of decomposition is typical of large projects and leads to many similar *makefile*s and lots of (*makefile*) code duplication.

Code duplication is bad, even *makefile* code duplication. It increases the maintenance costs of the software and leads to more bugs. It also makes it more difficult to understand algorithms and identify minor variations in them. So we would like to avoid code duplication in our *makefile*s as much as possible. This is most easily accomplished by moving the common pieces of a *makefile* into a common include file.

For example, the *codec makefile* contains:

```
lib_codec    := libcodec.a
sources      := codec.c
objects      := $(subst .c,.o,$(sources))
dependencies := $(subst .c,.d,$(sources))

include_dirs := .. ../../include
CPPFLAGS     += $(addprefix -I ,$(include_dirs))
vpath %.h $(include_dirs)

all: $(lib_codec)

$(lib_codec): $(objects)
        $(AR) $(ARFLAGS) $@ $^

.PHONY: clean
clean:
        $(RM) $(lib_codec) $(objects) $(dependencies)

ifneq "$(MAKECMDGOALS)" "clean"
  include $(dependencies)
endif

%.d: %.c
        $(CC) $(CFLAGS) $(CPPFLAGS) $(TARGET_ARCH) -M $< |        \
        sed 's,\($*\.o\) *:,\1 $@: ,' > $@.tmp
        mv $@.tmp $@
```

Almost all of this code is duplicated in the *db* and *ui makefiles*. The only lines that change for each library are the name of the library itself and the source files the library contains. When duplicate code is moved into *common.mk*, we can pare this *makefile* down to:

```
library := libcodec.a
sources := codec.c

include ../../common.mk
```

See what we have moved into the single, shared include file:

```
MV           := mv -f
RM           := rm -f
SED          := sed

objects      := $(subst .c,.o,$(sources))
dependencies := $(subst .c,.d,$(sources))
include_dirs := .. ../../include
CPPFLAGS     += $(addprefix -I ,$(include_dirs))

vpath %.h $(include_dirs)
```

```
.PHONY: library
library: $(library)

$(library): $(objects)
	$(AR) $(ARFLAGS) $@ $^

.PHONY: clean
clean:
	$(RM) $(objects) $(program) $(library) $(dependencies) $(extra_clean)

ifneq "$(MAKECMDGOALS)" "clean"
  -include $(dependencies)
endif

%.c %.h: %.y
	$(YACC.y) --defines $<
	$(MV) y.tab.c $*.c
	$(MV) y.tab.h $*.h

%.d: %.c
	$(CC) $(CFLAGS) $(CPPFLAGS) $(TARGET_ARCH) -M $< |       \
	$(SED) 's,\($*\.o\) *:,\1 $@: ,' > $@.tmp
	$(MV) $@.tmp $@
```

The variable include_dirs, which was different for each *makefile*, is now identical in all *makefiles* because we reworked the path source files use for included headers to make all libraries use the same include path.

The *common.mk* file even includes the default goal for the library include files. The original *makefiles* used the default target all. That would cause problems with nonlibrary *makefiles* that need to specify a different set of prerequisites for their default goal. So the shared code version uses a default target of library.

Notice that because this common file contains targets it must be included after the default target for nonlibrary *makefiles*. Also notice that the clean command script references the variables program, library, and extra_clean. For library *makefiles*, the program variable is empty; for program *makefiles*, the library variable is empty. The extra_clean variable was added specifically for the *db makefile*. This *makefile* uses the variable to denote code generated by yacc. The *makefile* is:

```
library     := libdb.a
sources     := scanner.c playlist.c
extra_clean := $(sources) playlist.h

.SECONDARY: playlist.c playlist.h scanner.c

include ../../common.mk
```

Using these techniques, code duplication can be kept to a minimum. As more *makefile* code is moved into the common *makefile*, it evolves into a generic *makefile* for the entire project. make variables and user-defined functions are used as customization points, allowing the generic *makefile* to be modified for each directory.

Nonrecursive make

Multidirectory projects can also be managed without recursive makes. The difference here is that the source manipulated by the *makefile* lives in more than one directory. To accommodate this, references to files in subdirectories must include the path to the file—either absolute or relative.

Often, the *makefile* managing a large project has many targets, one for each module in the project. For our mp3 player example, we would need targets for each of the libraries and each of the applications. It can also be useful to add phony targets for collections of modules such as the collection of all libraries. The default goal would typically build all of these targets. Often the default goal builds documentation and runs a testing procedure as well.

The most straightforward use of nonrecursive make includes targets, object file references, and dependencies in a single *makefile*. This is often unsatisfying to developers familiar with recursive make because information about the files in a directory is centralized in a single file while the source files themselves are distributed in the filesystem. To address this issue, the Miller paper on nonrecursive make suggests using one make include file for each directory containing file lists and module-specific rules. The top-level *makefile* includes these sub-*makefiles*.

Example 6-1 shows a *makefile* for our mp3 player that includes a module-level *makefile* from each subdirectory. Example 6-2 shows one of the module-level include files.

Example 6-1. A nonrecursive makefile

```
# Collect information from each module in these four variables.
# Initialize them here as simple variables.
programs    :=
sources     :=
libraries   :=
extra_clean :=

objects      = $(subst .c,.o,$(sources))
dependencies = $(subst .c,.d,$(sources))

include_dirs := lib include
CPPFLAGS     += $(addprefix -I ,$(include_dirs))
vpath %.h $(include_dirs)

MV  := mv -f
RM  := rm -f
SED := sed

all:

include lib/codec/module.mk
include lib/db/module.mk
```

Example 6-1. A nonrecursive makefile (continued)

```
include lib/ui/module.mk
include app/player/module.mk

.PHONY: all
all: $(programs)

.PHONY: libraries
libraries: $(libraries)

.PHONY: clean
clean:
        $(RM) $(objects) $(programs) $(libraries) \
            $(dependencies) $(extra_clean)

ifneq "$(MAKECMDGOALS)" "clean"
  include $(dependencies)
endif

%.c %.h: %.y
        $(YACC.y) --defines $<
        $(MV) y.tab.c $*.c
        $(MV) y.tab.h $*.h

%.d: %.c
        $(CC) $(CFLAGS) $(CPPFLAGS) $(TARGET_ARCH) -M $< | \
        $(SED) 's,\($(notdir $*)\.o\) *:,$(dir $@)\1 $@: ,' > $@.tmp
        $(MV) $@.tmp $@
```

Example 6-2. The lib/codec include file for a nonrecursive makefile

```
local_dir  := lib/codec
local_lib  := $(local_dir)/libcodec.a
local_src  := $(addprefix $(local_dir)/,codec.c)
local_objs := $(subst .c,.o,$(local_src))

libraries  += $(local_lib)
sources    += $(local_src)

$(local_lib): $(local_objs)
        $(AR) $(ARFLAGS) $@ $^
```

Thus, all the information specific to a module is contained in an include file in the module directory itself. The top-level *makefile* contains only a list of modules and include directives. Let's examine the *makefile* and *module.mk* in detail.

Each *module.mk* include file appends the local library name to the variable libraries and the local sources to sources. The local_ variables are used to hold constant values or to avoid duplicating a computed value. Note that each include file reuses these same local_ variable names. Therefore, it uses simple variables (those assigned with :=) rather than recursive ones so that builds combining multiple *makefiles* hold no risk of infecting the variables in each *makefile*. The library name and source file lists use a relative path as discussed earlier. Finally, the include file defines a rule for updating the local library. There is no problem with using the local_ variables in this rule because the target and prerequisite parts of a rule are immediately evaluated.

In the top-level *makefile*, the first four lines define the variables that accumulate each module's specific file information. These variables must be simple variables because each module will append to them using the same local variable name:

```
local_src  := $(addprefix $(local_dir)/,codec.c)
...
sources    += $(local_src)
```

If a recursive variable were used for sources, for instance, the final value would simply be the last value of local_src repeated over and over. An explicit assignment is required to initialize these simple variables, even though they are assigned null values, since variables are recursive by default.

The next section computes the object file list, objects, and dependency file list from the sources variable. These variables are recursive because at this point in the *makefile* the sources variable is empty. It will not be populated until later when the include files are read. In this *makefile*, it is perfectly reasonable to move the definition of these variables after the includes and change their type to simple variables, but keeping the basic file lists (e.g., sources, libraries, objects) together simplifies understanding the *makefile* and is generally good practice. Also, in other *makefile* situations, mutual references between variables require the use of recursive variables.

Next, we handle C language include files by setting CPPFLAGS. This allows the compiler to find the headers. We append to the CPPFLAGS variable because we don't know if the variable is really empty; command-line options, environment variables, or other make constructs may have set it. The vpath directive allows make to find the headers stored in other directories. The include_dirs variable is used to avoid duplicating the include directory list.

Variables for mv, rm, and sed are defined to avoid hard coding programs into the *makefile*. Notice the case of variables. We are following the conventions suggested in the make manual. Variables that are internal to the *makefile* are lowercased; variables that might be set from the command line are uppercased.

In the next section of the *makefile,* things get more interesting. We would like to begin the explicit rules with the default target, all. Unfortunately, the prerequisite for all is the variable programs. This variable is evaluated immediately, but is set by reading the module include files. So, we must read the include files before the all target is defined. Unfortunately again, the include modules contain targets, the first of which will be considered the default goal. To work through this dilemma, we can specify the all target with no prerequisites, source the include files, then add the prerequisites to all later.

The remainder of the *makefile* is already familiar from previous examples, but how make applies implicit rules is worth noting. Our source files now reside in subdirectories. When make tries to apply the standard %.o: %.c rule, the prerequisite will be a file with a relative path, say *lib/ui/ui.c*. make will automatically propagate that relative path to the target file and attempt to update *lib/ui/ui.o*. Thus, make automagically does the Right Thing.

There is one final glitch. Although make is handling paths correctly, not all the tools used by the *makefile* are. In particular, when using gcc, the generated dependency file does not include the relative path to the target object file. That is, the output of gcc -M is:

```
ui.o: lib/ui/ui.c include/ui/ui.h lib/db/playlist.h
```

rather than what we expect:

```
lib/ui/ui.o: lib/ui/ui.c include/ui/ui.h lib/db/playlist.h
```

This disrupts the handling of header file prerequisites. To fix this problem we can alter the sed command to add relative path information:

```
$(SED) 's,\($(notdir $*)\)\.o\) *:,$(dir $@)\1 $@: ,'
```

Tweaking the *makefile* to handle the quirks of various tools is a normal part of using make. Portable *makefiles* are often very complex due to vagaries of the diverse set of tools they are forced to rely upon.

We now have a decent nonrecursive *makefile*, but there are maintenance problems. The *module.mk* include files are largely similar. A change to one will likely involve a change to all of them. For small projects like our mp3 player it is annoying. For large projects with several hundred include files it can be fatal. By using consistent variable names and regularizing the contents of the include files, we position ourselves nicely to cure these ills. Here is the *lib/codec* include file after refactoring:

```
local_src := $(wildcard $(subdirectory)/*.c)

$(eval $(call make-library, $(subdirectory)/libcodec.a, $(local_src)))
```

Instead of specifying source files by name, we assume we want to rebuild all *.c* files in the directory. The make-library function now performs the bulk of the tasks for an include file. This function is defined at the top of our project *makefile* as:

```
# $(call make-library, library-name, source-file-list)
define make-library
  libraries += $1
  sources   += $2

  $1: $(call source-to-object,$2)
     $(AR) $(ARFLAGS) $$@ $$^
endef
```

The function appends the library and sources to their respective variables, then defines the explicit rule to build the library. Notice how the automatic variables use two dollar signs to defer actual evaluation of the $@ and $^ until the rule is fired. The source-to-object function translates a list of source files to their corresponding object files:

```
source-to-object = $(subst .c,.o,$(filter %.c,$1)) \
                   $(subst .y,.o,$(filter %.y,$1)) \
                   $(subst .l,.o,$(filter %.l,$1))
```

In our previous version of the *makefile*, we glossed over the fact that the actual parser and scanner source files are *playlist.y* and *scanner.l*. Instead, we listed the source files as the generated *.c* versions. This forced us to list them explicitly and to include an extra variable, extra_clean. We've fixed that issue here by allowing the sources variable to include *.y* and *.l* files directly and letting the source-to-object function do the work of translating them.

In addition to modifying source-to-object, we need another function to compute the yacc and lex output files so the clean target can perform proper clean up. The generated-source function simply accepts a list of sources and produces a list of intermediate files as output:

```
# $(call generated-source, source-file-list)
generated-source = $(subst .y,.c,$(filter %.y,$1)) \
                   $(subst .y,.h,$(filter %.y,$1)) \
                   $(subst .l,.c,$(filter %.l,$1))
```

Our other helper function, subdirectory, allows us to omit the variable local_dir.

```
subdirectory = $(patsubst %/makefile,%,                      \
                 $(word                                       \
                   $(words $(MAKEFILE_LIST)),$(MAKEFILE_LIST)))
```

As noted in the section "String Functions" in Chapter 4, we can retrieve the name of the current *makefile* from MAKEFILE_LIST. Using a simple patsubst, we can extract the relative path from the top-level *makefile*. This eliminates another variable and reduces the differences between include files.

Our final optimization (at least for this example), uses wildcard to acquire the source file list. This works well in most environments where the source tree is kept clean. However, I have worked on projects where this is not the case. Old code was kept in the source tree "just in case." This entailed real costs in terms of programmer time and anguish since old, dead code was maintained when it was found by global search and replace and new programmers (or old ones not familiar with a module) attempted to compile or debug code that was never used. If you are using a modern source code control system, such as CVS, keeping dead code in the source tree is unnecessary (since it resides in the repository) and using wildcard becomes feasible.

The include directives can also be optimzed:

```
modules := lib/codec lib/db lib/ui app/player
...
include $(addsuffix /module.mk,$(modules))
```

For larger projects, even this can be a maintenance problem as the list of modules grows to the hundreds or thousands. Under these circumstances, it might be preferable to define modules as a find command:

```
modules := $(subst /module.mk,,$(shell find . -name module.mk))
...
include $(addsuffix /module.mk,$(modules))
```

We strip the filename from the find output so the modules variable is more generally useful as the list of modules. If that isn't necessary, then, of course, we would omit the subst and addsuffix and simply save the output of find in modules. Example 6-3 shows the final *makefile*.

Example 6-3. A nonrecursive makefile, version 2

```
# $(call source-to-object, source-file-list)
source-to-object = $(subst .c,.o,$(filter %.c,$1)) \
                   $(subst .y,.o,$(filter %.y,$1)) \
                   $(subst .l,.o,$(filter %.l,$1))

# $(subdirectory)
subdirectory = $(patsubst %/module.mk,%,                        \
                  $(word                                        \
                     $(words $(MAKEFILE_LIST)),$(MAKEFILE_LIST)))

# $(call make-library, library-name, source-file-list)
define make-library
  libraries += $1
  sources   += $2

  $1: $(call source-to-object,$2)
        $(AR) $(ARFLAGS) $$@ $$^
endef

# $(call generated-source, source-file-list)
generated-source = $(subst .y,.c,$(filter %.y,$1))     \
                   $(subst .y,.h,$(filter %.y,$1))     \
                   $(subst .l,.c,$(filter %.l,$1))

# Collect information from each module in these four variables.
# Initialize them here as simple variables.
modules      := lib/codec lib/db lib/ui app/player
programs     :=
libraries    :=
sources      :=

objects      = $(call source-to-object,$(sources))
dependencies = $(subst .o,.d,$(objects))

include_dirs := lib include
CPPFLAGS     += $(addprefix -I ,$(include_dirs))
vpath %.h $(include_dirs)
```

Example 6-3. A nonrecursive makefile, version 2 (continued)

```
MV   := mv -f
RM   := rm -f
SED := sed

all:

include $(addsuffix /module.mk,$(modules))

.PHONY: all
all: $(programs)

.PHONY: libraries
libraries: $(libraries)

.PHONY: clean
clean:
        $(RM) $(objects) $(programs) $(libraries) $(dependencies)      \
             $(call generated-source, $(sources))

ifneq "$(MAKECMDGOALS)" "clean"
  include $(dependencies)
endif

%.c %.h: %.y
        $(YACC.y) --defines $<
        $(MV) y.tab.c $*.c
        $(MV) y.tab.h $*.h

%.d: %.c
        $(CC) $(CFLAGS) $(CPPFLAGS) $(TARGET_ARCH) -M $< | \
        $(SED) 's,\($(notdir $*)\.o\) *:,$(dir $@)\1 $@: ,' > $@.tmp
        $(MV) $@.tmp $@
```

Using one include file per module is quite workable and has some advantages, but I'm not convinced it is worth doing. My own experience with a large Java project indicates that a single top-level *makefile*, effectively inserting all the *module.mk* files directly into the *makefile*, provides a reasonable solution. This project included 997 separate modules, about two dozen libraries, and half a dozen applications. There were several *makefiles* for disjoint sets of code. These *makefiles* were roughly 2,500 lines long. A common include file containing global variables, user-defined functions, and pattern rules was another 2,500 lines.

Whether you choose a single *makefile* or break out module information into include files, the nonrecursive make solution is a viable approach to building large projects. It also solves many traditional problems found in the recursive make approach. The only drawback I'm aware of is the paradigm shift required for developers used to recursive make.

Components of Large Systems

For the purposes of this discussion, there are two styles of development popular today: the free software model and the commercial development model.

In the free software model, each developer is largely on his own. A project has a *makefile* and a *README* and developers are expected to figure it out with only a small amount of help. The principals of the project want things to work well and want to receive contributions from a large community, but they are mostly interested in contributions from the skilled and well-motivated. This is not a criticism. In this point of view, software should be written well, and not necessarily to a schedule.

In the commercial development model, developers come in a wide variety of skill levels and all of them must be able to develop software to contribute to the bottom line. Any developer who can't figure out how to do their job is wasting money. If the system doesn't compile or run properly, the development team as a whole may be idle, the most expensive possible scenario. To handle these issues, the development process is managed by an engineering support team that coordinates the build process, configuration of software tools, coordination of new development and maintenance work, and the management of releases. In this environment, efficiency concerns dominate the process.

It is the commercial development model that tends to create elaborate build systems. The primary reason for this is pressure to reduce the cost of software development by increasing programmer efficiency. This, in turn, should lead to increased profit. It is this model that requires the most support from make. Nevertheless, the techniques we discuss here apply to the free software model as well when their requirements demand it.

This section contains a lot of high-level information with very few specifics and no examples. That's because so much depends on the language and operating environment used. In Chapters 8 and 9, I will provide specific examples of how to implement many of these features.

Requirements

Of course requirements vary with every project and every work environment. Here we cover a wide range that are often considered important in many commercial development environments.

The most common feature desired by development teams is the separation of source code from binary code. That is, the object files generated from a compile should be placed in a separate binary tree. This, in turn, allows many other features to be added. Separate binary trees offer many advantages:

- It is easier to manage disk resources when the location of large binary trees can be specified.

- Many versions of a binary tree can be managed in parallel. For instance, a single source tree may have optimized, debug, and profiling binary versions available.

- Multiple platforms can be supported simultaneously. A properly implemented source tree can be used to compile binaries for many platforms in parallel.

- Developers can check out partial source trees and have the build system automatically "fill in" the missing files from a reference source and binary trees. This doesn't strictly require separating source and binary, but without the separation it is more likely that developer build systems would get confused about where binaries should be found.

- Source trees can be protected with read-only access. This provides added assurance that the builds reflect the source code in the repository.

- Some targets, such as clean, can be implemented trivially (and will execute dramatically faster) if a tree can be treated as a single unit rather than searching the tree for files to operate on.

Most of the above points are themselves important build features and may be project requirements.

Being able to maintain reference builds of a project is often an important system feature. The idea is that a clean check-out and build of the source is performed nightly, typically by a cron job. Since the resulting source and binary trees are unmodified with respect to the CVS source, I refer to these as reference source and binary trees. The resulting trees have many uses.

First, a reference source tree can be used by programmers and managers who need to look at the source. This may seem trivial, but when the number of files and releases grows it can be unwieldy or unreasonable to expect someone to check-out the source just to examine a single file. Also, while CVS repository browsing tools are common, they do not typically provide for easy searching of the entire source tree. For this, tags tables or even find/grep (or grep -R) are more appropriate.

Second, and most importantly, a reference binary tree indicates that the source builds cleanly. When developers begin each morning, they know if the system is broken or whole. If a batch-oriented testing framework is in place, the clean build can be used to run automated tests. Each day developers can examine the test report to determine the health of the system without wasting time running the tests themselves. The cost savings is compounded if a developer has only a modified version of the source because he avoids spending additional time performing a clean check-out and build. Finally, the reference build can be run by developers to test and compare the functionality of specific components.

The reference build can be used in other ways as well. For projects that consist of many libraries, the precompiled libraries from the nightly build can be used by programmers to link their own application with those libraries they are not modifying. This allows them to shorten their develoment cycle by omiting large portions of the source tree from their local compiles. Of course, easy access to the project source on a local file server is convenient if developers need to examine the code and do not have a complete checked out source tree.

With so many different uses, it becomes more important to verify the integrity of the reference source and binary trees. One simple and effective way to improve reliability is to make the source tree read-only. Thus, it is guaranteed that the reference source files accurately reflect the state of the repository at the time of check out. Doing this can require special care, because many different aspects of the build may attempt to causally write to the source tree. Especially when generating source code or writing temporary files. Making the source tree read-only also prevents casual users from accidentally corrupting the source tree, a most common occurrence.

Another common requirement of the project build system is the ability to easily handle different compilation, linking, and deployment configurations. The build system typically must be able to manage different versions of the project (which may be branches of the source repository).

Most large projects rely on significant third-party software, either in the form of linkable libraries or tools. If there are no other tools to manage configurations of the software (and often there are not), using the *makefile* and build system to manage this is often a reasonable choice.

Finally, when software is released to a customer, it is often repackaged from its development form. This can be as complex as constructing a *setup.exe* file for Windows or as simple as formatting an HTML file and bundling it with a jar. Sometimes this installer build operation is combined with the normal build process. I prefer to keep the build and the install generation as two separate stages because they seem to use radically different processes. In any case, it is likely that both of these operations will have an impact on the build system.

Filesystem Layout

Once you choose to support fmultiple binary trees, the question of filesystem layout arises. In environments that require multiple binary trees, there are often *a lot* of binary trees. To keep all these trees straight requires some thought.

A common way to organize this data is to designate a large disk for a binary tree "farm." At (or near) the top level of this disk is one directory for each binary tree.

One reasonable layout for these trees is to include in each directory name the vendor, hardware platform, operating system, and build parameters of the binary tree:

```
$ ls
hp-386-windows-optimized
hp-386-windows-debug
sgi-irix-optimzed
sgi-irix-debug
sun-solaris8-profiled
sun-solaris8-debug
```

When builds from many different times must be kept, it is usually best to include a date stamp (and even a timestamp) in the directory name. The format yymmdd or yymmddhhmm sorts well:

```
$ ls
hp-386-windows-optimized-040123
hp-386-windows-debug-040123
sgi-irix-optimzed-040127
sgi-irix-debug-040127
sun-solaris8-profiled-040127
sun-solaris8-debug-040127
```

Of course, the order of these filename components is up to your site. The top-level directory of these trees is a good place to hold the *makefile* and testing logs.

This layout is appropriate for storing many parallel developer builds. If a development team makes "releases," possibly for internal customers, you can consider adding an additional release farm, structured as a set of products, each of which may have a version number and timestamp as shown in Figure 6-2.

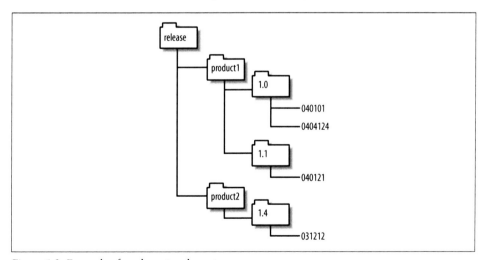

Figure 6-2. Example of a release tree layout

Here products might be libraries that are the output of a development team for use by other developers. Of course, they may also be products in the traditional sense.

Whatever your file layout or environment, many of the same criteria govern the implementation. It must be easy to identify each tree. Cleanup should be fast and obvious. It is useful to make it easy to move trees around and archive trees. In addition, the filesystem layout should closely match the process structure of the organization. This makes it easy for nonprogrammers such as managers, quality assurance, and technical publications to navigate the tree farm.

Automating Builds and Testing

It is typically important to be able to automate the build process as much as possible. This allows reference tree builds to be performed at night, saving developer time during the day. It also allows developers themselves to run builds on their own machines unattended.

For software that is "in production," there are often many outstanding requests for builds of different versions of different products. For the person in charge of satisfying these requests, the ability to fire off several builds and "walk away" is often critical to maintaining sanity and satisfying requests.

Automated testing presents its own issues. Many nongraphical applications can use simple scripting to manage the testing process. The GNU tool dejaGnu can also be used to test nongraphical utilities that require interaction. Of course, testing frameworks like JUnit (*http://www.junit.org*) also provide support for nongraphical unit testing.

Testing of graphical applications presents special problems. For X11-based systems, I have successfully performed unattended, cron-based testing using the virtual frame buffer, Xvfb. On Windows, I have not found a satisfactory solution to unattended testing. All approaches rely on leaving the testing account logged in and the screen unlocked.

## CHAPTER 7

Portable Makefiles

What do we mean by a portable *makefile*? As an extreme example, we want a *makefile* that runs without change on any system that GNU make runs on. But this is virtually impossible due to the enormous variety in operating systems. A more reasonable interpretation is a *makefile* that is easy to change for each new platform it is run on. An important added constraint is that the port to the new system does not break support for the previous platforms.

We can achieve this level of portability for *makefile*s using the same techniques as traditional programming: encapsulation and abstraction. By using variables and user-defined functions we can encapsulate applications and algorithms. By defining variables for command-line arguments and parameters, we can abstract out elements that vary from platform to platform from elements that are constant.

You then have to determine what tools each platform offers to get your job done, and what to use from each platform. The extreme in portability is to use only those tools and features that exist on all platforms of interest. This is typically called the "least common denominator" approach and obviously can leave you with very primitive functionality to work with.

Another version of the least common denominator approach is to choose a powerful set of tools and make sure to bring it with you to every platform, thus guaranteeing that the commands you invoke in the *makefile* work exactly the same everywhere. This can be hard to pull off, both administratively and in terms of getting your organization to cooperate with your fiddling with their systems. But it can be successful, and I'll show one example of that later with the Cygwin package for Windows. As you'll see, standardizing on tools does not solve every problem; there are always operating system differences to deal with.

Finally, you can accept differences between systems and work around them by careful choices of macros and functions. I'll show this approach in this chapter, too.

So, by judicious use of variables and user-defined functions, and by minimizing the use of exotic features and relying on standard tools, we can increase the portability of our *makefiles*. As noted previously, there is no such thing as perfect portability, so it is our job to balance effort versus portability. But before we explore specific techniques, let's review some of the issues of portable *makefiles*.

Portability Issues

Portability problems can be difficult to characterize since they span the entire spectrum from a total paradigm shift (such as traditional Mac OS versus System V Unix) to almost trivial bug fixes (such as a fix to a bug in the error exit status of a program). Nevertheless, here are some common portability problems that every *makefile* must deal with sooner or later:

Program names
> It is quite common for various platforms to use different names for the same or similar programs. The most common is the name of the C or C++ compiler (e.g., cc, xlc). It is also common for GNU versions of programs to be installed on a non-GNU system with the *g* prefix (e.g., gmake, gawk).

Paths
> The location of programs and files often varies between platforms. For instance, on Solaris systems the X directories are stored under */usr/X* while on many other systems the path is */usr/X11R6*. In addition, the distinction between */bin*, */usr/bin*, */sbin*, and */usr/sbin* is often rather fuzzy as you move from one system to another.

Options
> The command-line options to programs vary, particularly when an alternate implementation is used. Furthermore, if a platform is missing a utility or comes with a broken version, you may need to replace the utility with another that uses different command-line options.

Shell features
> By default, make executes command scripts with */bin/sh*, but sh implementations vary widely in their features. In particular, pre-POSIX shells are missing many features and will not accept the same syntax as a modern shell.
>
> The Open Group has a very useful white paper on the differences between the System V shell and the POSIX shell. It can be found at *http://www.unix-systems.org/whitepapers/shdiffs.html*. For those who want more details, the specification of the POSIX shell's command language can be found at *http://www.opengroup.org/onlinepubs/007904975/utilities/xcu_chap02.html*.

Program behavior
> Portable *makefiles* must contend with programs that simply behave differently. This is very common as different vendors fix or insert bugs and add features. There are also upgrades to utilities that may or may not have made it into a vendor's release. For instance, in 1987 the awk program underwent a major revision.

Nearly 20 years later, some systems still do not install this upgraded version as the standard awk.

Operating system

Finally, there are the portability problems associated with a completely different operating system such as Windows versus Unix or Linux versus VMS.

Cygwin

Although there is a native Win32 port of make, this is a small part of the Windows portability problem, because the shell this native port uses is *cmd.exe* (or *command.exe*). This, along with the absence of most of the Unix tools, makes cross-platform portability a daunting task. Fortunately, the Cygwin project (*http://www.cygwin.com*) has built a Linux-compatible library for Windows to which many programs[*] have been ported. For Windows developers who want Linux compatibility or access to GNU tools, I don't believe there is a better tool to be found.

I have used Cygwin for over 10 years on a variety of projects from a combined C++/Lisp CAD application to a pure Java workflow management system. The Cygwin tool set includes compilers and interpreters for many programming languages. However, Cygwin can be used profitably even when the applications themselves are implemented using non-Cygwin compilers and interpreters. The Cygwin tool set can be used solely as an aid to coordinating the development and build process. In other words, it is not necessary to write a "Cygwin" application or use Cygwin language tools to reap the benefits of the Cygwin environment.

Nevertheless, Linux is not Windows (thank goodness!) and there are issues involved when applying Cygwin tools to native Windows applications. Almost all of these issues revolve around the line endings used in files and the form of paths passed between Cygwin and Windows.

Line Termination

Windows filesystems use a two-character sequence carriage return followed by line feed (or CRLF) to terminate each line of a text file. POSIX systems use a single character, a line feed (LF or *newline*). Occasionally this difference can cause the unwary some confusion as programs report syntax errors or seek to the wrong location in a data file. However, the Cygwin library does a very good job of working through these issues. When Cygwin is installed (or alternatively when the mount command is used), you can choose whether Cygwin should translate files with CRLF endings. If a DOS file format is selected, Cygwin will translate CRLF to LF when reading and the reverse when writing text files so that Unix-based programs can properly handle

---

[*] My Cygwin /bin directory currently contains 1343 executables.

DOS text files. If you plan to use native language tools such as Visual C++ or Sun's Java SDK, choose the DOS file format. If you are going to use Cygwin compilers, choose Unix. (Your choice can be changed at any time.)

In addition, Cygwin comes with tools to translate files explicitly. The utilities `dos2unix` and `unix2dos` transform the line endings of a file, if necessary.

Filesystem

Cygwin provides a POSIX view of the Windows filesystem. The root directory of a POSIX filesystem is /, which maps to the directory in which Cygwin is installed. Windows drives are accessible through the pseudo-directory /cygdrive/letter. So, if Cygwin is installed in C:\usr\cygwin (my preferred location), the directory mappings shown in Table 7-1 would hold.

Table 7-1. Default Cygwin directory mapping

Native Windows path	Cygwin path	Alternate Cygwin path
c:\usr\cygwin	/	/cygdrive/c/usr/cygwin
c:\Program Files	/cygdrive/c/Program Files	
c:\usr\cygwin\bin	/bin	/cygdrive/c/usr/cygwin/bin

This can be a little confusing at first, but doesn't pose any problems to tools. Cygwin also includes a `mount` command that allows users to access files and directories more conveniently. One option to `mount`, `--change-cygdrive-prefix`, allows you to change the prefix. I find that changing the prefix to simply / is particularly useful because drive letters can be accessed more naturally:

```
$ mount --change-cygdrive-prefix /
$ ls /c
AUTOEXEC.BAT              Home           Program Files              hp
BOOT.INI                  I386           RECYCLER                   ntldr
CD                        IO.SYS         System Volume Information  pagefile.sys
CONFIG.SYS                MSDOS.SYS      Temp                       tmp
C_DILLA                   NTDETECT.COM   WINDOWS                    usr
Documents and Settings    PERSIST        WUTemp                     work
```

Once this change is made, our previous directory mapping would change to those shown in Table 7-2.

Table 7-2. Modified Cygwin directory mapping

Native Windows path	Cygwin path	Alternate Cygwin path
c:\usr\cygwin	/	/c/usr/cygwin
c:\Program Files	/c/Program Files	
c:\usr\cygwin\bin	/bin	/c/usr/cygwin/bin

If you need to pass a filename to a Windows program, such as the Visual C++ compiler, you can usually just pass the relative path to the file using POSIX-style forward slashes. The Win32 API does not distinguish between forward and backward slashes. Unfortunately, some utilities that perform their own command-line argument parsing treat all forward slashes as command options. One such utility is the DOS print command; another is the net command.

If absolute paths are used, the drive letter syntax is always a problem. Although Windows programs are usually happy with forward slashes, they are completely unable to fathom the /c syntax. The drive letter must always be tranformed back into c:. To accomplish this and the forward/backslash conversion, Cygwin provides the cygpath utility to translate between POSIX paths and Windows paths.

```
$ cygpath --windows /c/work/src/lib/foo.c
c:\work\src\lib\foo.c
$ cygpath --mixed /c/work/src/lib/foo.c
c:/work/src/lib/foo.c
$ cygpath --mixed --path "/c/work/src:/c/work/include"
c:/work/src;c:/work/include
```

The --windows option translates the POSIX path given on the command line into a Windows path (or vice versa with the proper argument). I prefer to use the --mixed option that produces a Windows path, but with forward slashes instead of backslashes (when the Windows utility accepts it). This plays much better with the Cygwin shell because the backslash is the escape character. The cygpath utility has many options, some of which provide portable access to important Windows paths:

```
$ cygpath --desktop
/c/Documents and Settings/Owner/Desktop
$ cygpath --homeroot
/c/Documents and Settings
$ cygpath --smprograms
/c/Documents and Settings/Owner/Start Menu/Programs
$ cygpath --sysdir
/c/WINDOWS/SYSTEM32
$ cygpath --windir
/c/WINDOWS
```

If you're using cygpath in a mixed Windows/Unix environment, you'll want to wrap these calls in a portable function:

```
ifdef COMSPEC
  cygpath-mixed       = $(shell cygpath -m "$1")
  cygpath-unix        = $(shell cygpath -u "$1")
  drive-letter-to-slash = /$(subst :,,$1)
else
  cygpath-mixed       = $1
  cygpath-unix        = $1
  drive-letter-to-slash = $1
endif
```

If all you need to do is map the *c:* drive letter syntax to the POSIX form, the `drive-letter-to-slash` function is faster than running the cygpath program.

Finally, Cygwin cannot hide all the quirks of Windows. Filenames that are invalid in Windows are also invalid in Cygwin. Thus, names such as *aux.h*, *com1*, and *prn* cannot be used in a POSIX path, even with an extension.

Program Conflicts

Several Windows programs have the same names as Unix programs. Of course, the Windows programs do not accept the same command-line arguments or behave in compatible ways with the Unix programs. If you accidentally invoke the Windows versions, the usual result is serious confusion. The most troublesome ones seem to be `find`, `sort`, `ftp`, and `telnet`. For maximum portability, you should be sure to provide full paths to these programs when porting between Unix, Windows, and Cygwin.

If your commitment to Cygwin is strong and you do not need to build using native Windows support tools, you can safely place the Cygwin */bin* directory at the front of your Windows path. This will guarantee access to Cygwin tools over Windows versions.

If your *makefile* is working with Java tools, be aware that Cygwin includes the GNU jar program that is incompatible with the standard Sun *jar* file format. Therefore, the Java jdk *bin* directory should be placed before the Cygwin */bin* directory in your Path variable to avoid using Cygwin's jar program.

Managing Programs and Files

The most common way to manage programs is to use a variable for program names or paths that are likely to change. The variables can be defined in a simple block, as we have seen:

```
MV ?= mv -f
RM ?= rm -f
```

or in a conditional block:

```
ifdef COMSPEC
  MV ?= move
  RM ?= del
else
  MV ?= mv -f
  RM ?= rm -f
endif
```

If a simple block is used, the values can be changed by resetting them on the command line, by editing the *makefile*, or (in this case because we used conditional assignment, ?=) by setting an environment variable. As mentioned previously, one

way to test for a Windows platform is to check for the COMSPEC variable, which is
used by all Windows operating systems. Sometimes only a path needs to change:

```
ifdef COMSPEC
  OUTPUT_ROOT := d:
  GCC_HOME    := c:/gnu/usr/bin
else
  OUTPUT_ROOT := $(HOME)
  GCC_HOME    := /usr/bin
endif

OUTPUT_DIR := $(OUTPUT_ROOT)/work/binaries
CC := $(GCC_HOME)/gcc
```

This style results in a *makefile* in which most programs are invoked via make variables. Until you get used to it, this can make the *makefile* a little harder to read.
However, variables are often more convenient to use in the *makefile* anyway, because
they can be considerably shorter than the literal program name, particularly when
full paths are used.

The same technique can be used to manage different command options. For
instance, the built-in compilation rules include a variable, TARGET_ARCH, that can be
used to set platform-specific flags:

```
ifeq "$(MACHINE)" "hpux-hppa"
  TARGET_ARCH := -mdisable-fpregs
endif
```

When defining your own program variables, you may need to use a similar
approach:

```
MV := mv $(MV_FLAGS)

ifeq "$(MACHINE)" "solaris-sparc"
  MV_FLAGS := -f
endif
```

If you are porting to many platforms, chaining the ifdef sections can become ugly
and difficult to maintain. Instead of using ifdef, place each set of platform-specific
variables in its own file whose name contains a platform indicator. For instance, if
you designate a platform by its uname parameters, you can select the appropriate make
include file like this:

```
MACHINE := $(shell uname -smo | sed 's/ /-/g')
include $(MACHINE)-defines.mk
```

Filenames with spaces present a particularly irritating problem for make. The assump-
tion that whitespace separates tokens during parsing is fundamental to make. Many
built-in functions such as word, filter, wildcard, and others assume their arguments
are space-separated words. Nevertheless, here are some tricks that may help in small

ways. The first trick, noted in the section "Supporting Multiple Binary Trees" in Chapter 8, is how to replace spaces with another character using subst:

```
space = $(empty) $(empty)

# $(call space-to-question,file-name)
space-to-question = $(subst $(space),?,$1)
```

The space-to-question function replaces all spaces with the globbing wildcard question mark. Now, we can implement wildcard and file-exists functions that can handle spaces:

```
# $(call wildcard-spaces,file-name)
wildcard-spaces = $(wildcard $(call space-to-question,$1))

# $(call file-exists
file-exists = $(strip                                            \
                     $(if $1,,$(warning $1 has no value))        \
                     $(call wildcard-spaces,$1))
```

The wildcard-spaces function uses space-to-question to allow the *makefile* to perform a wildcard operation on a pattern including spaces. We can use our wildcard-spaces function to implement file-exists. Of course, the use of the question mark may also cause wildcard-spaces to return files that do not correctly match the original wildcard pattern (e.g., "my document.doc" and "my-document.doc"), but this is the best we can do.

The space-to-question function can also be used to transform filenames with spaces in targets and prerequisites, since those allow globbing patterns to be used.

```
space := $(empty) $(empty)

# $(call space-to-question,file-name)
space-to-question = $(subst $(space),?,$1)

# $(call question-to-space,file-name)
question-to-space = $(subst ?,$(space),$1)

$(call space-to-question,foo bar): $(call space-to-question,bar baz)
        touch "$(call question-to-space,$@)"
```

Assuming the file "*bar baz*" exists, the first time this *makefile* is executed the prerequisite is found because the globbing pattern is evaluated. But the target globbing pattern fails because the target does not yet exist, so $@ has the value foo?bar. The command script then uses question-to-space to transform $@ back to the file with spaces that we really want. The next time the *makefile* is run, the target is found because the globbing pattern finds the target with spaces. A bit ugly, but I have found these tricks useful in real *makefiles*.

Source Tree Layout

Another aspect of portability is the ability to allow developers freedom to manage their development environment as they deem necessary. There will be problems if the build system requires the developers to always place their source, binaries, libraries, and support tools under the same directory or on the same Windows disk drive, for instance. Eventually, some developer low on disk space will be faced with the problem of having to partition these various files.

Instead, it makes sense to implement the *makefile* using variables to reference these collections of files and set reasonable defaults. In addition, each support library and tool can be referenced through a variable to allow developers to customize file locations as they find necessary. For the most likely customization variables, use the conditional assignment operator to allow developers a simple way of overriding the *makefile* with environment variables.

In addition, the ability to easily support multiple copies of the source and binary tree is a boon to developers. Even if they don't have to support different platforms or compilation options, developers often find themselves working with several copies of the source, either for debugging purposes or because they work on several projects in parallel. Two ways to support this have already been discussed: use a "top-level" environment variable to identify the root of the source and binary trees, or use the directory of the *makefile* and a fixed relative path to find the binary tree. Either of these allows developers the flexibility of supporting more than one tree.

Working with Nonportable Tools

As noted previously, one alternative to writing *makefile*s to the least common denominator is to adopt some standard tools. Of course, the goal is to make sure the standard tools are at least as portable as the application you are building. The obvious choice for portable tools are programs from the GNU project, but portable tools come from a wide variety of sources. Perl and Python are two other tools that come to mind.

In the absence of portable tools, encapsulating nonportable tools in make functions can sometimes do just as well. For instance, to support a variety of compilers for Enterprise JavaBeans (each of which has a slightly different invocation syntax), we can write a basic function to compile an EJB jar and parameterize it to allow one to plug in different compilers.

```
EJB_TMP_JAR = $(TMPDIR)/temp.jar

# $(call compile-generic-bean, bean-type, jar-name,
#                              bean-files-wildcard, manifest-name-opt )
define compile-generic-bean
  $(RM) $(dir $(META_INF))
  $(MKDIR) $(META_INF)
```

```
    $(if $(filter %.xml %.xmi, $3),                \
       cp $(filter %.xml %.xmi, $3) $(META_INF))
    $(call compile-$1-bean-hook,$2)
    cd $(OUTPUT_DIR) &&                             \
    $(JAR) -cf0 $(EJB_TMP_JAR)                      \
           $(call jar-file-arg,$(META_INF))         \
           $(call bean-classes,$3)
    $(call $1-compile-command,$2)
    $(call create-manifest,$(if $4,$4,$2),,)
  endef
```

The first argument to this general EJB compilation function is the type of bean compiler we are using, such as Weblogic, Websphere, etc. The remaining arguments are the jar name, the files forming the content of the jar (including configuration files), and an optional manifest file. The template function first creates a clean temporary area by deleting any old temporary directory and recreating it. Next, the function copies in the *xml* or *xmi* files present in the prerequisites into the $(META_INF) directory. At this point, we may need to perform custom operations to clean up the *META-INF* files or prepare the *.class* files. To support these operations, we include a hook function, compile-$1-bean-hook, that the user can define, if necessary. For instance, if the Websphere compiler required an extra control file, say an *xsl* file, we would write this hook:

```
# $(call compile-websphere-bean-hook, file-list)
define compile-websphere-bean-hook
  cp $(filter %.xsl, $1) $(META_INF)
endef
```

By simply defining this function, we make sure the call in compile-generic-bean will be expanded appropriately. If we do not choose to write a hook function, the call in compile-generic-bean expands to nothing.

Next, our generic function creates the jar. The helper function jar-file-arg decomposes a normal file path into a -C option and a relative path:

```
# $(call jar-file-arg, file-name)
define jar-file-arg
  -C "$(patsubst %/,%,$(dir $1))" $(notdir $1)
endef
```

The helper function bean-classes extracts the appropriate class files from a source file list (the jar file only needs the interface and home classes):

```
# $(call bean-classes, bean-files-list)
define bean-classes
  $(subst $(SOURCE_DIR)/,,                         \
    $(filter %Interface.class %Home.class, \
      $(subst .java,.class,$1)))
endef
```

Then the generic function invokes the compiler of choice with $(call $1-compile-command,$2):

```
define weblogic-compile-command
  cd $(TMPDIR) && \
  $(JVM) weblogic.ejbc -compiler $(EJB_JAVAC) $(EJB_TMP_JAR) $1
endef
```

Finally, our generic function adds the manifest.

Having defined compile-generic-bean, we wrap it in a compiler-specific function for each environment we want to support.

```
# $(call compile-weblogic-bean, jar-name,
#                              bean-files-wildcard, manifest-name-opt )
define compile-weblogic-bean
  $(call compile-generic-bean,weblogic,$1,$2,$3)
endef
```

A Standard Shell

It is worth reiterating here that one of the irksome incompatibilities one finds in moving from system to system is the capabilities of /bin/sh, the default shell used by make. If you find yourself tweaking the command scripts in your *makefile*, you should consider standardizing your shell. Of course, this is not reasonable for the typical open source project where the *makefile* is executed in uncontrolled environments. However, in a controlled setting, with a fixed set of specially configured machines, this is quite reasonable.

In addition to avoiding shell incompatibilities, many shells provide features that can avoid the use of numerous small utilities. For example, the bash shell includes enhanced shell variable expansion, such as %% and ##, that can help avoid the use of shell utilities, such as sed and expr.

Automake

The focus of this chapter has been on using GNU make and supporting tools effectively to achieve a portable build system. There are times, however, when even these modest requirements are beyond reach. If you cannot use the enhanced features of GNU make and are forced to rely on a least-common-denominator set of features, you should consider using the automake tool, *http://www.gnu.org/software/automake/automake.html*.

The automake tool accepts a stylized *makefile* as input and generates a portable old-style *makefile* as output. automake is built around a set of m4 macros that allow a very terse notation in the input file (called *makefile.am*). Typically, automake is used in conjunction with autoconf, a portability support package for C/C++ programs, but autoconf is not required.

While automake is a good solution for build systems that require maxium portability, the *makefiles* it generates cannot use any of the advanced features of GNU make with the exception of appending assignment, +=, for which it has special support. Furthermore, the input to automake bears little resemblance to normal *makefile* input. Thus, using automake (without autoconf) isn't terribly different from using the least-common-denominator approach.

## CHAPTER 8

C and C++

The issues and techniques shown in Chapter 6 are enhanced and applied in this chapter to C and C++ projects. We'll continue with the mp3 player example building on our nonrecursive *makefile*.

Separating Source and Binary

If we want to support a single source tree with multiple platforms and multiple builds per platform, separating the source and binary trees is necessary, so how do we do it? The make program was originally written to work well for files in a single directory. Although it has changed dramatically since then, it hasn't forgotten its roots. make works with multiple directories best when the files it is updating live in the current directory (or its subdirectories).

The Easy Way

The easiest way to get make to place binaries in a separate directory from sources is to start the make program from the binary directory. The output files are accessed using relative paths, as shown in the previous chapter, while the input files must be found either through explicit paths or through searching through vpath. In either case, we'll need to refer to the source directory in several places, so we start with a variable to hold it:

```
SOURCE_DIR := ../mp3_player
```

Building on our previous *makefile*, the source-to-object function is unchanged, but the subdirectory function now needs to take into account the relative path to the source.

```
# $(call source-to-object, source-file-list)
source-to-object = $(subst .c,.o,$(filter %.c,$1)) \
                   $(subst .y,.o,$(filter %.y,$1)) \
                   $(subst .l,.o,$(filter %.l,$1))
```

```
# $(subdirectory)
subdirectory = $(patsubst $(SOURCE_DIR)/%/module.mk,%, \
                $(word                                 \
                  $(words $(MAKEFILE_LIST)),$(MAKEFILE_LIST)))
```

In our new *makefile*, the files listed in the MAKEFILE_LIST will include the relative path to the source. So to extract the relative path to the module's directory, we must strip off the prefix as well as the *module.mk* suffix.

Next, to help make find the sources, we use the vpath feature:

```
vpath %.y $(SOURCE_DIR)
vpath %.l $(SOURCE_DIR)
vpath %.c $(SOURCE_DIR)
```

This allows us to use simple relative paths for our source files as well as our output files. When make needs a source file, it will search SOURCE_DIR if it cannot find the file in the current directory of the output tree. Next, we must update the include_dirs variable:

```
include_dirs := lib $(SOURCE_DIR)/lib $(SOURCE_DIR)/include
```

In addition to the source directories, this variable now includes the *lib* directory from the binary tree because the generated yacc and lex header files will be placed there.

The make include directive must be updated to access the *module.mk* files from their source directories since make does not use the vpath to find include files:

```
include $(patsubst %,$(SOURCE_DIR)/%/module.mk,$(modules))
```

Finally, we create the output directories themselves:

```
create-output-directories :=                              \
      $(shell for f in $(modules);                        \
              do                                          \
                $(TEST) -d $$f || $(MKDIR) $$f;           \
              done)
```

This assignment creates a dummy variable whose value is never used, but because of the simple variable assignment we are guaranteed that the directories will be created before make performs any other work. We must create the directories "by hand" because yacc, lex, and the dependency file generation will not create the output directories themselves.

Another way to ensure these directories are created is to add the directories as prerequisites to the dependency files (the *.d* files). This is a bad idea because the directory is not really a prerequisite. The yacc, lex, or dependency files do not depend on the *contents* of the directory, nor should they be regenerated just because the directory timestamp is updated. In fact, this would be a source of great inefficiency if the project were remade when a file was added or removed from an output directory.

The modifications to the *module.mk* file are even simpler:

```
local_src := $(addprefix $(subdirectory)/,playlist.y scanner.l)

$(eval $(call make-library, $(subdirectory)/libdb.a, $(local_src)))

.SECONDARY: $(call generated-source, $(local_src))

$(subdirectory)/scanner.d: $(subdirectory)/playlist.d
```

This version omits the wildcard to find the source. It is a straightforward matter to restore this feature and is left as an exercise for the reader. There is one glitch that appears to be a bug in the original *makefile*. When this example was run, I discovered that the *scanner.d* dependency file was being generated before *playlist.h*, which it depends upon. This dependency was missing from the original *makefile*, but it worked anyway purely by accident. Getting *all* the dependencies right is a difficult task, even in small projects.

Assuming the source is in the subdirectory *mp3_player*, here is how we build our project with the new *makefile*:

```
$ mkdir mp3_player_out
$ cd mp3_player_out
$ make --file=../mp3_player/makefile
```

The *makefile* is correct and works well, but it is rather annoying to be forced to change directories to the output directory and then be forced to add the --file (-f) option. This can be cured with a simple shell script:

```
#! /bin/bash
if [[ ! -d $OUTPUT_DIR ]]
then
  if ! mkdir -p $OUTPUT_DIR
  then
    echo "Cannot create output directory" > /dev/stderr
    exit 1
  fi
fi

cd $OUTPUT_DIR
make --file=$SOURCE_DIR/makefile "$@"
```

This script assumes the source and output directories are stored in the environment variables SOURCE_DIR and OUTPUT_DIR, respectively. This is a standard practice that allows developers to switch trees easily but still avoid typing paths too frequently.

One last caution. There is nothing in make or our *makefile* to prevent a developer from executing the *makefile* from the source tree, even though it should be executed from the binary tree. This is a common mistake and some command scripts might behave badly. For instance, the clean target:

```
.PHONY: clean
clean:
        $(RM) -r *
```

would delete the user's entire source tree! Oops. It seems prudent to add a check for this eventuality in the *makefile* at the highest level. Here is a reasonable check:

```
$(if $(filter $(notdir $(SOURCE_DIR)),$(notdir $(CURDIR))),\
    $(error Please run the makefile from the binary tree.))
```

This code tests if the name of the current working directory ($(notdir $(CURDIR))) is the same as the source directory ($(notdir $(SOURCE_DIR))). If so, print the error and exit. Since the if and error functions expand to nothing, we can place these two lines immediately after the definition of SOURCE_DIR.

The Hard Way

Some developers find having to cd into the binary tree so annoying that they will go to great lengths to avoid it, or maybe the *makefile* maintainer is working in an environment where shell script wrappers or aliases are unsuitable. In any case, the *makefile* can be modified to allow running make from the source tree and placing binary files in a separate output tree by prefixing all the output filenames with a path. At this point I usually go with absolute paths since this provides more flexibility, although it does exacerbate problems with command-line length limits. The input files continue to use simple relative paths from the *makefile* directory.

Example 8-1 shows the *makefile* modified to allow executing make from the source tree and writing binary files to a binary tree.

Example 8-1. A makefile separating source and binary that can be executed from the source tree

```
SOURCE_DIR := /test/book/examples/ch07-separate-binaries-1
BINARY_DIR := /test/book/out/mp3_player_out

# $(call source-dir-to-binary-dir, directory-list)
source-dir-to-binary-dir = $(addprefix $(BINARY_DIR)/, $1)

# $(call source-to-object, source-file-list)
source-to-object = $(call source-dir-to-binary-dir,       \
                   $(subst .c,.o,$(filter %.c,$1))         \
                   $(subst .y,.o,$(filter %.y,$1))         \
                   $(subst .l,.o,$(filter %.l,$1)))

# $(subdirectory)
subdirectory = $(patsubst %/module.mk,%,                  \
                 $(word                                    \
                   $(words $(MAKEFILE_LIST)),$(MAKEFILE_LIST)))

# $(call make-library, library-name, source-file-list)
define make-library
  libraries += $(BINARY_DIR)/$1
  sources   += $2

  $(BINARY_DIR)/$1: $(call source-dir-to-binary-dir,      \
                    $(subst .c,.o,$(filter %.c,$2)))       \
```

```
                        $(subst .y,.o,$(filter %.y,$2))     \
                        $(subst .l,.o,$(filter %.l,$2)))
        $(AR) $(ARFLAGS) $$@ $$^
endef


# $(call generated-source, source-file-list)
generated-source = $(call source-dir-to-binary-dir,       \
                        $(subst .y,.c,$(filter %.y,$1))    \
                        $(subst .y,.h,$(filter %.y,$1))    \
                        $(subst .l,.c,$(filter %.l,$1)))   \
                    $(filter %.c,$1)

# $(compile-rules)
define compile-rules
  $(foreach f, $(local_src),\
    $(call one-compile-rule,$(call source-to-object,$f),$f))
endef

# $(call one-compile-rule, binary-file, source-files)
define one-compile-rule
  $1: $(call generated-source,$2)
        $(COMPILE.c) -o $$@ $$<

  $(subst .o,.d,$1): $(call generated-source,$2)
        $(CC) $(CFLAGS) $(CPPFLAGS) $(TARGET_ARCH) -M $$< | \
        $(SED) 's,\($$(notdir $$*)\).o\) *:,$$(dir $$@)\1 $$@: ,' > $$@.tmp
        $(MV) $$@.tmp $$@

endef

modules      := lib/codec lib/db lib/ui app/player
programs     :=
libraries    :=
sources      :=

objects      = $(call source-to-object,$(sources))
dependencies = $(subst .o,.d,$(objects))

include_dirs := $(BINARY_DIR)/lib lib include
CPPFLAGS     += $(addprefix -I ,$(include_dirs))
vpath %.h $(include_dirs)

MKDIR := mkdir -p
MV    := mv -f
RM    := rm -f
SED   := sed
TEST  := test

create-output-directories :=                                  \
        $(shell for f in $(call source-dir-to-binary-dir,$(modules));  \
                do                                            \
```

Example 8-1. A makefile separating source and binary that can be executed from the source tree (continued)

```
                    $(TEST) -d $$f || $(MKDIR) $$f;                    \
               done)

all:

include $(addsuffix /module.mk,$(modules))

.PHONY: all
all: $(programs)

.PHONY: libraries
libraries: $(libraries)

.PHONY: clean
clean:
       $(RM) -r $(BINARY_DIR)

ifneq "$(MAKECMDGOALS)" "clean"
  include $(dependencies)
endif
```

In this version the source-to-object function is modified to prepend the path to the binary tree. This prefixing operation is performed several times, so write it as a function:

```
SOURCE_DIR := /test/book/examples/ch07-separate-binaries-1
BINARY_DIR := /test/book/out/mp3_player_out

# $(call source-dir-to-binary-dir, directory-list)
source-dir-to-binary-dir = $(addprefix $(BINARY_DIR)/, $1)

# $(call source-to-object, source-file-list)
source-to-object = $(call source-dir-to-binary-dir,          \
                    $(subst .c,.o,$(filter %.c,$1))           \
                    $(subst .y,.o,$(filter %.y,$1))           \
                    $(subst .l,.o,$(filter %.l,$1)))
```

The make-library function is similarly altered to prefix the output file with BINARY_DIR. The subdirectory function is restored to its previous version since the include path is again a simple relative path. One small snag; a bug in make 3.80 prevents calling source-to-object within the new version of make-library. This bug has been fixed in 3.81. We can work around the bug by hand expanding the source-to-object function.

Now we get to the truly ugly part. When the output file is not directly accessible from a path relative to the *makefile*, the implicit rules no longer fire. For instance, the basic compile rule %.o: %.c works well when the two files live in the same directory, or even if the C file is in a subdirectory, say *lib/codec/codec.c*. When the source file lives in a remote directory, we can instruct make to search for the source with the vpath feature. But when the object file lives in a remote directory, make has no way of determining where the object file resides and the target/prerequisite chain is broken.

The only way to inform make of the location of the output file is to provide an explicit rule linking the source and object files:

```
$(BINARY_DIR)/lib/codec/codec.o: lib/codec/codec.c
```

This must be done for every single object file.

Worse, this target/prerequisite pair is not matched against the implicit rule, %.o: %.c. That means we must also provide the command script, duplicating whatever is in the implicit database and possibly repeating this script many times. The problem also applies to the automatic dependency generation rule we've been using. Adding two explicit rules for every object file in a *makefile* is a maintenance nightmare, if done by hand. However, we can minimize the code duplication and maintenance by writing a function to generate these rules:

```
# $(call one-compile-rule, binary-file, source-files)
define one-compile-rule
  $1: $(call generated-source,$2)
        $(COMPILE.c) $$@ $$<

  $(subst .o,.d,$1): $(call generated-source,$2)
        $(CC) $(CFLAGS) $(CPPFLAGS) $(TARGET_ARCH) -M $$< | \
        $(SED) 's,\($$(notdir $$*)\.o\) *:,$$(dir $$@)\1 $$@: ,' > $$@.tmp
        $(MV) $$@.tmp $$@

endef
```

The first two lines of the function are the explicit rule for the object-to-source dependency. The prerequisites for the rule must be computed using the generated-source function we wrote in Chapter 6 because some of the source files are yacc and lex files that will cause compilation failures when they appear in the command script (expanded with $^, for instance). The automatic variables are quoted so they are expanded later when the command script is executed rather than when the user-defined function is evaluated by eval. The generated-source function has been modified to return C files unaltered as well as the generated source for yacc and lex:

```
# $(call generated-source, source-file-list)
generated-source = $(call source-dir-to-binary-dir,       \
                    $(subst .y,.c,$(filter %.y,$1))        \
                    $(subst .y,.h,$(filter %.y,$1))        \
                    $(subst .l,.c,$(filter %.l,$1)))       \
                $(filter %.c,$1)
```

With this change, the function now produces this output:

```
Argument                Result
lib/db/playlist.y       /c/mp3_player_out/lib/db/playlist.c
                        /c/mp3_player_out/lib/db/playlist.h
lib/db/scanner.l        /c/mp3_player_out/lib/db/scanner.c
app/player/play_mp3.c   app/player/play_mp3.c
```

The explicit rule for dependency generation is similar. Again, note the extra quoting (double dollar signs) required by the dependency script.

Our new function must now be expanded for each source file in a module:

```
# $(compile-rules)
define compile-rules
  $(foreach f, $(local_src),\
    $(call one-compile-rule,$(call source-to-object,$f),$f))
endef
```

This function relies on the global variable local_src used by the *module.mk* files. A more general approach would pass this file list as an argument, but in this project it seems unnecessary. These functions are easily added to our *module.mk* files:

```
local_src := $(subdirectory)/codec.c

$(eval $(call make-library,$(subdirectory)/libcodec.a,$(local_src)))

$(eval $(compile-rules))
```

We must use eval because the compile-rules function expands to more than one line of make code.

There is one last complication. If the standard C compilation pattern rule fails to match with binary output paths, the implicit rule for lex and our pattern rule for yacc will also fail. We can update these by hand easily. Since they are no longer applicable to other lex or yacc files, we can move them into *lib/db/module.mk*:

```
local_dir := $(BINARY_DIR)/$(subdirectory)
local_src := $(addprefix $(subdirectory)/,playlist.y scanner.l)

$(eval $(call make-library,$(subdirectory)/libdb.a,$(local_src)))

$(eval $(compile-rules))

.SECONDARY: $(call generated-source, $(local_src))

$(local_dir)/scanner.d: $(local_dir)/playlist.d

$(local_dir)/%.c $(local_dir)/%.h: $(subdirectory)/%.y
        $(YACC.y) --defines $<
        $(MV) y.tab.c $(dir $@)$*.c
        $(MV) y.tab.h $(dir $@)$*.h

$(local_dir)/scanner.c: $(subdirectory)/scanner.l
        @$(RM) $@
        $(LEX.l) $< > $@
```

The lex rule has been implemented as a normal explicit rule, but the yacc rule is a pattern rule. Why? Because the yacc rule is used to build two targets, a C file and a header file. If we used a normal explicit rule, make would execute the command script twice, once for the C file to be created and once for the header. But make assumes that a pattern rule with multiple targets updates both targets with a single execution.

If possible, instead of the *makefiles* shown in this section, I would use the simpler approach of compiling from the binary tree. As you can see, complications arise immediately (and seem to get worse and worse) when trying to compile from the source tree.

Read-Only Source

Once the source and binary trees are separate, the ability to make a reference source tree read-only often comes for free if the only files generated by the build are the binary files placed in the output tree. However, if source files are generated, then we must take care that they are placed in the binary tree.

In the simpler "compile from binary tree" approach, the generated files are written into the binary tree automatically because the yacc and lex programs are executed from the binary tree. In the "compile from source tree" approach, we are forced to provide explicit paths for our source and target files, so specifying the path to a binary tree file is no extra work, except that we must remember to do it.

The other obstacles to making the reference source tree read only are usually self-imposed. Often a legacy build system will include actions that create files in the source tree because the original author had not considered the advantages to a read-only source tree. Examples include generated documentation, log files, and temporary files. Moving these files to the output tree can sometimes be arduous, but if building multiple binary trees from a single source is necessary, the alternative is to maintain multiple, identical source trees and keep them in sync.

Dependency Generation

We gave a brief introduction to dependency generation in the section "Automatic Dependency Generation" in Chapter 2, but it left several problems unaddressed. Therefore, this section offers some alternatives to the simple solution already described.* In particular, the simple approach described earlier and in the GNU make manual suffer from these failings:

- It is inefficient. When make discovers that a dependency file is missing or out of date, it updates the *.d* file and restarts itself. Rereading the *makefile* can be inefficient if it performs many tasks during the reading of the *makefile* and the analysis of the dependency graph.

- make generates a warning when you build a target for the first time and each time you add new source files. At these times the dependency file associated with a

---

* Much of the material in this section was invented by Tom Tromey (*tromey@cygnus.com*) for the GNU automake utility and is taken from the excellent summary article by Paul Smith (the maintainer of GNU make) from his web site *http://make.paulandlesley.org*.

new source file does not yet exist, so when make attempts to read the dependency file it will produce a warning message before generating the dependency file. This is not fatal, merely irritating.

- If you remove a source file, make stops with a fatal error during subsequent builds. In this situation, there exists a dependency file containing the removed file as a prerequisite. Since make cannot find the removed file and doesn't know how to make it, make prints the message:

```
make: *** No rule to make target foo.h, needed by foo.d.  Stop.
```

Furthermore, make cannot rebuild the dependency file because of this error. The only recourse is to remove the dependency file by hand, but since these files are often hard to find, users typically delete all the dependency files and perform a clean build. This error also occurs when files are renamed.

Note that this problem is most noticeable with removed or renamed header files rather than *.c* files. This is because *.c* files will be removed from the list of dependency files automatically and will not trouble the build.

Tromey's Way

Let's address these problems individually.

How can we avoid restarting make?

On careful consideration, we can see that restarting make is unnecessary. If a dependency file is updated, it means that at least one of its prerequisites has changed, which means we must update the target. Knowing more than that isn't necessary in this execution of make because more dependency information won't change make's behavior. But we want the dependency file updated so that the next run of make will have complete dependency information.

Since we don't need the dependency file in this execution of make, we could generate the file at the same time as we update the target. We can do this by rewriting the compilation rule to also update the dependency file.

```
# $(call make-depend,source-file,object-file,depend-file)
define make-depend
  $(CC) $(CFLAGS) $(CPPFLAGS) $(TARGET_ARCH) -M $1 | \
  $(SED) 's,\($$(notdir $2)\) *:,$$(dir $2) $3: ,' > $3.tmp
  $(MV) $3.tmp $3
endef

%.o: %.c
        $(call make-depend,$<,$@,$(subst .o,.d,$@))
        $(COMPILE.c) -o $@ $<
```

We implement the dependency generation feature with the function make-depend that accepts the source, object, and dependency filenames. This provides maximum flexibility if we need to reuse the function later in a different context. When we modify our compilation rule this way, we must delete the %.d: %.c pattern rule we wrote to avoid generating the dependency files twice.

Now, the object file and dependency file are logically linked: if one exists the other must exist. Therefore, we don't really care if a dependency file is missing. If it is, the object file is also missing and both will be updated by the next build. So we can now ignore any warnings that result from missing .d files.

In the section "Include and Dependencies" in Chapter 3, I introduced an alternate form of include directive, -include (or sinclude), that ignores errors and does not generate warnings:

```
ifneq "$(MAKECMDGOALS)" "clean"
  -include $(dependencies)
endif
```

This solves the second problem, that of an annoying message when a dependency file does not yet exist.

Finally, we can avoid the warning when missing prerequisites are discovered with a little trickery. The trick is to create a target for the missing file that has no prerequisites and no commands. For example, suppose our dependency file generator has created this dependency:

```
target.o target.d: header.h
```

Now suppose that, due to code refactoring, *header.h* no longer exists. The next time we run the *makefile* we'll get the error:

```
make: *** No rule to make target header.h, needed by target.d.  Stop.
```

But if we add a target with no command for *header.h* to the dependency file, the error does not occur:

```
target.o target.d: header.h
header.h:
```

This is because, if *header.h* does not exist, it will simply be considered out of date and any targets that use it as a prerequisite will be updated. So the dependency file will be regenerated without *header.h* because it is no longer referenced. If *header.h* does exist, make considers it up to date and continues. So, all we need to do is ensure that every prerequisite has an associated empty rule. You may recall that we first encountered this kind of rule in the section "Phony Targets" in Chapter 2. Here is a version of make-depend that adds the new targets:

```
# $(call make-depend,source-file,object-file,depend-file)
define make-depend
  $(CC) $(CFLAGS) $(CPPFLAGS) $(TARGET_ARCH) -M $1 |        \
  $(SED) 's,\($$(notdir $2)\) *:,$$(dir $2) $3: ,' > $3.tmp
  $(SED) -e 's/#.*//'                                        \
         -e 's/^[^:]*: *//'                                  \
         -e 's/ *\\$$$$//'                                   \
         -e '/^$$$$/ d'                                      \
```

```
            -e 's/$$$$/ :/' $3.tmp >> $3.tmp
      $(MV) $3.tmp $3
    endef
```

We execute a new sed command on the dependency file to generate the additional rules. This chunk of sed code performs five transformations:

1. Deletes comments
2. Deletes the target file(s) and subsequent spaces
3. Deletes trailing spaces
4. Deletes blank lines
5. Adds a colon to the end of every line

(GNU sed is able to read from a file and append to it in a single command line, saving us from having to use a second temporary file. This feature may not work on other systems.) The new sed command will take input that looks like:

```
# any comments
target.o target.d: prereq1 prereq2 prereq3 \
    prereq4
```

and transform it into:

```
prereq1 prereq2 prereq3:
prereq4:
```

So make-depend appends this new output to the original dependency file. This solves the "No rule to make target" error.

makedepend Programs

Up to now we have been content to use the -M option provided by most compilers, but what if this option doesn't exist? Alternatively, are there better options than our simple -M?

These days most C compilers have some support for generating make dependencies from the source, but not long ago this wasn't true. In the early days of the X Window System project, they implemented a tool, makedepend, that computes the dependencies from a set of C or C++ sources. This tool is freely available over the Internet. Using makedepend is a little awkward because it is written to append its output to the *makefile*, which we do not want to do. The output of makedepend assumes the object files reside in the same directory as the source. This means that, again, our sed expression must change:

```
# $(call make-depend,source-file,object-file,depend-file)
define make-depend
  $(MAKEDEPEND) -f- $(CFLAGS) $(CPPFLAGS) $(TARGET_ARCH) $1 | \
  $(SED) 's,^.*/\([^/]*\.o\) *:,$(dir $2)\1 $3: ,' > $3.tmp
  $(SED) -e 's/#.*//'                                        \
         -e 's/^[^:]*: *//'                                  \
```

```
                -e 's/ *\\$$$$//'                              \
                -e '/^$$$$/ d'                                 \
                -e 's/$$$$/ :/' $3.tmp >> $3.tmp
        $(MV) $3.tmp $3
    endef
```

The -f- option tells makedepend to write its dependency information to the standard output.

An alternative to using makedepend or your native compiler is to use gcc. It sports a bewildering set of options for generating dependency information. The ones that seem most apropos for our current requirements are:

```
    ifneq "$(MAKECMDGOALS)" "clean"
      -include $(dependencies)
    endif

    # $(call make-depend,source-file,object-file,depend-file)
    define make-depend
      $(GCC)  -MM                \
              -MF $3            \
              -MP               \
              -MT $2            \
              $(CFLAGS)         \
              $(CPPFLAGS)       \
              $(TARGET_ARCH)  \
              $1
    endef

    %.o: %.c
            $(call make-depend,$<,$@,$(subst .o,.d,$@))
            $(COMPILE.c) $(OUTPUT_OPTION) $<
```

The -MM option causes gcc to omit "system" headers from the prerequisites list. This is useful because these files rarely, if ever, change and, as the build system gets more complex, reducing the clutter helps. Originally, this may have been done for performance reasons. With today's processors, the performance difference is barely measurable.

The -MF option specifies the dependency filename. This will be the object filename with the *.d* suffix substituted for *.o*. There is another gcc option, -MD or -MMD, that automatically generates the output filename using a similar substitution. Ideally we would prefer to use this option, but the substitution fails to include the proper relative path to the object file directory and instead places the *.d* file in the current directory. So, we are forced to do the job ourselves using -MF.

The -MP option instructs gcc to include phony targets for each prerequisite. This completely eliminates the messy five-part sed expression in our make-depend function. It seems that the automake developers who invented the phony target technique caused this option to be added to gcc.

Finally, the -MT option specifies the string to use for the target in the dependency file. Again, without this option, gcc fails to include the relative path to the object file output directory.

By using gcc, we can reduce the four commands previously required for dependency generation to a single command. Even when proprietary compilers are used it may be possible to use gcc for dependency management.

Supporting Multiple Binary Trees

Once the *makefile* is modified to write binary files into a separate tree, supporting many trees becomes quite simple. For interactive or developer-invoked builds, where a developer initiates a build from the keyboard, there is little or no preparation required. The developer creates the output directory, cd's to it and invokes make on the *makefile*.

```
$ mkdir -p ~/work/mp3_player_out
$ cd ~/work/mp3_player_out
$ make -f ~/work/mp3_player/makefile
```

If the process is more involved than this, then a shell script wrapper is usually the best solution. This wrapper can also parse the current directory and set an environment variable like BINARY_DIR for use by the *makefile*.

```
#! /bin/bash

# Assume we are in the source directory.
curr=$PWD
export SOURCE_DIR=$curr
while [[ $SOURCE_DIR ]]
do
  if [[ -e $SOURCE_DIR/[Mm]akefile ]]
  then
    break;
  fi
  SOURCE_DIR=${SOURCE_DIR%/*}
done

# Print an error if we haven't found a makefile.
if [[ ! $SOURCE_DIR ]]
then
  printf "run-make: Cannot find a makefile" > /dev/stderr
  exit 1
fi

# Set the output directory to a default, if not set.
if [[ ! $BINARY_DIR ]]
then
  BINARY_DIR=${SOURCE_DIR}_out
fi
```

```
# Create the output directory
mkdir --parents $BINARY_DIR

# Run the make.
make --directory="$BINARY_DIR" "$@"
```

This particular script is a bit fancier. It searches for the *makefile* first in the current directory and then in the parent directory on up the tree until a *makefile* is found. It then checks that the variable for the binary tree is set. If not, it is set by appending "_out" to the source directory. The script then creates the output directory and executes make.

If the build is being performed on different platforms, some method for differentiating between platforms is required. The simplest approach is to require the developer to set an environment variable for each type of platform and add conditionals to the *makefile* and source based on this variable. A better approach is to set the platform type automatically based on the output of uname.

```
space := $(empty) $(empty)
export MACHINE := $(subst $(space),-,$(shell uname -smo))
```

If the builds are being invoked automatically from cron, I've found that a helper shell script is a better approach than having cron invoke make itself. A wrapper script provides better support for setup, error recovery, and finalization of an automated build. The script is also an appropriate place to set variables and command-line parameters.

Finally, if a project supports a fixed set of trees and platforms, you can use directory names to automatically identify the current build. For example:

```
ALL_TREES := /builds/hp-386-windows-optimized \
             /builds/hp-386-windows-debug      \
             /builds/sgi-irix-optimzed         \
             /builds/sgi-irix-debug            \
             /builds/sun-solaris8-profiled     \
             /builds/sun-solaris8-debug

BINARY_DIR := $(foreach t,$(ALL_TREES),\
                 $(filter $(ALL_TREES)/%,$(CURDIR)))

BUILD_TYPE := $(notdir $(subst -,/,$(BINARY_DIR)))

MACHINE_TYPE := $(strip                          \
                  $(subst /,-,                    \
                    $(patsubst %/,%,              \
                      $(dir                       \
                        $(subst -,/,             \
                          $(notdir $(BINARY_DIR)))))))
```

The ALL_TREES variable holds a list of all valid binary trees. The foreach loop matches the current directory against each of the valid binary trees. Only one can match. Once the binary tree has been identified, we can extract the build type (e.g., optimized, debug, or profiled) from the build directory name. We retrieve the last component of the directory name by transforming the dash-separated words into slash-separated words and grabbing the last word with notdir. Similarly, we retrieve the machine type by grabbing the last word and using the same technique to remove the last dash component.

Partial Source Trees

On really large projects, just checking out and maintaining the source can be a burden on developers. If a system consists of many modules and a particular developer is modifying only a localized part of it, checking out and compiling the entire project can be a large time sink. Instead, a centrally managed build, performed nightly, can be used to fill in the holes in a developer's source and binary trees.

Doing so requires two types of search. First, when a missing header file is required by the compiler, it must be instructed to search in the reference source tree. Second, when the *makefile* requires a missing library, it must be told to search in the reference binary tree. To help the compiler find source, we can simply add additional -I options after the -I options specifying local directories. To help make find libraries, we can add additional directories to the vpath.

```
SOURCE_DIR      := ../mp3_player
REF_SOURCE_DIR := /reftree/src/mp3_player
REF_BINARY_DIR := /binaries/mp3_player
...
include_dirs := lib $(SOURCE_DIR)/lib $(SOURCE_DIR)/include
CPPFLAGS      += $(addprefix -I ,$(include_dirs))            \
                 $(addprefix -I $(REF_SOURCE_DIR)/,$(include_dirs))
vpath %.h       $(include_dirs)                              \
                 $(addprefix $(REF_SOURCE_DIR)/,$(include_dirs))

vpath %.a       $(addprefix $(REF_BINARY_DIR)/lib/, codec db ui)
```

This approach assumes that the "granularity" of a CVS check out is a library or program module. In this case, the make can be contrived to skip missing library and program directories if a developer has chosen not to check them out. When it comes time to use these libraries, the search path will automatically fill in the missing files.

In the *makefile*, the modules variable lists the set of subdirectories to be searched for *module.mk* files. If a subdirectory is not checked out, this list must be edited to remove the subdirectory. Alternatively, the *modules* variable can be set by wildcard:

```
modules := $(dir $(wildcard lib/*/module.mk))
```

This expression will find all the subdirectories containing a *module.mk* file and return the directory list. Note that because of how the dir function works, each directory will contain a trailing slash.

It is also possible for make to manage partial source trees at the individual file level, building libraries by gathering some object files from a local developer tree and missing files from a reference tree. However, this is quite messy and developers are not happy with it, in my experience.

Reference Builds, Libraries, and Installers

At this point we've pretty much covered everything needed to implement reference builds. Customizing the single top-level *makefile* to support the feature is straightforward. Simply replace the simple assignments to SOURCE_DIR and BINARY_DIR with ?= assignments. The scripts you run from cron can use this basic approach:

1. Redirect output and set the names of log files
2. Clean up old builds and clean the reference source tree
3. Check out fresh source
4. Set the source and binary directory variables
5. Invoke make
6. Scan the logs for errors
7. Compute tags files, and possibly update the locate database*
8. Post information on the success or failure of the build

It is convenient, in the reference build model, to maintain a set of old builds in case a rogue check-in corrupts the tree. I usually keep 7 or 14 nightly builds. Of course, the nightly build script logs its output to files stored near the builds themselves and the script purges old builds and logs. Scanning the logs for errors is usually done with an awk script. Finally, I usually have the script maintain a *latest* symbolic link. To determine if the build is valid, I include a validate target in each *makefile*. This target performs simple validation that the targets were built.

```
.PHONY: validate_build
validate_build:
        test $(foreach f,$(RELEASE_FILES),-s $f -a) -e .
```

This command script simply tests if a set of expected files exists and is not empty. Of course, this doesn't take the place of testing, but is a convenient sanity check for a build. If the test returns failure, the make returns failure and the nightly build script can leave the *latest* symbolic link pointing to the old build.

Third-party libraries are always a bit of a hassle to manage. I subscribe to the commonly held belief that it is bad to store large binary files in CVS. This is because CVS cannot store deltas as diffs and the underlying RCS files can grow to enormous size.

---

* The locate database is a compilation of all the filenames present on a filesystem. It is a fast way of performing a find by name. I have found this database invaluable for managing large source trees and like to have it updated nightly after the build has completed.

Very large files in the CVS repository can slow down many common CVS operations, thus affecting all development.

If third-party libraries are not stored in CVS, they must be managed some other way. My current preference is to create a library directory in the reference tree and record the library version number in the directory name, as shown in Figure 8-1.

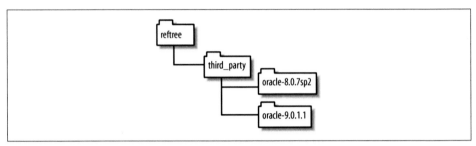

Figure 8-1. Directory layout for third-party libraries

These directory names are referenced by the *makefile*:

```
ORACLE_9011_DIR ?= /reftree/third_party/oracle-9.0.1.1/Ora90
ORACLE_9011_JAR ?= $(ORACLE_9011_DIR)/jdbc/lib/classes12.jar
```

When the vendor updates its libraries, create a new directory in the reference tree and declare new variables in the *makefile*. This way the *makefile*, which is properly maintained with tags and branches, always explicitly reflects the versions being used.

Installers are also a difficult issue. I believe that separating the basic build process from creating the installer image is a good thing. Current installer tools are complex and fragile. Folding them into the (also often complex and fragile) build system yields difficult-to-maintain systems. Instead, the basic build can write its results into a "release" directory that contains all (or most of) the data required by the installer build tool. This tool may be driven from its own *makefile* that ultimately yields an executable setup image.

## CHAPTER 9

Java

Many Java developers like Integrated Development Environments (IDEs) such as Eclipse. Given such well-known alternatives as Java IDEs and Ant, readers could well ask why they should even think of using make on Java projects. This chapter explores the value of make in these situations; in particular, it presents a generalized *makefile* that can be dropped into just about any Java project with minimal modification and carry out all the standard rebuilding tasks.

Using make with Java raises several issues and introduces some opportunities. This is primarily due to three factors: the Java compiler, javac, is extremely fast; the standard Java compiler supports the @filename syntax for reading "command-line parameters" from a file; and if a Java package is specified, the Java language specifies a path to the .*class* file.

Standard Java compilers are very fast. This is primarily due to the way the import directive works. Similar to a #include in C, this directive is used to allow access to externally defined symbols. However, rather than rereading source code, which then needs to be reparsed and analyzed, Java reads the class files directly. Because the symbols in a class file cannot change during the compilation process, the class files are cached by the compiler. In even medium-sized projects, this means the Java compiler can avoid rereading, parsing, and analyzing literally millions of lines of code compared with C. A more modest performance improvement is due to the bare minimum of optimization performed by most Java compilers. Instead, Java relies on sophisticated just-in-time (JIT) optimizations performed by the Java virtual machine (JVM) itself.

Most large Java projects make extensive use of Java's *package* feature. A class is declared to be encapsulated in a package that forms a scope around the symbols defined by the file. Package names are hierarchical and implicitly define a file structure. For instance, the package a.b.c would implicitly define a directory structure *a/b/c*. Code declared to be within the a.b.c package would be compiled to class files in the *a/b/c* directory. This means that make's normal algorithm for associating a binary file with its source fails. But it also means that there is no need to specify a -o option to indicate where output files should be placed. Indicating the root of the output tree, which is the same for all files, is sufficient. This, in turn, means that source files from different directories can be compiled with the same command-line invocation.

The standard Java compilers all support the @filename syntax that allows command-line parameters to be read from a file. This is significant in conjunction with the package feature because it means that the entire Java source for a project can be compiled with a single execution of the Java compiler. This is a major performance improvement because the time it takes to load and execute the compiler is a major contributor to build times.

In summary, by composing the proper command line, compiling 400,000 lines of Java takes about three minutes on a 2.5-GHz Pentium 4 processor. Compiling an equivalent C++ application would require hours.

Alternatives to make

As previously mentioned, the Java developer community enthusiastically adopts new technologies. Let's see how two of these, Ant and IDEs, relate to make.

Ant

The Java community is very active, producing new tools and APIs at an impressive rate. One of these new tools is Ant, a build tool intended to replace make in the Java development process. Like make, Ant uses a description file to indicate the targets and prerequisites of a project. Unlike make, Ant is written in Java and Ant build files are written in XML.

To give you a feel for the XML build file, here is an excerpt from the Ant build file:

```
<target name="build"
        depends="prepare, check_for_optional_packages"
        description="--> compiles the source code">
  <mkdir dir="${build.dir}"/>
  <mkdir dir="${build.classes}"/>
  <mkdir dir="${build.lib}"/>

  <javac srcdir="${java.dir}"
         destdir="${build.classes}"
         debug="${debug}"
         deprecation="${deprecation}"
         target="${javac.target}"
         optimize="${optimize}" >
    <classpath refid="classpath"/>
  </javac>

  ...

  <copy todir="${build.classes}">
    <fileset dir="${java.dir}">
```

```
        <include name="**/*.properties"/>
        <include name="**/*.dtd"/>
      </fileset>
    </copy>
  </target>
```

As you can see, a target is introduced with an XML <target> tag. Each target has a name and dependency list specified with <name> and <depends> attributes, respectively. Actions are performed by Ant *tasks*. A task is written in Java and bound to an XML tag. For instance, the task of creating a directory is specified with the <mkdir> tag and triggers the execution of the Java method Mkdir.execute, which eventually calls File.mkdir. As far as possible, all tasks are implemented using the Java API.

An equivalent build file using make syntax would be:

```
# compiles the source code
build: $(all_javas) prepare check_for_optional_packages
        $(MKDIR) -p $(build.dir) $(build.classes) $(build.lib)
        $(JAVAC) -sourcepath $(java.dir)                         \
                -d $(build.classes)                              \
                $(debug)                                         \
                $(deprecation)                                   \
                -target $(javac.target)                          \
                $(optimize)                                      \
                -classpath $(classpath)                          \
                @$<
        ...
        $(FIND) . \( -name '*.properties' -o -name '*.dtd' \) | \
        $(TAR) -c -f - -T - | $(TAR) -C $(build.classes) -x -f -
```

This snippet of make uses techniques that this book hasn't discussed yet. Suffice to say that the prerequisite *all.javas*, which is the value of the variable *all_javas*, contains a list of all java files to be compiled. The Ant tasks <mkdir>, <javac>, and <copy> also perform dependency checking. That is, if the directory already exists, mkdir is not executed. Likewise, if the Java class files are newer than the source files, the source files are not compiled. Nevertheless, the make command script performs essentially the same functions. Ant includes a generic task, called <exec>, to run a local program.

Ant is a clever and fresh approach to build tools; however, it presents some issues worth considering:

- Although Ant has found wide acceptance in the Java community, it is still relatively unknown elsewhere. Also, it seems doubtful that its popularity will spread much beyond Java (for the reasons listed here). make, on the other hand, has consistently been applied to a broad range of fields including software development, document processing and typesetting, and web site and workstation maintenance, to name a few. Understanding make is important for anyone who needs to work on a variety of software systems.

- The choice of XML as the description language is appropriate for a Java-based tool. But XML is not particularly pleasant to write or to read (for many). Good XML editors can be difficult to find and often do not integrate well with existing tools (either my integrated development environment includes a good XML editor or I must leave my IDE and find a separate tool). As you can see from the previous example, XML and the Ant dialect, in particular, are verbose compared with make and shell syntax. And the XML is filled with its own idiosyncrasies.

- When writing Ant build files you must contend with another layer of indirection. The Ant <mkdir> task does not invoke the underlying mkdir program for your system. Instead, it executes the Java mkdir( ) method of the java.io.File class. This may or may not do what you expect. Essentially, any knowledge a programmer brings to Ant about the behavior of common tools is suspect and must be checked against the Ant documentation, Java documentation, or the Ant source. In addition, to invoke the Java compiler, for instance, I may be forced to navigate through a dozen or more unfamiliar XML attributes, such as <srcdir>, <debug>, etc., that are not documented in the compiler manual. In contrast, the make script is completely transparent, that is, I can typically type the commands directly into a shell to see how they behave.

- Although Ant is certainly portable, so is make. As shown in Chapter 7, writing portable *makefiles*, like writing portable Ant files, requires experience and knowledge. Programmers have been writing portable *makefiles* for two decades. Furthermore, the Ant documentation notes that there are portability issues with symbolic links on Unix and long filenames on Windows, that MacOS X is the only supported Apple operating system, and that support for other platforms is not guaranteed. Also, basic operations like setting the execution bit on a file cannot be performed from the Java API. An external program must be used. Portability is never easy or complete.

- The Ant tool does not explain precisely what it is doing. Since Ant tasks are not generally implemented by executing shell commands, the Ant tool has a difficult time displaying its actions. Typically, the display consists of natural language prose from print statements added by the task author. These print statements cannot be executed by a user from a shell. In contrast, the lines echoed by make are usually command lines that a user can copy and paste into a shell for reexecution. This means the Ant build is less useful to developers trying to understand the build process and tools. Also, it is not possible for a developer to reuse parts of a task, impromptu, at the keyboard.

- Last and most importantly, Ant shifts the build paradigm from a scripted to a nonscripted programming language. Ant tasks are written in Java. If a task does not exist or does not do what you want, you must either write your own task in Java or use the <exec> task. (Of course, if you use the <exec> task often, you would do far better to simply use make with its macros, functions, and more compact syntax.)

Scripting languages, on the other hand, were invented and flourish precisely to address this type of issue. make has existed for nearly 30 years and can be used in the most complex situations without extending its implementation. Of course, there have been a handful of extensions in those 30 years. Many of them conceived and implemented in GNU make.

Ant is a marvelous tool that is widely accepted in the Java community. However, before embarking on a new project, consider carefully if Ant is appropriate for your development environment. This chapter will hopefully prove to you that make can powerfully meet your Java build needs.

IDEs

Many Java developers use Integrated Development Environments (IDEs) that bundle an editor, compiler, debugger, and code browser in a single (typically) graphical environment. Examples include the open source Eclipse (*http://www.eclipse.org*) and Emacs JDEE (*http://jdee.sunsite.dk*), and, from commercial vendors, Sun Java Studio (*http://wwws.sun.com/software/sundev/jde*) and JBuilder (*http://www.borland.com/jbuilder*). These environments typically have the notion of a project-build process that compiles the necessary files and enables the application execution.

If the IDEs support all this, why should we consider using make? The most obvious reason is portability. If there is ever a need to build the project on another platform, the build may fail when ported to the new target. Although Java itself is portable across platforms, the support tools are often not. For instance, if the configuration files for your project include Unix- or Windows-style paths, these may generate errors when the build is run on the other operating system. A second reason to use make is to support unattended builds. Some IDEs support batch building and some do not. The quality of support for this feature also varies. Finally, the build support included is often limited. If you hope to implement customized release directory structures, integrate help files from external applications, support automated testing, and handle branching and parallel lines of development, you may find the integrated build support inadequate.

In my own experience, I have found the IDEs to be fine for small scale or localized development, but production builds require the more comprehensive support that make can provide. I typically use an IDE to write and debug code, and write a *makefile* for production builds and releases. During development I use the IDE to compile the project to a state suitable for debugging. But if I change many files or modify files that are input to code generators, then I run the *makefile*. The IDEs I've used do not have good support for external source code generation tools. Usually the result of an IDE build is not suitable for release to internal or external customers. For that task I use make.

A Generic Java Makefile

Example 9-1 shows a generic *makefile* for Java; I'll explain each of its parts later in the chapter.

Example 9-1. Generic makefile for Java

```
# A generic makefile for a Java project.

VERSION_NUMBER := 1.0

# Location of trees.
SOURCE_DIR  := src
OUTPUT_DIR  := classes

# Unix tools
AWK         := awk
FIND        := /bin/find
MKDIR       := mkdir -p
RM          := rm -rf
SHELL       := /bin/bash

# Path to support tools
JAVA_HOME    := /opt/j2sdk1.4.2_03
AXIS_HOME    := /opt/axis-1_1
TOMCAT_HOME  := /opt/jakarta-tomcat-5.0.18
XERCES_HOME  := /opt/xerces-1_4_4
JUNIT_HOME   := /opt/junit3.8.1

# Java tools
JAVA        := $(JAVA_HOME)/bin/java
JAVAC       := $(JAVA_HOME)/bin/javac

JFLAGS      := -sourcepath $(SOURCE_DIR)        \
               -d $(OUTPUT_DIR)                 \
               -source 1.4

JVMFLAGS    := -ea                              \
               -esa                             \
               -Xfuture

JVM         := $(JAVA) $(JVMFLAGS)

JAR         := $(JAVA_HOME)/bin/jar
JARFLAGS    := cf

JAVADOC     := $(JAVA_HOME)/bin/javadoc
JDFLAGS     := -sourcepath $(SOURCE_DIR)        \
               -d $(OUTPUT_DIR)                 \
               -link http://java.sun.com/products/jdk/1.4/docs/api

# Jars
COMMONS_LOGGING_JAR    := $(AXIS_HOME)/lib/commons-logging.jar
```

Example 9-1. Generic makefile for Java (continued)

```makefile
LOG4J_JAR             := $(AXIS_HOME)/lib/log4j-1.2.8.jar
XERCES_JAR            := $(XERCES_HOME)/xerces.jar
JUNIT_JAR             := $(JUNIT_HOME)/junit.jar

# Set the Java classpath
class_path := OUTPUT_DIR             \
             XERCES_JAR              \
             COMMONS_LOGGING_JAR     \
             LOG4J_JAR               \
             JUNIT_JAR

# space - A blank space
space := $(empty) $(empty)

# $(call build-classpath, variable-list)
define build-classpath
$(strip                                      \
  $(patsubst :%,%,                           \
    $(subst : ,:,                            \
      $(strip                                \
        $(foreach j,$1,$(call get-file,$j):)))))
endef

# $(call get-file, variable-name)
define get-file
  $(strip                                    \
    $($1)                                     \
    $(if $(call file-exists-eval,$1),,       \
      $(warning The file referenced by variable \
                '$1' ($($1)) cannot be found)))
endef

# $(call file-exists-eval, variable-name)
define file-exists-eval
  $(strip                                    \
    $(if $($1),,$(warning '$1' has no value)) \
    $(wildcard $($1)))
endef

# $(call brief-help, makefile)
define brief-help
  $(AWK) '$$1 ~ /^[^.][-A-Za-z0-9]*:/          \
        { print substr($$1, 1, length($$1)-1) }' $1 | \
  sort |                                     \
  pr -T -w 80 -4
endef

# $(call file-exists, wildcard-pattern)
file-exists = $(wildcard $1)

# $(call check-file, file-list)
define check-file
```

Example 9-1. Generic makefile for Java (continued)

```
  $(foreach f, $1,                                        \
    $(if $(call file-exists, $($f)),,                     \
       $(warning $f ($($f)) is missing)))
endef

# #(call make-temp-dir, root-opt)
define make-temp-dir
  mktemp -t $(if $1,$1,make).XXXXXXXXXX
endef

# MANIFEST_TEMPLATE - Manifest input to m4 macro processor
MANIFEST_TEMPLATE := src/manifest/manifest.mf
TMP_JAR_DIR       := $(call make-temp-dir)
TMP_MANIFEST      := $(TMP_JAR_DIR)/manifest.mf

# $(call add-manifest, jar, jar-name, manifest-file-opt)
define add-manifest
  $(RM) $(dir $(TMP_MANIFEST))
  $(MKDIR) $(dir $(TMP_MANIFEST))
  m4 --define=NAME="$(notdir $2)"                         \
     --define=IMPL_VERSION=$(VERSION_NUMBER)              \
     --define=SPEC_VERSION=$(VERSION_NUMBER)              \
     $(if $3,$3,$(MANIFEST_TEMPLATE))                     \
     > $(TMP_MANIFEST)
  $(JAR) -ufm $1 $(TMP_MANIFEST)
  $(RM) $(dir $(TMP_MANIFEST))
endef

# $(call make-jar,jar-variable-prefix)
define make-jar
  .PHONY: $1 $$($1_name)
  $1: $($1_name)
  $$($1_name):
        cd $(OUTPUT_DIR); \
        $(JAR) $(JARFLAGS) $$(notdir $$@) $$($1_packages)
        $$(call add-manifest, $$@, $$($1_name), $$($1_manifest))
endef

# Set the CLASSPATH
export CLASSPATH := $(call build-classpath, $(class_path))

# make-directories - Ensure output directory exists.
make-directories := $(shell $(MKDIR) $(OUTPUT_DIR))

# help - The default goal
.PHONY: help
help:
        @$(call brief-help, $(CURDIR)/Makefile)

# all - Perform all tasks for a complete build
.PHONY: all
all: compile jars javadoc
```

Example 9-1. Generic makefile for Java (continued)

```
# all_javas - Temp file for holding source file list
all_javas := $(OUTPUT_DIR)/all.javas

# compile - Compile the source
.PHONY: compile
compile: $(all_javas)
        $(JAVAC) $(JFLAGS) @$<

# all_javas - Gather source file list
.INTERMEDIATE: $(all_javas)
$(all_javas):
        $(FIND) $(SOURCE_DIR) -name '*.java' > $@

# jar_list - List of all jars to create
jar_list := server_jar ui_jar

# jars - Create all jars
.PHONY: jars
jars: $(jar_list)

# server_jar - Create the $(server_jar)
server_jar_name     := $(OUTPUT_DIR)/lib/a.jar
server_jar_manifest := src/com/company/manifest/foo.mf
server_jar_packages := com/company/m com/company/n

# ui_jar - create the $(ui_jar)
ui_jar_name     := $(OUTPUT_DIR)/lib/b.jar
ui_jar_manifest := src/com/company/manifest/bar.mf
ui_jar_packages := com/company/o com/company/p

# Create an explicit rule for each jar
# $(foreach j, $(jar_list), $(eval $(call make-jar,$j)))
$(eval $(call make-jar,server_jar))
$(eval $(call make-jar,ui_jar))

# javadoc - Generate the Java doc from sources
.PHONY: javadoc
javadoc: $(all_javas)
        $(JAVADOC) $(JDFLAGS) @$<

.PHONY: clean
clean:
        $(RM) $(OUTPUT_DIR)

.PHONY: classpath
classpath:
        @echo CLASSPATH='$(CLASSPATH)'

.PHONY: check-config
check-config:
        @echo Checking configuration...
        $(call check-file, $(class_path) JAVA_HOME)
```

Example 9-1. Generic makefile for Java (continued)

```
.PHONY: print
print:
        $(foreach v, $(V), \
          $(warning $v = $($v)))
```

Compiling Java

Java can be compiled with make in two ways: the traditional approach, one javac execution per source file; or the fast approach outlined previously using the @filename
syntax.

The Fast Approach: All-in-One Compile

Let's start with the fast approach. As you can see in the generic *makefile*:

```
# all_javas - Temp file for holding source file list
all_javas := $(OUTPUT_DIR)/all.javas

# compile - Compile the source
.PHONY: compile
compile: $(all_javas)
        $(JAVAC) $(JFLAGS) @$<

# all_javas - Gather source file list
.INTERMEDIATE: $(all_javas)
$(all_javas):
        $(FIND) $(SOURCE_DIR) -name '*.java' > $@
```

The phony target compile invokes javac once to compile all the source of the project.

The $(all_javas) prerequisite is a file, *all.javas*, containing a list of Java files, one
filename per line. It is not necessary for each file to be on its own line, but this way it
is much easier to filter files with grep -v if the need ever arises. The rule to create *all.
javas* is marked .INTERMEDIATE so that make will remove the file after each run and
thus create a new one before each compile. The command script to create the file is
straightforward. For maximum maintainability we use the find command to retrieve
all the java files in the source tree. This command can be a bit slow, but is guaranteed to work correctly with virtually no modification as the source tree changes.

If you have a list of source directories readily available in the *makefile*, you can use
faster command scripts to build *all.javas*. If the list of source directories is of medium
length so that the length of the command line does not exceed the operating system's limits, this simple script will do:

```
$(all_javas):
        shopt -s nullglob; \
        printf "%s\n" $(addsuffix /*.java,$(PACKAGE_DIRS)) > $@
```

This script uses shell wildcards to determine the list of Java files in each directory. If, however, a directory contains no Java files, we want the wildcard to yield the empty string, not the original globbing pattern (the default behavior of many shells). To achieve this effect, we use the bash option shopt -s nullglob. Most other shells have similar options. Finally, we use globbing and printf rather than ls -1 because these are built-in to bash, so our command script executes only a single program regardless of the number of package directories.

Alternately, we can avoid shell globbing by using wildcard:

```
$(all_javas):
        print "%s\n" $(wildcard \
                        $(addsuffix /*.java,$(PACKAGE_DIRS))) > $@
```

If you have very many source directories (or very long paths), the above script may exceed the command-line length limit of the operating system. In that case, the following script may be preferable:

```
.INTERMEDIATE: $(all_javas)
$(all_javas):
        shopt -s nullglob;              \
        for f in $(PACKAGE_DIRS);       \
        do                              \
          printf "%s\n" $$f/*.java;     \
        done > $@
```

Notice that the compile target and the supporting rule follow the nonrecursive make approach. No matter how many subdirectories there are, we still have one *makefile* and one execution of the compiler. If you want to compile all of the source, this is as fast as it gets.

Also, we completely discarded all dependency information. With these rules, make neither knows nor cares about which file is newer than which. It simply compiles everything on every invocation. As an added benefit, we can execute the *makefile* from the source tree, instead of the binary tree. This may seem like a silly way to organize the *makefile* considering make's abilities to manage dependencies, but consider this:

- The alternative (which we will explore shortly) uses the standard dependency approach. This invokes a new javac process for each file, adding a lot of overhead. But, if the project is small, compiling all the source files will not take significantly longer than compiling a few files because the javac compiler is so fast and process creation is typically slow. Any build that takes less than 15 seconds is basically equivalent regardless of how much work it does. For instance, compiling approximately 500 source files (from the Ant distribution) takes 14 seconds on my 1.8-GHz Pentium 4 with 512 MB of RAM. Compiling one file takes five seconds.

- Most developers will be using some kind of development environment that provides fast compilation for individual files. The *makefile* will most likely be used when changes are more extensive, complete rebuilds are required, or unattended builds are necessary.

- As we shall see, the effort involved in implementing and maintaining dependencies is equal to the separate source and binary tree builds for C/C++ (described in Chapter 8). Not a task to be underestimated.

As we will see in later examples, the PACKAGE_DIRS variable has uses other than simply building the *all.javas* file. But maintaining this variables can be a labor-intensive, and potentially difficult, step. For smaller projects, the list of directories can be maintained by hand in the *makefile*, but when the number grows beyond a hundred directories, hand editing becomes error-prone and irksome. At this point, it might be prudent to use find to scan for these directories:

```
# $(call find-compilation-dirs, root-directory)
find-compilation-dirs =                          \
  $(patsubst %/,%,                               \
    $(sort                                       \
      $(dir                                      \
        $(shell $(FIND) $1 -name '*.java'))))

PACKAGE_DIRS := $(call find-compilation-dirs, $(SOURCE_DIR))
```

The find command returns a list of files, dir discards the file leaving only the directory, sort removes duplicates from the list, and patsubst strips the trailing slash. Notice that find-compilation-dirs finds the list of files to compile, only to discard the filenames, then the *all.javas* rule uses wildcards to restore the filenames. This seems wasteful, but I have often found that a list of the packages containing source code is very useful in other parts of the build, for instance to scan for EJB configuration files. If your situation does not require a list of packages, then by all means use one of the simpler methods previously mentioned to build *all.javas*.

Compiling with Dependencies

To compile with full dependency checking, you first need a tool to extract dependency information from the Java source files, something similar to cc -M. Jikes (*http://www.ibm.com/developerworks/opensource/jikes*) is an open source Java compiler that supports this feature with the -makefile or +M option. Jikes is not ideal for separate source and binary compilation because it always writes the dependency file in the same directory as the source file, but it is freely available and it works. On the plus side, it generates the dependency file while compiling, avoiding a separate pass.

Here is a dependency processing function and a rule to use it:

```
%.class: %.java
        $(JAVAC) $(JFLAGS) +M $<
        $(call java-process-depend,$<,$@)

# $(call java-process-depend, source-file, object-file)
define java-process-depend
```

```
    $(SED) -e 's/^.*\.class *:/$2 $(subst .class,.d,$2):/'    \
            $(subst .java,.u,$1) > $(subst .class,.tmp,$2)
    $(SED) -e 's/#.*//'                                        \
           -e 's/^[^:]*: *//'                                  \
           -e 's/ *\\$$$$//'                                   \
           -e '/^$$$$/ d'                                      \
           -e 's/$$$$/ :/' $(subst .class,.tmp,$2)             \
           >> $(subst .class,.tmp,$2)
    $(MV) $(subst .class,.tmp,$2).tmp  $(subst .class,.d,$2)
endef
```

This requires that the *makefile* be executed from the binary tree and that the vpath be set to find the source. If you want to use the Jikes compiler only for dependency generation, resorting to a different compiler for actual code generation, you can use the +B option to prevent Jikes from generating bytecodes.

In a simple timing test compiling 223 Java files, the single line compile described previously as the fast approach required 9.9 seconds on my machine. The same 223 files compiled with individual compilation lines required 411.6 seconds or 41.5 times longer. Furthermore, with separate compilation, any build that required compiling more than four files was slower than compiling all the source files with a single compile line. If the dependency generation and compilation were performed by separate programs, the discrepancy would increase.

Of course, development environments vary, but it is important to carefully consider your goals. Minimizing the number of files compiled will not always minimize the time it takes to build a system. For Java in particular, full dependency checking and minimizing the number of files compiled does not appear to be necessary for normal program development.

Setting CLASSPATH

One of the most important issues when developing software with Java is setting the CLASSPATH variable correctly. This variable determines which code is loaded when a class reference is resolved. To compile a Java application correctly, the *makefile* must include the proper CLASSPATH. The CLASSPATH can quickly become long and complex as Java packages, APIs, and support tools are added to a system. If the CLASSPATH can be difficult to set properly, it makes sense to set it in one place.

A technique I've found useful is to use the *makefile* to set the CLASSPATH for itself and other programs. For instance, a target classpath can return the CLASSPATH to the shell invoking the *makefile*:

```
.PHONY: classpath
classpath:
        @echo "export CLASSPATH='$(CLASSPATH)'"
```

Developers can set their CLASSPATH with this (if they use bash):

```
$ eval $(make classpath)
```

The CLASSPATH in the Windows environment can be set with this invocation:

```
.PHONY: windows_classpath
windows_classpath:
        regtool set /user/Environment/CLASSPATH "$(subst /,\\,$(CLASSPATH))"
        control sysdm.cpl,@1,3 &
        @echo "Now click Environment Variables, then OK, then OK again."
```

The program regtool is a utility in the Cygwin development system that manipulates the Windows Registry. Simply setting the Registry doesn't cause the new values to be read by Windows, however. One way to do this is to visit the Environment Variable dialog box and simply exit by clicking OK.

The second line of the command script causes Windows to display the System Properties dialog box with the Advanced tab active. Unfortunately, the command cannot display the Environment Variables dialog box or activate the OK button, so the last line prompts the user to complete the task.

Exporting the CLASSPATH to other programs, such as Emacs JDEE or JBuilder project files, is not difficult.

Setting the CLASSPATH itself can also be managed by make. It is certainly reasonable to set the CLASSPATH variable in the obvious way with:

```
CLASSPATH = /third_party/toplink-2.5/TopLink.jar:/third_party/…
```

For maintainability, using variables is preferred:

```
CLASSPATH = $(TOPLINK_25_JAR):$(TOPLINKX_25_JAR):…
```

But we can do better than this. As you can see in the generic *makefile*, we can build the CLASSPATH in two stages: first list the elements in the path as make variables, then transform those variables into the string value of the environment variable:

```
# Set the Java classpath
class_path := OUTPUT_DIR                \
              XERCES_JAR                \
              COMMONS_LOGGING_JAR       \
              LOG4J_JAR                 \
              JUNIT_JAR
…
# Set the CLASSPATH
export CLASSPATH := $(call build-classpath, $(class_path))
```

(The CLASSPATH in Example 9-1 is meant to be more illustrative than useful.) A well-written build-classpath function solves several irritating problems:

- It is very easy to compose a CLASSPATH in pieces. For instance, if different applications servers are used, the CLASSPATH might need to change. The different versions of the CLASSPATH could then be enclosed in ifdef sections and selected by setting a make variable.

- Casual maintainers of the *makefile* do not have to worry about embedded blanks, newlines, or line continuation, because the build-classpath function handles them.

- The path separator can be selected automatically by the build-classpath function. Thus, it is correct whether run on Unix or Windows.

- The validity of path elements can be verified by the build-classpath function. In particular, one irritating problem with make is that undefined variables collapse to the empty string without an error. In most cases this is very useful, but occasionally it gets in the way. In this case, it quietly yields a bogus value for the CLASSPATH variable.* We can solve this problem by having the build-classpath function check for the empty valued elements and warn us. The function can also check that each file or directory exists.

- Finally, having a hook to process the CLASSPATH can be useful for more advanced features, such as help accommodating embedded spaces in path names and search paths.

Here is an implementation of build-classpath that handles the first three issues:

```
# $(call build-classpath, variable-list)
define build-classpath
$(strip                                         \
  $(patsubst %:,%,                              \
    $(subst : ,:,                               \
      $(strip                                   \
        $(foreach c,$1,$(call get-file,$c):)))))
endef

# $(call get-file, variable-name)
define get-file
  $(strip                                       \
    $($1)                                        \
    $(if $(call file-exists-eval,$1),,          \
      $(warning The file referenced by variable \
                '$1' ($($1)) cannot be found)))
endef

# $(call file-exists-eval, variable-name)
define file-exists-eval
  $(strip                                       \
    $(if $($1),,$(warning '$1' has no value))   \
    $(wildcard $($1)))
endef
```

The build-classpath function iterates through the words in its argument, verifying each element and concatenating them with the path separator (: in this case). Selecting the path separator automatically is easy now. The function then strips spaces added by the get-file function and foreach loop. Next, it strips the final separator

---

* We could try using the --warn-undefined-variables option to identify this situation, but this also flags many other empty variables that are desirable.

added by the foreach loop. Finally, the whole thing is wrapped in a strip so errant spaces introduced by line continuation are removed.

The get-file function returns its filename argument, then tests whether the variable refers to an existing file. If it does not, it generates a warning. It returns the value of the variable regardless of the existence of the file because the value may be useful to the caller. On occasion, get-file may be used with a file that will be generated, but does not yet exist.

The last function, file-exists-eval, accepts a variable name containing a file reference. If the variable is empty, a warning is issued; otherwise, the wildcard function is used to resolve the value into a file (or a list of files for that matter).

When the build-classpath function is used with some suitable bogus values, we see these errors:

```
Makefile:37: The file referenced by variable 'TOPLINKX_25_JAR'
             (/usr/java/toplink-2.5/TopLinkX.jar) cannot be found
...
Makefile:37: 'XERCES_142_JAR' has no value
Makefile:37: The file referenced by variable
             'XERCES_142_JAR' () cannot be found
```

This represents a great improvement over the silence we would get from the simple approach.

The existence of the get-file function suggests that we could generalize the search for input files.

```
# $(call get-jar, variable-name)
define get-jar
  $(strip                                                      \
    $(if $($1),,$(warning '$1' is empty))                      \
    $(if $(JAR_PATH),,$(warning JAR_PATH is empty))            \
    $(foreach d, $(dir $($1)) $(JAR_PATH),                     \
      $(if $(wildcard $d/$(notdir $($1))),                     \
        $(if $(get-jar-return),,                               \
          $(eval get-jar-return := $d/$(notdir $($1))))))      \
    $(if $(get-jar-return),                                    \
      $(get-jar-return)                                        \
      $(eval get-jar-return :=),                               \
      $($1)                                                    \
      $(warning get-jar: File not found '$1' in $(JAR_PATH))))
endef
```

Here we define the variable JAR_PATH to contain a search path for files. The first file found is returned. The parameter to the function is a variable name containing the path to a jar. We want to look for the jar file first in the path given by the variable, then in the JAR_PATH. To accomplish this, the directory list in the foreach loop is composed of the directory from the variable, followed by the JAR_PATH. The two other uses of the parameter are enclosed in notdir calls so the jar name can be composed from a path from this list. Notice that we cannot exit from a foreach loop.

Instead, therefore, we use eval to set a variable, get-jar-return, to remember the first file we found. After the loop, we return the value of our temporary variable or issue a warning if nothing was found. We must remember to reset our return value variable before terminating the macro.

This is essentially reimplementing the vpath feature in the context of setting the CLASSPATH. To understand this, recall that the vpath is a search path used implicitly by make to find prerequisites that cannot be found from the current directory by a relative path. In these cases, make searches the vpath for the prerequisite file and inserts the completed path into the $^, $?, and $+ automatic variables. To set the CLASSPATH, we want make to search a path for each jar file and insert the completed path into the CLASSPATH variable. Since make has no built-in support for this, we've added our own. You could, of course, simply expand the jar path variable with the appropriate jar filenames and let Java do the searching, but CLASSPATHs already get long quickly. On some operating systems, environment variable space is limited and long CLASSPATHs are in danger of being truncated. On Windows XP, there is a limit of 1023 characters for a single environment variable. In addition, even if the CLASSPATH is not truncated, the Java virtual machine must search the CLASSPATH when loading classes, thus slowing down the application.

Managing Jars

Building and managing jars in Java presents different issues from C/C++ libraries. There are three reasons for this. First, the members of a jar include a relative path, so the precise filenames passed to the jar program must be carefully controlled. Second, in Java there is a tendency to merge jars so that a single jar can be released to represent a program. Finally, jars include other files than classes, such as manifests, property files, and XML.

The basic command to create a jar in GNU make is:

```
JAR      := jar
JARFLAGS := -cf

$(FOO_JAR): prerequisites...
        $(JAR) $(JARFLAGS) $@ $^
```

The jar program can accept directories instead of filenames, in which case, all the files in the directory trees are included in the jar. This can be very convenient, especially when used with the -C option for changing directories:

```
JAR      := jar
JARFLAGS := -cf

.PHONY: $(FOO_JAR)
$(FOO_JAR):
        $(JAR) $(JARFLAGS) $@ -C $(OUTPUT_DIR) com
```

Here the jar itself is declared .PHONY. Otherwise subsequent runs of the *makefile* would not recreate the file, because it has no prerequisites. As with the ar command described in an earlier chapter, there seems little point in using the update flag, -u, since it takes the same amount of time or longer as recreating the jar from scratch, at least for most updates.

A jar often includes a manifest that identifies the vendor, API and version number the jar implements. A simple manifest might look like:

```
Name: JAR_NAME
Specification-Title: SPEC_NAME
Implementation-Version: IMPL_VERSION
Specification-Vendor: Generic Innovative Company, Inc.
```

This manifest includes three placeholders, JAR_NAME, SPEC_NAME, and IMPL_VERSION, that can be replaced at jar creation time by make using sed, m4, or your favorite stream editor. Here is a function to process a manifest:

```
MANIFEST_TEMPLATE := src/manifests/default.mf
TMP_JAR_DIR       := $(call make-temp-dir)
TMP_MANIFEST      := $(TMP_JAR_DIR)/manifest.mf

# $(call add-manifest, jar, jar-name, manifest-file-opt)
define add-manifest
  $(RM) $(dir $(TMP_MANIFEST))
  $(MKDIR) $(dir $(TMP_MANIFEST))
  m4 --define=NAME="$(notdir $2)"                 \
     --define=IMPL_VERSION=$(VERSION_NUMBER)      \
     --define=SPEC_VERSION=$(VERSION_NUMBER)      \
     $(if $3,$3,$(MANIFEST_TEMPLATE))             \
     > $(TMP_MANIFEST)
  $(JAR) -ufm $1 $(TMP_MANIFEST)
  $(RM) $(dir $(TMP_MANIFEST))
endef
```

The add-manifest function operates on a manifest file similar to the one shown previously. The function first creates a temporary directory, then expands the sample manifest. Next, it updates the jar, and finally deletes the temporary directory. Notice that the last parameter to the function is optional. If the manifest file path is empty, the function uses the value from MANIFEST_TEMPLATE.

The generic *makefile* bundles these operations into a generic function to write an explicit rule for creating a jar:

```
# $(call make-jar,jar-variable-prefix)
define make-jar
  .PHONY: $1 $$($1_name)
  $1: $($1_name)
  $$($1_name):
        cd $(OUTPUT_DIR); \
        $(JAR) $(JARFLAGS) $$(notdir $$@) $$($1_packages)
        $$(call add-manifest, $$@, $$($1_name), $$($1_manifest))
endef
```

It accepts a single argument, the prefix of a make variable, that identifies a set of variables describing four jar parameters: the target name, the jar name, the packages in the jar, and the jar's manifest file. For example, for a jar named *ui.jar*, we would write:

```
ui_jar_name     := $(OUTPUT_DIR)/lib/ui.jar
ui_jar_manifest := src/com/company/ui/manifest.mf
ui_jar_packages := src/com/company/ui \
                   src/com/company/lib

$(eval $(call make-jar,ui_jar))
```

By using variable name composition, we can shorten the calling sequence of our function and allow for a very flexible implementation of the function.

If we have many jar files to create, we can automate this further by placing the jar names in a variable:

```
jar_list := server_jar ui_jar

.PHONY: jars $(jar_list)
jars: $(jar_list)

$(foreach j, $(jar_list),\
  $(eval $(call make-jar,$j)))
```

Occasionally, we need to expand a jar file into a temporary directory. Here is a simple function to do that:

```
# $(call burst-jar, jar-file, target-directory)
define burst-jar
  $(call make-dir,$2)
  cd $2; $(JAR) -xf $1
endef
```

Reference Trees and Third-Party Jars

To use a single, shared reference tree to support partial source trees for developers, simply have the nightly build create jars for the project and include those jars in the CLASSPATH of the Java compiler. The developer can check out the parts of the source tree he needs and run the compile (assuming the source file list is dynamically created by something like find). When the Java compiler requires symbols from a missing source file, it will search the CLASSPATH and discover the *.class* file in the jar.

Selecting third-party jars from a reference tree is also simple. Just place the path to the jar in the CLASSPATH. The *makefile* can be a valuable tool for managing this process as previously noted. Of course, the get-file function can be used to automatically select beta or stable, local or remote jars by simply setting the JAR_PATH variable.

Enterprise JavaBeans

Enterprise JavaBeans™ is a powerful technique to encapsulate and reuse business logic in the framework of remote method invocation. EJB sets up Java classes used to implement server APIs that are ultimately used by remote clients. These objects and services are configured using XML-based control files. Once the Java classes and XML control files are written, they must be bundled together in a jar. Then a special EJB compiler builds stubs and ties to implement the RPC support code.

The following code can be plugged into Example 9-1 to provide generic EJB support:

```
EJB_TMP_JAR = $(EJB_TMP_DIR)/temp.jar
META_INF    = $(EJB_TMP_DIR)/META-INF

# $(call compile-bean, jar-name,
#                      bean-files-wildcard, manifest-name-opt)
define compile-bean
  $(eval EJB_TMP_DIR := $(shell mktemp -d $(TMPDIR)/compile-bean.XXXXXXXX))
  $(MKDIR) $(META_INF)
  $(if $(filter %.xml, $2),cp $(filter %.xml, $2) $(META_INF))
  cd $(OUTPUT_DIR) &&                         \
  $(JAR) -cfO $(EJB_TMP_JAR)                   \
         $(call jar-file-arg,$(META_INF))      \
         $(filter-out %.xml, $2)
  $(JVM) weblogic.ejbc $(EJB_TMP_JAR) $1
  $(call add-manifest,$(if $3,$3,$1),,)
  $(RM) $(EJB_TMP_DIR)
endef

# $(call jar-file-arg, jar-file)
jar-file-arg = -C "$(patsubst %/,%,$(dir $1))" $(notdir $1)
```

The compile-bean function accepts three parameters: the name of the jar to create, the list of files in the jar, and an optional manifest file. The function first creates a clean temporary directory using the mktemp program and saves the directory name in the variable EJB_TMP_DIR. By embedding the assignment in an eval, we ensure that EJB_TMP_DIR is reset to a new temporary directory once for each expansion of compile-bean. Since compile-bean is used in the command script part of a rule, the function is expanded only when the command script is executed. Next, it copies any XML files in the bean file list into the *META-INF* directory. This is where EJB configuration files live. Then, the function builds a temporary jar that is used as input to the EJB compiler. The jar-file-arg function converts filenames of the form *dir1/dir2/dir3* into -C dir1/dir2 dir3 so the relative path to the file in the jar is correct. This is the appropriate format for indicating the *META-INF* directory to the jar command. The bean file list contains *.xml* files that have already been placed in the *META-INF* directory, so we filter these files out. After building the temporary jar, the WebLogic EJB compiler is invoked, generating the output jar. A manifest is then added to the compiled jar. Finally, our temporary directory is removed.

Using the new function is straightforward:

```
bean_files = com/company/bean/FooInterface.class      \
             com/company/bean/FooHome.class           \
             src/com/company/bean/ejb-jar.xml         \
             src/com/company/bean/weblogic-ejb-jar.xml

.PHONY: ejb_jar $(EJB_JAR)
ejb_jar: $(EJB_JAR)
$(EJB_JAR):
        $(call compile-bean, $@, $(bean_files), weblogic.mf)
```

The bean_files list is a little confusing. The *.class* files it references will be accessed relative to the *classes* directory, while the *.xml* files will be accessed relative to the directory of the *makefile*.

This is fine, but what if you have lots of bean files in your bean jar. Can we build the file list automatically? Certainly:

```
src_dirs := $(SOURCE_DIR)/com/company/...

bean_files =                                    \
  $(patsubst $(SOURCE_DIR)/%,%,                  \
    $(addsuffix /*.class,                        \
      $(sort                                     \
        $(dir                                    \
          $(wildcard                             \
            $(addsuffix /*Home.java,$(src_dirs))))))) \
  src/com/company/bean/ejb-jar.xml              \
  src/com/company/bean/weblogic-ejb-jar.xml

.PHONY: ejb_jar $(EJB_JAR)
ejb_jar: $(EJB_JAR)
$(EJB_JAR):
        $(call compile-bean, $@, $(bean_files), weblogic.mf)
```

This assumes that all the directories with EJB source are contained in the src_dirs variable (there can also be directories that do not contain EJB source) and that any file ending in *Home.java* identifies a package containing EJB code. The expression for setting the bean_files variable first adds the wildcard suffix to the directories, then invokes wildcard to gather the list of *Home.java* files. The filenames are discarded to leave the directories, which are sorted to remove duplicates. The wildcard /*.class suffix is added so that the shell will expand the list to the actual class files. Finally, the source directory prefix (which is not valid in the *classes* tree) is removed. Shell wildcard expansion is used instead of make's wildcard because we can't rely on make to perform its expansion after the class files have been compiled. If make evaluated the wildcard function too early it would find no files and directory caching would prevent it from ever looking again. The wildcard in the source tree is perfectly safe because (we assume) no source files will be added while make is running.

The above code works when we have a small number of bean jars. Another style of development places each EJB in its own jar. Large projects may have dozens of jars. To handle this case automatically, we need to generate an explicit rule for each EJB jar. In this example, EJB source code is self-contained: each EJB is located in a single directory with its associated XML files. EJB directories can be identified by files that end with *Session.java*.

The basic approach is to search the source tree for EJBs, then build an explicit rule to create each EJB and write these rules into a file. The EJB rules file is then included in our *makefile*. The creation of the EJB rules file is triggered by make's own dependency handling of include files.

```
# session_jars - The EJB jars with their relative source path.
session_jars =
  $(subst .java,.jar,                        \
    $(wildcard                               \
      $(addsuffix /*Session.java, $(COMPILATION_DIRS))))

# EJBS - A list of all EJB jars we need to build.
EJBS = $(addprefix $(TMP_DIR)/,$(notdir $(session_jars)))

# ejbs - Create all EJB jar files.
.PHONY: ejbs
ejbs: $(EJBS)
$(EJBS):
        $(call compile-bean,$@,$^,)
```

We find the *Session.java* files by calling a `wildcard` on all the compilation directories. In this example, the jar file is the name of the Session file with the *.jar* suffix. The jars themselves will be placed in a temporary binary directory. The `EJBS` variable contains the list of jars with their binary directory path. These EJB jars are the targets we want to update. The actual command script is our `compile-bean` function. The tricky part is that the file list is recorded in the prerequisites for each jar file. Let's see how they are created.

```
-include $(OUTPUT_DIR)/ejb.d

# $(call ejb-rule, ejb-name)
ejb-rule = $(TMP_DIR)/$(notdir $1):             \
            $(addprefix $(OUTPUT_DIR)/,         \
              $(subst .java,.class,             \
                $(wildcard $(dir $1)*.java))) \
            $(wildcard $(dir $1)*.xml)

# ejb.d - EJB dependencies file.
$(OUTPUT_DIR)/ejb.d: Makefile
        @echo Computing ejb dependencies...
        @for f in $(session_jars);            \
        do                                    \
          echo "\$$(call ejb-rule,$$f)";      \
        done > $@
```

The dependencies for each EJB jar are recorded in a separate file, *ejb.d*, that is included by the *makefile*. The first time make looks for this include file it does not exist. So make invokes the rule for updating the include file. This rule writes one line for each EJB, something like:

```
$(call ejb-rule,src/com/company/foo/FooSession.jar)
```

The function ejb-rule will expand to the target jar and its list of prerequisites, something like:

```
classes/lib/FooSession.jar: classes/com/company/foo/FooHome.class \
            classes/com/company/foo/FooInterface.class            \
            classes/com/company/foo/FooSession.class              \
            src/com/company/foo/ejb-jar.xml                       \
            src/com/company/foo/ejb-weblogic-jar.xml
```

In this way, a large number of jars can be managed in make without incurring the overhead of maintaining a set of explicit rules by hand.

## CHAPTER 10

Improving the Performance of make

make plays a critical role in the development process. It combines the elements of a project to create an application while allowing the developer to avoid the subtle errors caused by accidentally omitting steps of the build. However, if developers avoid using make, because they feel the *makefile* is too slow, all the benefits of make are lost. It is important, therefore, to ensure that the *makefile* be crafted to be as efficient as possible.

Performance issues are always tricky, but become even more so when the perception of users and different paths through the code are considered. Not every target of a *makefile* is worth optimizing. Even radical optimizations might not be worth the effort depending on your environment. For instance, reducing the time of an operation from 90 minutes to 45 minutes may be immaterial since even the faster time is a "go get lunch" operation. On the other hand, reducing a task from 2 minutes to 1 might be received with cheers if developers are twiddling their thumbs during that time.

When writing a *makefile* for efficient execution, it is important to know the costs of various operations and to know what operations are being performed. In the following sections, we will perform some simple benchmarking to quantify these general comments and present techniques to help identify bottlenecks.

A complementary approach to improving performance is to take advantage of parallelism and local network topology. By running more than one command script at a time (even on a uniprocessor), build times can be reduced.

Benchmarking

Here we measure the performance of some basic operations in make. Table 10-1 shows the results of these measurements. We'll explain each test and suggest how they might affect *makefiles* you write.

Table 10-1. *Cost of operations*

Operation	Executions	Seconds per execution (Windows)	Executions per second (Windows)	Seconds per execution (Linux)	Executions per second (Linux)
make (bash)	1000	0.0436	22	0.0162	61
make (ash)	1000	0.0413	24	0.0151	66
make (sh)	1000	0.0452	22	0.0159	62
assignment	10,000	0.0001	8130	0.0001	10,989
subst (short)	10,000	0.0003	3891	0.0003	3846
subst (long)	10,000	0.0018	547	0.0014	704
sed (bash)	1000	0.0910	10	0.0342	29
sed (ash)	1000	0.0699	14	0.0069	144
sed (sh)	1000	0.0911	10	0.0139	71
shell (bash)	1000	0.0398	25	0.0261	38
shell (ash)	1000	0.0253	39	0.0018	555
shell (sh)	1000	0.0399	25	0.0050	198

The Windows tests were run on a 1.9-GHz Pentium 4 (approximately 3578 Bogo-Mips)* with 512 MB RAM running Windows XP. The Cygwin version of make 3.80 was used, started from an rxvt window. The Linux tests were run on a 450-MHz Pentium 2 (891 BogoMips) with 256 MB of RAM running Linux RedHat 9.

The subshell used by make can have a significant effect on the overall performance of the *makefile*. The bash shell is a complex, fully featured shell, and therefore large. The ash shell is a much smaller, with fewer features but adequate for most tasks. To complicate matters, if bash is invoked from the filename */bin/sh*, it alters its behavior significantly to conform more closely to the standard shell. On most Linux systems the file */bin/sh* is a symbolic link to bash, while in Cygwin */bin/sh* is really *ash*. To account for these differences, some of the tests were run three times, each time using a different shell. The shell used is indicated in parentheses. When "(sh)" appears, it means that bash was linked to the file named */bin/sh*.

The first three tests, labeled make, give an indication of how expensive it is to run make if there is nothing to do. The *makefile* contains:

```
SHELL := /bin/bash
.PHONY: x
x:
        $(MAKE) --no-print-directory --silent --question make-bash.mk; \
        ...this command repeated 99 more times...
```

The word "bash" is replaced with the appropriate shell name as required.

---

* See *http://www.clifton.nl/bogomips.html* for an explanation of BogoMips.

We use the `--no-print-directory` and `--silent` commands to eliminate unnecessary computation that might skew the timing test and to avoid cluttering the timing output values with irrelevant text. The `--question` option tells make to simply check the dependencies without executing any commands and return an exit status of zero if the files are up to date. This allows make to do as little work as possible. No commands will be executed by this *makefile* and dependencies exist for only one `.PHONY` target. The command script executes make 100 times. This *makefile*, called *make-bash.mk*, is executed 10 times by a parent *makefile* with this code:

```
define ten-times
  TESTS += $1
  .PHONY: $1
  $1:
        @echo $(MAKE) --no-print-directory --silent $2; \
        time $(MAKE) --no-print-directory --silent $2; \
        time $(MAKE) --no-print-directory --silent $2; \
        time $(MAKE) --no-print-directory --silent $2; \
        time $(MAKE) --no-print-directory --silent $2; \
        time $(MAKE) --no-print-directory --silent $2; \
        time $(MAKE) --no-print-directory --silent $2; \
        time $(MAKE) --no-print-directory --silent $2; \
        time $(MAKE) --no-print-directory --silent $2; \
        time $(MAKE) --no-print-directory --silent $2; \
        time $(MAKE) --no-print-directory --silent $2
endef

.PHONY: all
all:

$(eval $(call ten-times, make-bash, -f make-bash.mk))

all: $(TESTS)
```

The time for these 1,000 executions is then averaged.

As you can see from the table, the Cygwin make ran at roughly 22 executions per second or 0.044 seconds per run, while the Linux version (even on a drastically slower CPU) performed roughly 61 executions per second or 0.016 seconds per run. To verify these results, the native Windows version of make was also tested and did not yield any dramatic speed up. Conclusion: while process creation in Cygwin make is slightly slower than a native Windows make, both are dramatically slower than Linux. It also suggests that use of recursive make on a Windows platform may perform significantly slower than the same build run on Linux.

As you would expect, the shell used in this test had no effect on execution time. Because the command script contained no shell special characters, the shell was not invoked at all. Rather, make executed the commands directly. This can be verified by setting the `SHELL` variable to a completely bogus value and noting that the test still runs correctly. The difference in performance between the three shells must be attributed to normal system variance.

The next benchmark measures the speed of variable assignment. This calibrates the most elementary make operation. The *makefile*, called *assign.mk*, contains:

```
# 10000 assignments
z := 10
…repeated 10000 times…
.PHONY: x
x: ;
```

This *makefile* is then run using our ten-times function in the parent *makefile*.

The assignment is obviously very fast. Cygwin make will execute 8130 assignments per second while the Linux system can do 10,989. I believe the performance of Windows for most of these operations is actually better than the benchmark indicates because the cost of creating the make process 10 times cannot be reliably factored out of the time. Conclusion: because it is unlikely that the average *makefile* would perform 10,000 assignments, the cost of variable assignment in an average *makefile* is negligible.

The next two benchmarks measure the cost of a subst function call. The first uses a short 10-character string with three substitutions:

```
# 10000 subst on a 10 char string
dir := ab/cd/ef/g
x := $(subst /, ,$(dir))
…repeated 10000 times…
.PHONY: x
x: ;
```

This operation takes roughly twice as long as a simple assignment, or 3891 operations per second on Windows. Again, the Linux system appears to outperform the Windows system by a wide margin. (Remember, the Linux system is running at less than one quarter the clock speed of the Windows system.)

The longer substitution operates on a 1000-character string with roughly 100 substitutions:

```
# Ten character file
dir := ab/cd/ef/g
# 1000 character path
p100 := $(dir);$(dir);$(dir);$(dir);$(dir);…
p1000 := $(p100)$(p100)$(p100)$(p100)$(p100)…

# 10000 subst on a 1000 char string
x := $(subst ;, ,$(p1000))
…repeated 10000 times…
.PHONY: x
x: ;
```

The next three benchmarks measure the speed of the same substitution using sed. The benchmark contains:

```
# 100 sed using bash
SHELL := /bin/bash
```

```
.PHONY: sed-bash
sed-bash:
        echo '$(p1000)' | sed 's/;/ /g' > /dev/null
        …repeated 100 times…
```

As usual, this *makefile* is executed using the ten-times function. On Windows, sed execution takes about 50 times longer than the subst function. On our Linux system, sed is only 24 times slower.

When we factor in the cost of the shell, we see that ash on Windows does provide a useful speed-up. With ash, the sed is only 39 times slower than subst! (wink) On Linux, the shell used has a much more profound effect. Using ash, the sed is only five times slower than subst. Here we also notice the curious effect of renaming bash to sh. On Cygwin, there is no difference between a bash named /bin/bash and one named /bin/sh, but on Linux, a bash linked to /bin/sh performs significantly better.

The final benchmark simply invokes the make shell command to evaluate the cost of running a subshell. The *makefile* contains:

```
# 100 $(shell ) using bash
SHELL := /bin/bash
x := $(shell :)
…repeated 100 times…
.PHONY: x
x: ;
```

There are no surprises here. The Windows system is slower than Linux, with ash having an edge over bash. The performance gain of ash is more pronounced—about 50% faster. The Linux system performs best with ash and slowest with bash (when named "bash").

Benchmarking is a never-ending task, however, the measurements we've made can provide some useful insight. Create as many variables as you like if they help clarify the structure of the *makefile* because they are essentially free. Built-in make functions are preferred over running commands even if you are required by the structure of your code to reexecute the make function repeatedly. Avoid recursive make or unnecessary process creation on Windows. While on Linux, use ash if you are creating many processes.

Finally, remember that in most *makefiles*, the time a *makefile* takes to run is due almost entirely to the cost of the programs run, not make or the structure of the *makefile*. Usually, reducing the number of programs run will be most helpful in reducing the execution time of a *makefile*.

Identifying and Handling Bottlenecks

Unnecessary delays in *makefiles* come from several sources: poor structuring of the *makefile*, poor dependency analysis, and poor use of make functions and variables.

These problems can be masked by make functions such as shell that invoke commands without echoing them, making it difficult to find the source of the delay.

Dependency analysis is a two-edged sword. On the one hand, if complete dependency analysis is performed, the analysis itself may incur significant delays. Without special compiler support, such as supplied by gcc or jikes, creating a dependency file requires running another program, nearly doubling compilation time.* The advantage of complete dependency analysis is that it allows make to perform fewer compiles. Unfortunately, developers may not believe this benefit is realized and write *makefiles* with less complete dependency information. This compromise almost always leads to an increase in development problems, leading other developers to overcompensate by compiling more code than would be required with the original, complete dependency information.

To formulate a dependency analysis strategy, begin by understanding the dependencies inherent in the project. Once complete dependency information is understood, you can choose how much to represent in the *makefile* (computed or hardcoded) and what shortcuts can be taken during the build. Although none of this is exactly simple, it is straightforward.

Once you've determined your *makefile* structure and necessary dependencies, implementing an efficient *makefile* is usually a matter of avoiding some simple pitfalls.

Simple Variables Versus Recursive

One of the most common performance-related problems is using recursive variables instead of simple variables. For example, because the following code uses the = operator instead of :=, it will execute the date command every time the DATE variable is used:

```
DATE = $(shell date +%F)
```

The +%F option instructs date to return the date in "yyyy-mm-dd" format, so for most users the repeated execution of date would never be noticed. Of course, developers working around midnight might get a surprise!

Because make doesn't echo commands executed from the shell function, it can be difficult to determine what is actually being run. By resetting the SHELL variable to /bin/sh -x, you can trick make into revealing all the commands it executes.

---

* In practice, compilation time grows linearly with the size of the input text and this time is almost always dominated by disk I/O. Similarly, the time to compute dependencies using the simple -M option is linear and bound by disk I/O.

This *makefile* creates its output directory before performing any actions. The name of the output directory is composed of the word "out" and the date:

```
DATE = $(shell date +%F)
OUTPUT_DIR = out-$(DATE)

make-directories := $(shell [ -d $(OUTPUT_DIR) ] || mkdir -p $(OUTPUT_DIR))

all: ;
```

When run with a debugging shell, we can see:

```
$ make SHELL='/bin/sh -x'
+ date +%F
+ date +%F
+ '[' -d out-2004-03-30 ']'
+ mkdir -p out-2004-03-30
make: all is up to date.
```

This clearly shows us that the date command was executed twice. If you need to perform this kind of shell trace often, you can make it easier to access with:

```
ifdef DEBUG_SHELL
  SHELL = /bin/sh -x
endif
```

Disabling @

Another way commands are hidden is through the use of the silent command modifier, @. It can be useful at times to be able to disable this feature. You can make this easy by defining a variable, QUIET, to hold the @ sign and use the variable in commands:

```
ifndef VERBOSE
  QUIET := @
endif
…
target:
        $(QUIET) echo Building target...
```

When it becomes necessary to see commands hidden by the silent modifier, simply define VERBOSE on the command line:

```
$ make VERBOSE=1
echo Building target...
Building target...
```

Lazy Initialization

When simple variables are used in conjunction with the shell function, make evaluates all the shell function calls as it reads the *makefile*. If there are many of these, or if they perform expensive computations, make can feel sluggish. The responsiveness of make can be measured by timing make when invoked with a nonexistent target:

```
$ time make no-such-target
make: *** No rule to make target no-such-target.  Stop.
```

```
real    0m0.058s
user    0m0.062s
sys     0m0.015s
```

This code times the overhead that make will add to any command executed, even trivial or erroneous commands.

Because recursive variables reevaluate their righthand side every time they are expanded, there is a tendency to express complex calculations as simple variables. However, this decreases the responsiveness of make for all targets. It seems that there is a need for another kind of variable, one whose righthand side is evaluated only once the first time the variable is evaluated, but not before.

An example illustrating the need for this type of initialization is the find-compilation-dirs function introduced in the section "The Fast Approach: All-in-One Compile" in Chapter 9:

```
# $(call find-compilation-dirs, root-directory)
find-compilation-dirs =                     \
  $(patsubst %/,%,                          \
    $(sort                                  \
      $(dir                                 \
        $(shell $(FIND) $1 -name '*.java')))))

PACKAGE_DIRS := $(call find-compilation-dirs, $(SOURCE_DIR))
```

Ideally, we would like to perform this find operation only once per execution, but only when the PACKAGE_DIRS variable is actually used. This might be called *lazy initialization*. We can build such a variable using eval like this:

```
PACKAGE_DIRS = $(redefine-package-dirs) $(PACKAGE_DIRS)

redefine-package-dirs = \
    $(eval PACKAGE_DIRS := $(call find-compilation-dirs, $(SOURCE_DIR)))
```

The basic approach is to define PACKAGE_DIRS first as a recursive variable. When expanded, the variable evaluates the expensive function, here find-compilation-dirs, and redefines itself as a simple variable. Finally, the (now simple) variable value is returned from the original recursive variable definition.

Let's go over this in detail:

1. When make reads these variables, it simply records their righthand side because the variables are recursive.

2. The first time the PACKAGE_DIRS variable is used, make retrieves the righthand side and expands the first variable, redefine-package-dirs.

3. The value of redefine-package-dirs is a single function call, eval.

4. The body of the eval redefines the recursive variable, PACKAGE_DIRS, as a simple variable whose value is the set of directories returned by find-compilation-dirs. Now PACKAGE_DIRS has been initialized with the directory list.

5. The redefine-package-dirs variable is expanded to the empty string (because eval expands to the empty string).

6. Now make continues to expand the original righthand side of PACKAGE_DIRS. The only thing left to do is expand the variable PACKAGE_DIRS. make looks up the value of the variable, sees a simple variable, and returns its value.

The only really tricky part of this code is relying on make to evaluate the righthand side of a recursive variable from left to right. If, for instance, make decided to evaluate $(PACKAGE_DIRS) before $(redefine-package-dirs), the code would fail.

The procedure I just described can be refactored into a function, lazy-init:

```
# $(call lazy-init,variable-name,value)
define lazy-init
  $1 = $$(redefine-$1) $$($1)
  redefine-$1 = $$(eval $1 := $2)
endef

# PACKAGE_DIRS - a lazy list of directories
$(eval                                    \
  $(call lazy-init,PACKAGE_DIRS, \
    $$(call find-compilation-dirs,$(SOURCE_DIRS)))))
```

Parallel make

Another way to improve the performance of a build is to take advantage of the parallelism inherent in the problem the *makefile* is solving. Most *makefile*s perform many tasks that are easily carried out in parallel, such as compiling C source to object files or creating libraries out of object files. Furthermore, the very structure of a well-written *makefile* provides all the information necessary to automatically control the concurrent processes.

Example 10-1 shows our mp3_player program executed with the jobs option, --jobs=2 (or -j 2). Figure 10-1 shows the same make run in a pseudo UML sequence diagram. Using --jobs=2 tells make to update two targets in parallel when that is possible. When make updates targets in parallel, it echos commands in the order in which they are executed, interleaving them in the output. This can make reading the output from parallel make more difficult. Let's look at this output more carefully.

Example 10-1. Output of make when --jobs = 2

```
$ make -f ../ch07-separate-binaries/makefile --jobs=2

1  bison -y  --defines ../ch07-separate-binaries/lib/db/playlist.y

2  flex  -t ../ch07-separate-binaries/lib/db/scanner.l > lib/db/scanner.c

3  gcc  -I lib -I ../ch07-separate-binaries/lib -I ../ch07-separate-binaries/include  -M
   ../ch07-separate-binaries/app/player/play_mp3.c | \
```

Example 10-1. Output of make when --jobs = 2 (continued)

```
    sed 's,\(play_mp3\.o\) *:,app/player/\1 app/player/play_mp3.d: ,' > app/player/play_
mp3.d.tmp

  4  mv -f y.tab.c lib/db/playlist.c

  5  mv -f y.tab.h lib/db/playlist.h

  6  gcc  -I lib -I ../ch07-separate-binaries/lib -I ../ch07-separate-binaries/include  -M
     ../ch07-separate-binaries/lib/codec/codec.c | \
     sed 's,\(codec\.o\) *:,lib/codec/\1 lib/codec/codec.d: ,' > lib/codec/codec.d.tmp

  7  mv -f app/player/play_mp3.d.tmp app/player/play_mp3.d

  8  gcc  -I lib -I ../ch07-separate-binaries/lib -I ../ch07-separate-binaries/include  -M
     lib/db/playlist.c | \
     sed 's,\(playlist\.o\) *:,lib/db/\1 lib/db/playlist.d: ,' > lib/db/playlist.d.tmp

  9  mv -f lib/codec/codec.d.tmp lib/codec/codec.d

 10  gcc  -I lib -I ../ch07-separate-binaries/lib -I ../ch07-separate-binaries/include  -M
     ../ch07-separate-binaries/lib/ui/ui.c | \
     sed 's,\(ui\.o\) *:,lib/ui/\1 lib/ui/ui.d: ,' > lib/ui/ui.d.tmp

 11  mv -f lib/db/playlist.d.tmp lib/db/playlist.d

 12  gcc  -I lib -I ../ch07-separate-binaries/lib -I ../ch07-separate-binaries/include  -M
     lib/db/scanner.c | \
     sed 's,\(scanner\.o\) *:,lib/db/\1 lib/db/scanner.d: ,' > lib/db/scanner.d.tmp

 13  mv -f lib/ui/ui.d.tmp lib/ui/ui.d

 14  mv -f lib/db/scanner.d.tmp lib/db/scanner.d

 15  gcc  -I lib -I ../ch07-separate-binaries/lib -I ../ch07-separate-binaries/include  -c
     -o app/player/play_mp3.o ../ch07-separate-binaries/app/player/play_mp3.c

 16  gcc  -I lib -I ../ch07-separate-binaries/lib -I ../ch07-separate-binaries/include  -c
     -o lib/codec/codec.o ../ch07-separate-binaries/lib/codec/codec.c

 17  gcc  -I lib -I ../ch07-separate-binaries/lib -I ../ch07-separate-binaries/include  -c
     -o lib/db/playlist.o lib/db/playlist.c

 18  gcc  -I lib -I ../ch07-separate-binaries/lib -I ../ch07-separate-binaries/include  -c
     -o lib/db/scanner.o lib/db/scanner.c
     ../ch07-separate-binaries/lib/db/scanner.l: In function yylex:
     ../ch07-separate-binaries/lib/db/scanner.l:9: warning: return makes integer from
pointer without a cast

 19  gcc  -I lib -I ../ch07-separate-binaries/lib -I ../ch07-separate-binaries/include  -c
     -o lib/ui/ui.o ../ch07-separate-binaries/lib/ui/ui.c

 20  ar rv lib/codec/libcodec.a lib/codec/codec.o
```

Example 10-1. Output of make when --jobs = 2 (continued)

```
   ar: creating lib/codec/libcodec.a
   a - lib/codec/codec.o

21 ar rv lib/db/libdb.a lib/db/playlist.o lib/db/scanner.o
   ar: creating lib/db/libdb.a
   a - lib/db/playlist.o
   a - lib/db/scanner.o

22 ar rv lib/ui/libui.a lib/ui/ui.o
   ar: creating lib/ui/libui.a
   a - lib/ui/ui.o

23 gcc  app/player/play_mp3.o lib/codec/libcodec.a lib/db/libdb.a lib/ui/libui.a  -o
   app/player/play_mp3
```

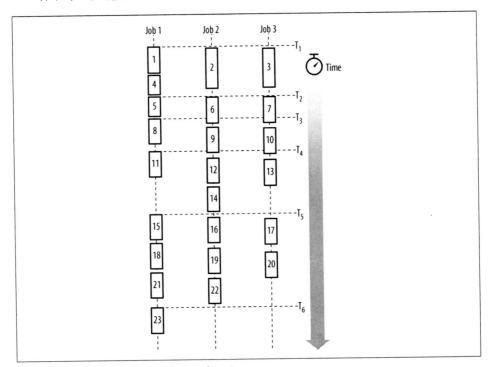

Figure 10-1. Diagram of make when --jobs = 2

First, make must build the generated source and dependency files. The two generated source files are the output of yacc and lex. This accounts for commands 1 and 2. The third command generates the dependency file for *play_mp3.c* and is clearly begun before the dependency files for either *playlist.c* or *scanner.c* are completed (by commands 4, 5, 8, 9, 12, and 14). Therefore, this make is running three jobs in parallel, even though the command-line option requests two jobs.

The mv commands, 4 and 5, complete the *playlist.c* source code generation started with command 1. Command 6 begins another dependency file. Each command script is always executed by a single make, but each target and prerequisite forms a separate job. Therefore, command 7, which is the second command of the dependency generation script, is being executed by the same make process as command 3. While command 6 is probably being executed by a make spawned immediately following the completion of the make that executed commands 1-4-5 (processing the yacc grammar), but before the generation of the dependency file in command 8.

The dependency generation continues in this fashion until command 14. All dependency files must be complete before make can move on to the next phase of processing, re-reading the *makefile*. This forms a natural synchronization point that make automatically obeys.

Once the *makefile* is reread with the dependency information, make can continue the build process in parallel again. This time make chooses to compile all the object files before building each of the archive libraries. This order is nondeterministic. That is, if the *makefile* is run again, it may be that the *libcodec.a* library might be built before the *playlist.c* is compiled, since that library doesn't require any objects other than *codec.o*. Thus, the example represents one possible execution order amongst many.

Finally, the program is linked. For this *makefile*, the link phase is also a natural synchronization point and will always occur last. If, however, the goal was not a single program but many programs or libraries, the last command executed might also vary.

Running multiple jobs on a multiprocessor obviously makes sense, but running more than one job on a uniprocessor can also be very useful. This is because of the latency of disk I/O and the large amount of cache on most systems. For instance, if a process, such as gcc, is idle waiting for disk I/O it may be that data for another task such as mv, yacc, or ar is currently in memory. In this case, it would be good to allow the task with available data to proceed. In general, running make with two jobs on a uniprocessor is almost always faster than running one job, and it is not uncommon for three or even four tasks to be faster than two.

The --jobs option can be used without a number. If so, make will spawn as many jobs as there are targets to be updated. This is usually a bad idea, because a large number of jobs will usually swamp a processor and can run much slower than even a single job.

Another way to manage multiple jobs is to use the system load average as a guide. The load average is the number of runnable processes averaged over some period of time, typically 1 minute, 5 minutes, and 15 minutes. The load average is expressed as a floating point number. The --load-average (or -l) option gives make a threshold above which new jobs cannot be spawned. For example, the command:

```
$ make --load-average=3.5
```

tells make to spawn new jobs only when the load average is less than or equal to 3.5. If the load average is greater, make waits until the average drops below this number, or until all the other jobs finish.

When writing a *makefile* for parallel execution, attention to proper prerequisites is even more important. As mentioned previously, when --jobs is 1, a list of prerequisites will usually be evaluated from left to right. When --jobs is greater than 1, these prerequisites may be evaluated in parallel. Therefore, any dependency relationship that was implicitly handled by the default left to right evaluation order must be made explicit when run in parallel.

Another hazard of parallel make is the problem of shared intermediate files. For example, if a directory contains both *foo.y* and *bar.y*, running yacc twice in parallel could result in one of them getting the other's instance of *y.tab.c* or *y.tab.h* or both moved into its own *.c* or *.h* file. You face a similar hazard with any procedure that stores temporary information in a scratch file that has a fixed name.

Another common idiom that hinders parallel execution is invoking a recursive make from a shell for loop:

```
dir:
        for d in $(SUBDIRS);      \
        do                        \
          $(MAKE) --directory=$$d; \
        done
```

As mentioned in the section "Recursive make" in Chapter 6, make cannot execute these recursive invocations in parallel. To achieve parallel execution, declare the directories .PHONY and make them targets:

```
.PHONY: $(SUBDIRS)
$(SUBDIRS):
        $(MAKE) --directory=$@
```

Distributed make

GNU make supports a little known (and only slightly tested) build option for managing builds that uses multiple systems over a network. The feature relies upon the Customs library distributed with Pmake. Pmake is an alternate version of make written in about 1989 by Adam de Boor (and maintained ever since by Andreas Stolcke) for the Sprite operating system. The Customs library helps to distribute a make execution across many machines in parallel. As of version 3.77, GNU make has included support for the Customs library for distributing make.

To enable Customs library support, you must rebuild make from sources. The instructions for this process are in the *README.customs* file in the make distribution. First, you must download and build the pmake distribution (the URL is in the README), then build make with the --with-customs option.

The heart of the Customs library is the customs daemon that runs on each host participating in the distributed make network. These hosts must all share a common view of the filesystem, such as NFS provides. One instance of the customs daemon is designated the master. The master monitors hosts in the participating hosts list and allocates jobs to each member. When make is run with the `--jobs` flag greater than 1, make contacts the master and together they spawn jobs on available hosts in the network.

The Customs library supports a wide range of features. Hosts can be grouped by architecture and rated for performance. Arbitrary attributes can be assigned to hosts and jobs can be allocated to hosts based on combinations of attributes and boolean operators. Additionally, host status such as idle time, free disk space, free swap space, and current load average can also be accounted for when processing jobs.

If your project is implemented in C, C++, or Objective-C you should also consider distcc (*http://distcc.samba.org*) for distributing compiles across several hosts. distcc was written by Martin Pool and others to speedup Samba builds. It is a robust and complete solution for projects written in C, C++, or Objective-C. The tool is used by simply replacing the C compiler with the distcc program:

```
$ make --jobs=8 CC=distcc
```

For each compilation, distcc uses the local compiler to preprocess the output, then ships the expanded source to an available remote machine for compilation. Finally, the remote host returns the resulting object file to the master. This approach removes the necessity for having a shared filesystem, greatly simplifying installation and configuration.

The set of worker or *volunteer* hosts can be specified in several ways. The simplest is to list the volunteer hosts in an environment variable before starting distcc:

```
$ export DISTCC_HOSTS='localhost wasatch oops'
```

distcc is very configurable with options for handling host lists, integrating with the native compiler, managing compression, search paths, and handling failure and recovery.

ccache is another tool for improving compilation performance, written by Samba project leader Andrew Tridgell. The idea is simple, cache the results of previous compiles. Before performing a compile, check if the cache already contains the resulting object files. This does not require multiple hosts, or even a network. The author reports a 5 to 10 times speed up in common compilations. The easiest way to use ccache is to prefix your compiler command with ccache:

```
$ make CC='ccache gcc'
```

ccache can be used together with distcc for even greater performance improvements. In addition, both tools are available in the Cygwin tool set.

CHAPTER 11

Example Makefiles

The *makefiles* shown throughout this book are industrial strength and quite suitable for adapting to your most advanced needs. But it's still worthwhile looking at some *makefiles* from real-life projects to see what people have done with make under the stress of providing deliverables. Here, we discuss several example *makefiles* in detail. The first example is the *makefile* to build this book. The second is the *makefile* used to build the 2.6.7 Linux kernel.

The Book Makefile

Writing a book on programming is in itself an interesting exercise in building systems. The text of the book consists of many files, each of which needs various preprocessing steps. The examples are real programs that should be run and their output collected, post-processed, and included in the main text (so that they don't have to be cut and pasted, with the risk of introducing errors). During composition, it is useful to be able to view the text in different formats. Finally, delivering the material requires packaging. Of course, all of this must be repeatable and relatively easy to maintain.

Sounds like a job for make! This is one of the great beauties of make. It can be applied to an amazing variety of problems. This book was written in DocBook format (i.e., XML). Applying make to T_EX, L_AT_EX, or troff is standard procedure when using those tools.

Example 11-1 shows the entire *makefile* for the book. It is about 440 lines long. The *makefile* is divided into these basic tasks:

- Managing the examples
- Preprocessing the XML
- Generating various output formats
- Validating the source
- Basic maintenance

Example 11-1. The makefile to build the book

```
# Build the book!
#
# The primary targets in this file are:
#
# show_pdf      Generate the pdf and start a viewer
# pdf           Generate the pdf
# print         Print the pdf
# show_html     Generate the html and start a viewer
# html          Generate the html
# xml           Generate the xml
# release       Make a release tarball
# clean         Clean up generated files
#

BOOK_DIR      := /test/book
SOURCE_DIR    := text
OUTPUT_DIR    := out
EXAMPLES_DIR  := examples

QUIET          = @

SHELL          =  bash
AWK           := awk
CP            := cp
EGREP         := egrep
HTML_VIEWER   := cygstart
KILL          := /bin/kill
M4            := m4
MV            := mv
PDF_VIEWER    := cygstart
RM            := rm -f
MKDIR         := mkdir -p
LNDIR         := lndir
SED           := sed
SORT          := sort
TOUCH         := touch
XMLTO         := xmlto
XMLTO_FLAGS    = -o $(OUTPUT_DIR) $(XML_VERBOSE)
process-pgm   := bin/process-includes
make-depend   := bin/make-depend

m4-macros     := text/macros.m4

# $(call process-includes, input-file, output-file)
#   Remove tabs, expand macros, and process include directives.
define process-includes
  expand $1 |                                             \
  $(M4) --prefix-builtins --include=text $(m4-macros) - |     \
  $(process-pgm) > $2
endef

# $(call file-exists, file-name)
#   Return non-null if a file exists.
```

Example 11-1. The makefile to build the book (continued)

```
file-exists = $(wildcard $1)

# $(call maybe-mkdir, directory-name-opt)
#    Create a directory if it doesn't exist.
#    If directory-name-opt is omitted use $@ for the directory-name.
maybe-mkdir = $(if $(call file-exists,              \
                    $(if $1,$1,$(dir $@))),,         \
               $(MKDIR) $(if $1,$1,$(dir $@)))

# $(kill-acroread)
#    Terminate the acrobat reader.
define kill-acroread
  $(QUIET) ps -W |                                   \
  $(AWK) 'BEGIN { FIELDWIDTHS = "9 47 100" }         \
         /AcroRd32/ {                                \
                     print "Killing " $$3;           \
                     system( "$(KILL) -f " $$1 )     \
                   }'
endef

# $(call source-to-output, file-name)
#    Transform a source tree reference to an output tree reference.
define source-to-output
$(subst $(SOURCE_DIR),$(OUTPUT_DIR),$1)
endef

# $(call run-script-example, script-name, output-file)
#    Run an example makefile.
define run-script-example
  ( cd $(dir $1);                                    \
    $(notdir $1) 2>&1 |                              \
    if $(EGREP) --silent '\$$\(MAKE\)' [mM]akefile;  \
    then                                             \
      $(SED) -e 's/^++*/$$/';                         \
    else                                             \
      $(SED) -e 's/^++*/$$/'                          \
             -e '/ing directory /d'                  \
             -e 's/\[[0-9]\]//';                      \
    fi )                                             \
  > $(TMP)/out.$$$$ &                                 \
  $(MV) $(TMP)/out.$$$$ $2
endef

# $(call generic-program-example,example-directory)
#    Create the rules to build a generic example.
define generic-program-example
  $(eval $1_dir      := $(OUTPUT_DIR)/$1)
  $(eval $1_make_out := $($1_dir)/make.out)
  $(eval $1_run_out  := $($1_dir)/run.out)
  $(eval $1_clean    := $($1_dir)/clean)
  $(eval $1_run_make := $($1_dir)/run-make)
  $(eval $1_run_run  := $($1_dir)/run-run)
  $(eval $1_sources  := $(filter-out %/CVS, $(wildcard $(EXAMPLES_DIR)/$1/*)))
```

Example 11-1. The makefile to build the book (continued)

```
  $($1_run_out): $($1_make_out) $($1_run_run)
        $$(call run-script-example, $($1_run_run), $$@)

  $($1_make_out): $($1_clean) $($1_run_make)
        $$(call run-script-example, $($1_run_make), $$@)

  $($1_clean): $($1_sources) Makefile
        $(RM) -r $($1_dir)
        $(MKDIR) $($1_dir)
        $(LNDIR) -silent ../../$(EXAMPLES_DIR)/$1 $($1_dir)
        $(TOUCH) $$@

  $($1_run_make):
        printf "#! /bin/bash -x\nmake\n" > $$@
endef


# Book output formats.
BOOK_XML_OUT     := $(OUTPUT_DIR)/book.xml
BOOK_HTML_OUT    := $(subst xml,html,$(BOOK_XML_OUT))
BOOK_FO_OUT      := $(subst xml,fo,$(BOOK_XML_OUT))
BOOK_PDF_OUT     := $(subst xml,pdf,$(BOOK_XML_OUT))
ALL_XML_SRC      := $(wildcard $(SOURCE_DIR)/*.xml)
ALL_XML_OUT      := $(call source-to-output,$(ALL_XML_SRC))
DEPENDENCY_FILES := $(call source-to-output,$(subst .xml,.d,$(ALL_XML_SRC)))


# xml/html/pdf - Produce the desired output format for the book.
.PHONY: xml html pdf
xml:  $(OUTPUT_DIR)/validate
html: $(BOOK_HTML_OUT)
pdf:  $(BOOK_PDF_OUT)

# show_pdf - Generate a pdf file and display it.
.PHONY: show_pdf show_html print
show_pdf: $(BOOK_PDF_OUT)
        $(kill-acroread)
        $(PDF_VIEWER) $(BOOK_PDF_OUT)

# show_html - Generate an html file and display it.
show_html: $(BOOK_HTML_OUT)
        $(HTML_VIEWER) $(BOOK_HTML_OUT)

# print - Print specified pages from the book.
print: $(BOOK_FO_OUT)
        $(kill-acroread)
        java -Dstart=15 -Dend=15 $(FOP) $< -print > /dev/null

# $(BOOK_PDF_OUT) - Generate the pdf file.
$(BOOK_PDF_OUT): $(BOOK_FO_OUT) Makefile

# $(BOOK_HTML_OUT) - Generate the html file.
$(BOOK_HTML_OUT): $(ALL_XML_OUT) $(OUTPUT_DIR)/validate Makefile
```

Example 11-1. The makefile to build the book (continued)

```
# $(BOOK_FO_OUT) - Generate the fo intermediate output file.
.INTERMEDIATE: $(BOOK_FO_OUT)
$(BOOK_FO_OUT): $(ALL_XML_OUT) $(OUTPUT_DIR)/validate Makefile

# $(BOOK_XML_OUT) - Process all the xml input files.
$(BOOK_XML_OUT): Makefile


###################################################################
# FOP Support
#
FOP := org.apache.fop.apps.Fop

# DEBUG_FOP - Define this to see fop processor output.
ifndef DEBUG_FOP
  FOP_FLAGS  := -q
  FOP_OUTPUT := | $(SED) -e '/not implemented/d'        \
                         -e '/relative-align/d'         \
                         -e '/xsl-footnote-separator/d'
endif

# CLASSPATH - Compute the appropriate CLASSPATH for fop.
export CLASSPATH
CLASSPATH = $(patsubst %;,%,                             \
              $(subst ; ,;,                              \
                $(addprefix c:/usr/xslt-process-2.2/java/,   \
                  $(addsuffix .jar;,                     \
                    xalan                                \
                    xercesImpl                           \
                    batik                                \
                    fop                                  \
                    jimi-1.0                             \
                    avalon-framework-cvs-20020315))))

# %.pdf - Pattern rule to produce pdf output from fo input.
%.pdf: %.fo
        $(kill-acroread)
        java -Xmx128M $(FOP) $(FOP_FLAGS) $< $@ $(FOP_OUTPUT)

# %.fo - Pattern rule to produce fo output from xml input.
PAPER_SIZE := letter
%.fo: %.xml
        XSLT_FLAGS="--stringparam paper.type $(PAPER_SIZE)" \
        $(XMLTO) $(XMLTO_FLAGS) fo $<

# %.html - Pattern rule to produce html output from xml input.
%.html: %.xml
        $(XMLTO) $(XMLTO_FLAGS) html-nochunks $<

# fop_help - Display fop processor help text.
.PHONY: fop_help
fop_help:
        -java org.apache.fop.apps.Fop -help
        -java org.apache.fop.apps.Fop -print help
```

Example 11-1. The makefile to build the book (continued)

```
##################################################################
# release - Produce a release of the book.
#
RELEASE_TAR   := mpwm-$(shell date +%F).tar.gz
RELEASE_FILES := README Makefile *.pdf bin examples out text

.PHONY: release
release: $(BOOK_PDF_OUT)
        ln -sf $(BOOK_PDF_OUT) .
        tar --create                       \
            --gzip                         \
            --file=$(RELEASE_TAR)          \
            --exclude=CVS                  \
            --exclude=semantic.cache       \
            --exclude=*~                   \
            $(RELEASE_FILES)
        ls -l $(RELEASE_TAR)


##################################################################
# Rules for Chapter 1 examples.
#

# Here are all the example directories.
EXAMPLES :=                                \
                ch01-bogus-tab             \
                ch01-cw1                   \
                ch01-hello                 \
                ch01-cw2                   \
                ch01-cw2a                  \
                ch02-cw3                   \
                ch02-cw4                   \
                ch02-cw4a                  \
                ch02-cw5                   \
                ch02-cw5a                  \
                ch02-cw5b                  \
                ch02-cw6                   \
                ch02-make-clean            \
                ch03-assert-not-null       \
                ch03-debug-trace           \
                ch03-debug-trace-1         \
                ch03-debug-trace-2         \
                ch03-filter-failure        \
                ch03-find-program-1        \
                ch03-find-program-2        \
                ch03-findstring-1          \
                ch03-grep                  \
                ch03-include               \
                ch03-invalid-variable      \
                ch03-kill-acroread         \
                ch03-kill-program          \
                ch03-letters               \
                ch03-program-variables-1   \
```

Example 11-1. The makefile to build the book (continued)

```
                    ch03-program-variables-2      \
                    ch03-program-variables-3      \
                    ch03-program-variables-5      \
                    ch03-scoping-issue            \
                    ch03-shell                    \
                    ch03-trailing-space           \
                    ch04-extent                   \
                    ch04-for-loop-1               \
                    ch04-for-loop-2               \
                    ch04-for-loop-3               \
                    ch06-simple                   \
                    appb-defstruct                \
                    appb-arithmetic

# I would really like to use this foreach loop, but a bug in 3.80
# generates a fatal error.
#$(foreach e,$(EXAMPLES),$(eval $(call generic-program-example,$e)))

# Instead I expand the foreach by hand here.
$(eval $(call generic-program-example,ch01-bogus-tab))
$(eval $(call generic-program-example,ch01-cw1))
$(eval $(call generic-program-example,ch01-hello))
$(eval $(call generic-program-example,ch01-cw2))
$(eval $(call generic-program-example,ch01-cw2a))
$(eval $(call generic-program-example,ch02-cw3))
$(eval $(call generic-program-example,ch02-cw4))
$(eval $(call generic-program-example,ch02-cw4a))
$(eval $(call generic-program-example,ch02-cw5))
$(eval $(call generic-program-example,ch02-cw5a))
$(eval $(call generic-program-example,ch02-cw5b))
$(eval $(call generic-program-example,ch02-cw6))
$(eval $(call generic-program-example,ch02-make-clean))
$(eval $(call generic-program-example,ch03-assert-not-null))
$(eval $(call generic-program-example,ch03-debug-trace))
$(eval $(call generic-program-example,ch03-debug-trace-1))
$(eval $(call generic-program-example,ch03-debug-trace-2))
$(eval $(call generic-program-example,ch03-filter-failure))
$(eval $(call generic-program-example,ch03-find-program-1))
$(eval $(call generic-program-example,ch03-find-program-2))
$(eval $(call generic-program-example,ch03-findstring-1))
$(eval $(call generic-program-example,ch03-grep))
$(eval $(call generic-program-example,ch03-include))
$(eval $(call generic-program-example,ch03-invalid-variable))
$(eval $(call generic-program-example,ch03-kill-acroread))
$(eval $(call generic-program-example,ch03-kill-program))
$(eval $(call generic-program-example,ch03-letters))
$(eval $(call generic-program-example,ch03-program-variables-1))
$(eval $(call generic-program-example,ch03-program-variables-2))
$(eval $(call generic-program-example,ch03-program-variables-3))
$(eval $(call generic-program-example,ch03-program-variables-5))
$(eval $(call generic-program-example,ch03-scoping-issue))
$(eval $(call generic-program-example,ch03-shell))
```

Example 11-1. The makefile to build the book (continued)

```
$(eval $(call generic-program-example,ch03-trailing-space))
$(eval $(call generic-program-example,ch04-extent))
$(eval $(call generic-program-example,ch04-for-loop-1))
$(eval $(call generic-program-example,ch04-for-loop-2))
$(eval $(call generic-program-example,ch04-for-loop-3))
$(eval $(call generic-program-example,ch06-simple))
$(eval $(call generic-program-example,ch10-echo-bash))
$(eval $(call generic-program-example,appb-defstruct))
$(eval $(call generic-program-example,appb-arithmetic))


################################################################
# validate
#
# Check for 1) unexpanded m4 macros; b) tabs; c) FIXME comments; d)
# RM: responses to Andy; e) duplicate m4 macros
#
validation_checks := $(OUTPUT_DIR)/chk_macros_tabs          \
                     $(OUTPUT_DIR)/chk_fixme                \
                     $(OUTPUT_DIR)/chk_duplicate_macros     \
                     $(OUTPUT_DIR)/chk_orphaned_examples

.PHONY: validate-only
validate-only: $(OUTPUT_DIR)/validate
$(OUTPUT_DIR)/validate: $(validation_checks)
        $(TOUCH) $@


$(OUTPUT_DIR)/chk_macros_tabs: $(ALL_XML_OUT)
        # Looking for macros and tabs...
        $(QUIET)! $(EGREP) --ignore-case                    \
                        --line-number                       \
                        --regexp='\b(m4_|mp_)'              \
                        --regexp='\011'                    \
                        $^
        $(TOUCH) $@

$(OUTPUT_DIR)/chk_fixme: $(ALL_XML_OUT)
        # Looking for RM: and FIXME...
        $(QUIET)$(AWK)                                       \
                '/FIXME/ { printf "%s:%s: %s\n", FILENAME, NR, $$0 }  \
                /^ *RM:/ {                                  \
                        if ( $$0 !~ /RM: Done/ )            \
                        printf "%s:%s: %s\n", FILENAME, NR, $$0  \
                }' $(subst $(OUTPUT_DIR)/,$(SOURCE_DIR)/,$^)
        $(TOUCH) $@

$(OUTPUT_DIR)/chk_duplicate_macros: $(SOURCE_DIR)/macros.m4
        # Looking for duplicate macros...
        $(QUIET)! $(EGREP) --only-matching              \
                "\`[^']+'," $< |                        \
        $(SORT) |                                       \
        uniq -c |                                       \
```

Example 11-1. The makefile to build the book (continued)

```
        $(AWK) '$$1 > 1 { printf "$<:0: %s\n", $$0 }' | \
        $(EGREP) "^"
        $(TOUCH) $@

ALL_EXAMPLES := $(TMP)/all_examples

$(OUTPUT_DIR)/chk_orphaned_examples: $(ALL_EXAMPLES) $(DEPENDENCY_FILES)
        $(QUIET)$(AWK) -F/ '/(EXAMPLES|OUTPUT)_DIR/ { print $$3 }'      \
                $(filter %.d,$^) |                                      \
        $(SORT) -u |                                                    \
        comm -13 - $(filter-out %.d,$^)
        $(TOUCH) $@

.INTERMEDIATE: $(ALL_EXAMPLES)
$(ALL_EXAMPLES):
        # Looking for unused examples...
        $(QUIET) ls -p $(EXAMPLES_DIR) |          \
        $(AWK) '/CVS/ { next }                    \
                /\// { print substr($$0, 1, length - 1) }' > $@

#################################################################
# clean
#
clean:
        $(kill-acroread)
        $(RM) -r $(OUTPUT_DIR)
        $(RM) $(SOURCE_DIR)/*~ $(SOURCE_DIR)/*.log semantic.cache
        $(RM) book.pdf

#################################################################
# Dependency Management
#
# Don't read or remake includes if we are doing a clean.
#
ifneq "$(MAKECMDGOALS)" "clean"
  -include $(DEPENDENCY_FILES)
endif

vpath %.xml $(SOURCE_DIR)
vpath %.tif $(SOURCE_DIR)
vpath %.eps $(SOURCE_DIR)

$(OUTPUT_DIR)/%.xml: %.xml $(process-pgm) $(m4-macros)
        $(call process-includes, $<, $@)

$(OUTPUT_DIR)/%.tif: %.tif
        $(CP) $< $@

$(OUTPUT_DIR)/%.eps: %.eps
        $(CP) $< $@

$(OUTPUT_DIR)/%.d: %.xml $(make-depend)
        $(make-depend) $< > $@
```

Example 11-1. The makefile to build the book (continued)

```
###################################################################
# Create Output Directory
#
# Create the output directory if necessary.
#
DOCBOOK_IMAGES := $(OUTPUT_DIR)/release/images
DRAFT_PNG      := /usr/share/docbook-xsl/images/draft.png

ifneq "$(MAKECMDGOALS)" "clean"
  _CREATE_OUTPUT_DIR :=                                          \
    $(shell                                                      \
      $(MKDIR) $(DOCBOOK_IMAGES) &                               \
      $(CP) $(DRAFT_PNG) $(DOCBOOK_IMAGES);                      \
      if ! [[ $(foreach d,                                       \
               $(notdir                                          \
                 $(wildcard $(EXAMPLES_DIR)/ch*)),               \
               -e $(OUTPUT_DIR)/$d &) -e . ]];                   \
    then                                                         \
      echo Linking examples... > /dev/stderr;                   \
      $(LNDIR) $(BOOK_DIR)/$(EXAMPLES_DIR) $(BOOK_DIR)/$(OUTPUT_DIR); \
    fi)
endif
```

The *makefile* is written to run under Cygwin with no serious attempt at portability to Unix. Nevertheless, I believe there are few, if any, incompatibilities with Unix that cannot be resolved by redefining a variable or possibly introducing an additional variable.

The global variables section first defines the location of the root directory and the relative locations of the text, examples, and output directories. Each nontrivial program used by the *makefile* is defined as a variable.

Managing Examples

The first task, managing the examples, is the most complex. Each example is stored in its own directory under *book/examples/chn-<title>*. Examples consist of a *makefile* along with any supporting files and directories. To process an example we first create a directory of symbolic links to the output tree and work there so that no artifacts of running the *makefile* are left in the source tree. Furthermore, most of the examples require setting the current working directory to that of the *makefile*, in order to generate the expected output. After symlinking the source, we execute a shell script, run-make, to invoke the *makefile* with the appropriate arguments. If no shell script is present in the source tree, we can generate a default version. The output of the run-make script is saved in *make.out*. Some examples produce an executable, which must also be run. This is accomplished by running the script run-run and saving its output in the file *run.out*.

Creating the tree of symbolic links is performed by this code at the end of the *makefile*:

```
ifneq "$(MAKECMDGOALS)" "clean"
  _CREATE_OUTPUT_DIR :=                                                    \
    $(shell                                                               \
      ...
      if ! [[ $(foreach d,                                               \
                $(notdir                                                  \
                  $(wildcard $(EXAMPLES_DIR)/ch*)),                       \
                -e $(OUTPUT_DIR)/$d &&) -e . ]];                          \
      then                                                                \
        echo Linking examples... > /dev/stderr;                          \
        $(LNDIR) $(BOOK_DIR)/$(EXAMPLES_DIR) $(BOOK_DIR)/$(OUTPUT_DIR); \
      fi)
endif
```

The code consists of a single, simple variable assignment wrapped in an `ifneq` conditional. The conditional is there to prevent `make` from creating the output directory structure during a `make clean`. The actual variable is a dummy whose value is never used. However, the `shell` function on the right-hand side is executed immediately when `make` reads the *makefile*. The `shell` function checks if each example directory exists in the output tree. If any is missing, the `lndir` command is invoked to update the tree of symbolic links.

The test used by the `if` is worth examining more closely. The test itself consists of one `-e` test (i.e., does the file exist?) for each example directory. The actual code goes something like this: use `wildcard` to determine all the examples and strip their directory part with `notdir`, then for each example directory produce the text `-e $(OUTPUT_DIR)/`*dir* `&&`. Now, concatenate all these pieces, and embed them in a `bash` `[[...]]` test. Finally, negate the result. One extra test, `-e .`, is included to allow the `foreach` loop to simply add `&&` to every clause.

This is sufficient to ensure that new directories are always added to the build when they are discovered.

The next step is to create rules that will update the two output files, *make.out* and *run.out*. This is done for each example *.out* file with a user-defined function:

```
# $(call generic-program-example,example-directory)
#   Create the rules to build a generic example.
define generic-program-example
  $(eval $1_dir      := $(OUTPUT_DIR)/$1)
  $(eval $1_make_out := $($1_dir)/make.out)
  $(eval $1_run_out  := $($1_dir)/run.out)
  $(eval $1_clean    := $($1_dir)/clean)
  $(eval $1_run_make := $($1_dir)/run-make)
  $(eval $1_run_run  := $($1_dir)/run-run)
  $(eval $1_sources  := $(filter-out %/CVS, $(wildcard $(EXAMPLES_DIR)/$1/*)))

  $($1_run_out): $($1_make_out) $($1_run_run)
          $$(call run-script-example, $($1_run_run), $$@)
```

```
    $($1_make_out): $($1_clean) $($1_run_make)
          $$(call run-script-example, $($1_run_make), $$@)

    $($1_clean): $($1_sources) Makefile
          $(RM) -r $($1_dir)
          $(MKDIR) $($1_dir)
          $(LNDIR) -silent ../../$(EXAMPLES_DIR)/$1 $($1_dir)
          $(TOUCH) $$@

    $($1_run_make):
          printf "#! /bin/bash -x\nmake\n" > $$@
endef
```

This function is intended to be invoked once for each example directory:

```
$(eval $(call generic-program-example,ch01-bogus-tab))
$(eval $(call generic-program-example,ch01-cw1))
$(eval $(call generic-program-example,ch01-hello))
$(eval $(call generic-program-example,ch01-cw2))
```

The variable definitions at the beginning of the function are mostly for convenience and to improve readability. Further improvement comes from performing the assignments inside eval so their value can be used immediately by the macro without extra quoting.

The heart of the function is the first two targets: $($1_run_out) and $($1_make_out). These update the *run.out* and *make.out* targets for each example, respectively. The variable names are composed from the example directory name and the indicated suffix, *_run_out* or *_make_out*.

The first rule says that *run.out* depends upon *make.out* and the *run-run* script. That is, rerun the example program if make has been run or the *run-run* control script has been updated. The target is updated with the run-script-example function:

```
# $(call run-script-example, script-name, output-file)
#   Run an example makefile.
define run-script-example
  ( cd $(dir $1);                                        \
    $(notdir $1) 2>&1 |                                  \
    if $(EGREP) --silent '\$$\(MAKE\)' [mM]akefile;      \
    then                                                 \
      $(SED) -e 's/^++*/$$/';                             \
    else                                                 \
      $(SED) -e 's/^++*/$$/'                              \
             -e '/ing directory /d'                      \
             -e 's/\[[0-9]\]//';                          \
    fi )                                                 \
  > $(TMP)/out.$$$$ &&                                   \
  $(MV) $(TMP)/out.$$$$ $2
endef
```

This function requires the path to the script and the output filename. It changes to the script's directory and runs the script, piping both the standard output and error output through a filter to clean them up.*

The *make.out* target is similar but has an added complication. If new files are added to an example, we would like to detect the situation and rebuild the example. The _CREATE_OUTPUT_DIR code rebuilds symlinks only if a new directory is discovered, not when new files are added. To detect this situation, we drop a timestamp file in each example directory indicating when the last lndir was performed. The $($1_clean) target updates this timestamp file and depends upon the actual source files in the examples directory (not the symlinks in the output directory). If make's dependency analysis discovers a newer file in the examples directory than the *clean* timestamp file, the command script will delete the symlinked output directory, recreate it, and drop a new *clean* timestamp file. This action is also performed when the *makefile* itself is modified.

Finally, the *run-make* shell script invoked to run the *makefile* is typically a two-line script.

```
#! /bin/bash -x
make
```

It quickly became tedious to produce these boilerplate scripts, so the $($1_run_make) target was added as a prerequisite to $($1_make_out) to create it. If the prerequisite is missing, the *makefile* generates it in the output tree.

The generic-program-example function, when executed for each example directory, creates all the rules for running examples and preparing the output for inclusion in the XML files. These rules are triggered by computed dependencies included in the *makefile*. For example, the dependency file for Chapter 1 is:

```
out/ch01.xml: $(EXAMPLES_DIR)/ch01-hello/Makefile
out/ch01.xml: $(OUTPUT_DIR)/ch01-hello/make.out
out/ch01.xml: $(EXAMPLES_DIR)/ch01-cw1/count_words.c
out/ch01.xml: $(EXAMPLES_DIR)/ch01-cw1/lexer.l
out/ch01.xml: $(EXAMPLES_DIR)/ch01-cw1/Makefile
out/ch01.xml: $(OUTPUT_DIR)/ch01-cw1/make.out
out/ch01.xml: $(EXAMPLES_DIR)/ch01-cw2/lexer.l
out/ch01.xml: $(OUTPUT_DIR)/ch01-cw2/make.out
out/ch01.xml: $(OUTPUT_DIR)/ch01-cw2/run.out
out/ch01.xml: $(OUTPUT_DIR)/ch01-bogus-tab/make.out
```

---

* The cleaning process gets complex. The *run-run* and *run-make* scripts often use bash -x to allow the actual make command line to be echoed. The -x option puts ++ before each command in the output, which the cleaning script transforms into a simple $ representing the shell prompt. However, commands are not the only information to appear in the output. Because make is running the example and eventually starts another make, simple *makefiles* include extra, unwanted output such as the messages Entering directory… and Leaving directory… as well as displaying a make level number in messages. For simple *makefiles* that do not recursively invoke make, we strip this inappropriate output to present the output of make as if it were run from a top-level shell.

These dependencies are generated by a simple awk script, imaginatively named make-depend:

```
#! /bin/awk -f

function generate_dependency( prereq )
{
  filename = FILENAME
  sub( /text/, "out", filename )
  print filename ": " prereq
}

/^ *include-program/ {
  generate_dependency( "$(EXAMPLES_DIR)/" $2 )
}

/^ *mp_program\(/ {
  match( $0, /\((.*)\)/, names )
  generate_dependency( "$(EXAMPLES_DIR)/" names[1] )
}

/^ *include-output/ {
  generate_dependency( "$(OUTPUT_DIR)/" $2 )
}

/^ *mp_output\(/ {
  match( $0, /\((.*)\)/, names )
  generate_dependency( "$(OUTPUT_DIR)/" names[1] )
}

/graphic fileref/ {
  match( $0, /"(.*)"/, out_file )
  generate_dependency( out_file[1] );
}
```

The script searches for patterns like:

```
mp_program(ch01-hello/Makefile)
mp_output(ch01-hello/make.out)
```

(The mp_program macro uses the program listing format, while the mp_output macro uses the program output format.) The script generates the dependency from the source filename and the filename parameter.

Finally, the generation of dependency files is triggered by a make include statement, in the usual fashion:

```
# $(call source-to-output, file-name)
#    Transform a source tree reference to an output tree reference.
define source-to-output
$(subst $(SOURCE_DIR),$(OUTPUT_DIR),$1)
endef
...
ALL_XML_SRC      := $(wildcard $(SOURCE_DIR)/*.xml)
DEPENDENCY_FILES := $(call source-to-output,$(subst .xml,.d,$(ALL_XML_SRC)))
```

```
...
ifneq "$(MAKECMDGOALS)" "clean"
  -include $(DEPENDENCY_FILES)
endif

vpath %.xml $(SOURCE_DIR)
...
$(OUTPUT_DIR)/%.d: %.xml $(make-depend)
        $(make-depend) $< > $@
```

This completes the code for handling examples. Most of the complexity stems from the desire to include the actual source of the *makefiles* as well as the actual output from make and the example programs. I suspect there is also a little bit of the "put up or shut up" syndrome here. If I believe make is so great, it should be able to handle this complex task and, by golly, it can.

XML Preprocessing

At the risk of branding myself as a philistine for all posterity, I must admit I don't like XML very much. I find it awkward and verbose. So, when I discovered that the manuscript must be written in DocBook, I looked for more traditional tools that would help ease the pain. The m4 macro processor and awk were two tools that helped immensely.

There were two problems with DocBook and XML that m4 was perfect for: avoiding the verbose syntax of XML and managing the XML identifiers used in cross-referencing. For instance, to emphasize a word in DocBook, you must write:

```
<emphasis>not</emphasis>
```

Using m4, I wrote a simple macro that allowed me to instead write:

```
mp_em(not)
```

Ahh, that feels better. In addition, I introduced many symbolic formatting styles appropriate for the material, such as mp_variable and mp_target. This allowed me to select a trivial format, such as literal, and change it later to whatever the production department preferred without having to perform a global search and replace.

I'm sure the XML aficionados will probably send me boat loads of email telling me how to do this with entities or some such, but remember Unix is about getting the job done now with the tools at hand, and as Larry Wall loves to say, "there's more than one way to do it." Besides, I'm afraid learning too much XML will rot my brain.

The second task for m4 was handling the XML identifiers used for cross-referencing. Each chapter, section, example, and table is labeled with an identifier:

```
<sect1 id="MPWM-CH-7-SECT-1">
```

References to a chapter must use this identifier. This is clearly an issue from a programming standpoint. The identifiers are complex constants sprinkled throughout the "code." Furthermore, the symbols themselves have no meaning. I have no idea what section 1 of Chapter 7 might have been about. By using m4, I could avoid duplicating complex literals, and provide a more meaningful name:

```
<sect1 id="mp_se_makedepend">
```

Most importantly, if chapters or sections shift, as they did many times, the text could be updated by changing a few constants in a single file. The advantage was most noticeable when sections were renumbered in a chapter. Such an operation might require a half dozen global search and replace operations across all files if I hadn't used symbolic references.

Here is an example of several m4 macros[*]:

```
m4_define(`mp_tag',       `<$1>`$2'</$1>')
m4_define(`mp_lit',       `mp_tag(literal, `$1')')

m4_define(`mp_cmd',       `mp_tag(command,`$1')')
m4_define(`mp_target', `mp_lit($1)')

m4_define(`mp_all',       `mp_target(all)')
m4_define(`mp_bash',      `mp_cmd(bash)')

m4_define(`mp_ch_examples',      `MPWM-CH-11')
m4_define(`mp_se_book',          `MPWM-CH-11.1')
m4_define(`mp_ex_book_makefile',`MPWM-CH-11-EX-1')
```

The other preprocessing task was to implement an include feature for slurping in the example text previously discussed. This text needed to have its tabs converted to spaces (since O'Reilly's DocBook converter cannot handle tabs and *makefiles* have lots of tabs!), must be wrapped in a [CDATA[...]] to protect special characters, and finally, has to trim the extra newlines at the beginning and end of examples. I accomplished this with another little awk program called process-includes:

```
#! /usr/bin/awk -f
function expand_cdata( dir )
{
  start_place = match( $1, "include-" )
  if ( start_place > 0 )
  {
    prefix = substr( $1, 1, start_place - 1 )
  }
  else
  {
    print "Bogus include '" $0 "'" > "/dev/stderr"
  }

  end_place = match( $2, "(</(programlisting|screen)>.*)$", tag )
```

---

[*] The mp prefix stands for Managing Projects (the book's title), macro processor, or make pretty. Take your pick.

```
    if ( end_place > 0 )
    {
      file = dir substr( $2, 1, end_place - 1 )
    }
    else
    {
      print "Bogus include '" $0 "'" > "/dev/stderr"
    }

    command = "expand " file

    printf "%s>&33;&91;CDATA[", prefix
    tail = 0
    previous_line = ""
    while ( (command | getline line) > 0 )
    {
      if ( tail )
        print previous_line;

      tail = 1
      previous_line = line
    }

    printf "%s&93;&93;&62;%s\n", previous_line, tag[1]
    close( command )
}

/include-program/ {
  expand_cdata( "examples/" )
  next;
}

/include-output/ {
  expand_cdata( "out/" )
  next;
}

/<(programlisting|screen)> *$/ {
  # Find the current indentation.
  offset = match( $0, "<(programlisting|screen)>" )

  # Strip newline from tag.
  printf $0

  # Read the program...
  tail = 0
  previous_line = ""
  while ( (getline line) > 0 )
  {
    if ( line ~ "</(programlisting|screen)>" )
    {
      gsub( /^ */, "", line )
      break
    }
```

```
   if ( tail )
     print previous_line

   tail = 1
   previous_line = substr( line, offset + 1 )
  }

 printf "%s%s\n", previous_line, line

 next
}

{
  print
}
```

In the *makefile*, we copy the XML files from the source tree to the output tree, transforming tabs, macros, and include files in the process:

```
process-pgm := bin/process-includes
m4-macros   := text/macros.m4

# $(call process-includes, input-file, output-file)
#   Remove tabs, expand macros, and process include directives.
define process-includes
  expand $1 |                                              \
  $(M4) --prefix-builtins --include=text $(m4-macros) - | \
  $(process-pgm) > $2
endef

vpath %.xml $(SOURCE_DIR)

$(OUTPUT_DIR)/%.xml: %.xml $(process-pgm) $(m4-macros)
        $(call process-includes, $<, $@)
```

The pattern rule indicates how to get an XML file from the source tree into the output tree. It also says that all the output XML files should be regenerated if the macros or the include processor change.

Generating Output

So far, nothing we've covered has actually formatted any text or created anything
that can be printed or displayed. Obviously, a very important feature if the *makefile*
is to format a book. There were two formats that I was interested in: HTML and
PDF.

I figured out how to format to HTML first. There's a great little program, xsltproc,
and its helper script, xmlto, that I used to do the job. Using these tools, the process
was fairly simple:

```
# Book output formats.
BOOK_XML_OUT    := $(OUTPUT_DIR)/book.xml
BOOK_HTML_OUT   := $(subst xml,html,$(BOOK_XML_OUT))
```

```
ALL_XML_SRC       := $(wildcard $(SOURCE_DIR)/*.xml)
ALL_XML_OUT       := $(call source-to-output,$(ALL_XML_SRC))

# html - Produce the desired output format for the book.
.PHONY: html
html: $(BOOK_HTML_OUT)

# show_html - Generate an html file and display it.
.PHONY: show_html
show_html: $(BOOK_HTML_OUT)
        $(HTML_VIEWER) $(BOOK_HTML_OUT)

# $(BOOK_HTML_OUT) - Generate the html file.
$(BOOK_HTML_OUT): $(ALL_XML_OUT) $(OUTPUT_DIR)/validate Makefile

# %.html - Pattern rule to produce html output from xml input.
%.html: %.xml
        $(XMLTO) $(XMLTO_FLAGS) html-nochunks $<
```

The pattern rule does most of the work of converting an XML file into an HTML file. The book is organized as a single top-level file, *book.xml*, that includes each chapter. The top-level file is represented by BOOK_XML_OUT. The HTML counterpart is BOOK_HTML_OUT, which is a target. The BOOK_HTML_OUT file has its included XML files a prerequisites. For convenience, there are two phony targets, html and show_html, that create the HTML file and display it in the local browser, respectively.

Although easy in principle, generating PDF was considerably more complex. The xsltproc program is able to produce PDF directly, but I was unable to get it to work. All this work was done on Windows with Cygwin and the Cygwin version of xsltproc wanted POSIX paths. The custom version of DocBook I was using and the manuscript itself contained Windows-specific paths. This difference, I believe, gave xsltproc fits that I could not quell. Instead, I chose to use xsltproc to generate XML formatting objects and the Java program FOP (*http://xml.apache.org/fop*) for generating the PDF.

Thus, the code to generate PDF is somewhat longer:

```
# Book output formats.
BOOK_XML_OUT      := $(OUTPUT_DIR)/book.xml
BOOK_FO_OUT       := $(subst xml,fo,$(BOOK_XML_OUT))
BOOK_PDF_OUT      := $(subst xml,pdf,$(BOOK_XML_OUT))
ALL_XML_SRC       := $(wildcard $(SOURCE_DIR)/*.xml)
ALL_XML_OUT       := $(call source-to-output,$(ALL_XML_SRC))

# pdf - Produce the desired output format for the book.
.PHONY: pdf
pdf:  $(BOOK_PDF_OUT)

# show_pdf - Generate a pdf file and display it.
.PHONY: show_pdf
show_pdf: $(BOOK_PDF_OUT)
        $(kill-acroread)
        $(PDF_VIEWER) $(BOOK_PDF_OUT)
```

```
# $(BOOK_PDF_OUT) - Generate the pdf file.
$(BOOK_PDF_OUT): $(BOOK_FO_OUT) Makefile

# $(BOOK_FO_OUT) - Generate the fo intermediate output file.
.INTERMEDIATE: $(BOOK_FO_OUT)
$(BOOK_FO_OUT): $(ALL_XML_OUT) $(OUTPUT_DIR)/validate Makefile

# FOP Support
FOP := org.apache.fop.apps.Fop

# DEBUG_FOP - Define this to see fop processor output.
ifndef DEBUG_FOP
  FOP_FLAGS   := -q
  FOP_OUTPUT := | $(SED) -e '/not implemented/d'       \
                         -e '/relative-align/d'        \
                         -e '/xsl-footnote-separator/d'
endif

# CLASSPATH - Compute the appropriate CLASSPATH for fop.
export CLASSPATH
CLASSPATH = $(patsubst %;,%,                              \
              $(subst ; ,;,                              \
                $(addprefix c:/usr/xslt-process-2.2/java/, \
                  $(addsuffix .jar;,                     \
                    xalan                                \
                    xercesImpl                           \
                    batik                                \
                    fop                                  \
                    jimi-1.0                             \
                    avalon-framework-cvs-20020315))))

# %.pdf - Pattern rule to produce pdf output from fo input.
%.pdf: %.fo
        $(kill-acroread)
        java -Xmx128M $(FOP) $(FOP_FLAGS) $< $@ $(FOP_OUTPUT)

# %.fo - Pattern rule to produce fo output from xml input.
PAPER_SIZE := letter
%.fo: %.xml
        XSLT_FLAGS="--stringparam paper.type $(PAPER_SIZE)" \
        $(XMLTO) $(XMLTO_FLAGS) fo $<

# fop_help - Display fop processor help text.
.PHONY: fop_help
fop_help:
        -java org.apache.fop.apps.Fop -help
        -java org.apache.fop.apps.Fop -print help
```

As you can see, there are now two pattern rules reflecting the two-stage process I used. The *.xml* to *.fo* rule invokes xmlto. The *.fo* to *.pdf* rule first kills any running Acrobat reader (because the program locks the PDF file, preventing FOP from writing the file), then runs FOP. FOP is a very chatty program, and scrolling through hundreds of lines of pointless warnings got old fast, so I added a simple sed filter,

FOP_OUTPUT, to remove the irritating warnings. Occasionally, however, those warnings had some real data in them, so I added a debugging feature, DEBUG_FOP, to disable my filter. Finally, like the HTML version, I added two convenience targets, pdf and show_pdf, to kick the whole thing off.

Validating the Source

What with DocBook's allergy to tabs, macro processors, include files and comments from editors, making sure the source text is correct and complete is not easy. To help, I implemented four validation targets that check for various forms of correctness.

```
validation_checks := $(OUTPUT_DIR)/chk_macros_tabs        \
                     $(OUTPUT_DIR)/chk_fixme               \
                     $(OUTPUT_DIR)/chk_duplicate_macros    \
                     $(OUTPUT_DIR)/chk_orphaned_examples

.PHONY: validate-only
validate-only: $(OUTPUT_DIR)/validate
$(OUTPUT_DIR)/validate: $(validation_checks)
        $(TOUCH) $@
```

Each target generates a timestamp file, and they are all prerequisites of a top-level timestamp file, *validate*.

```
$(OUTPUT_DIR)/chk_macros_tabs: $(ALL_XML_OUT)
        # Looking for macros and tabs...
        $(QUIET)! $(EGREP) --ignore-case         \
                           --line-number         \
                           --regexp='\b(m4_|mp_)'  \
                           --regexp='\011'       \
                           $^
        $(TOUCH) $@
```

This first check looks for m4 macros that were not expanded during preprocessing. This indicates either a misspelled macro or a macro that has never been defined. The check also scans for tab characters. Of course, neither of these situations should ever happen, but they did! One interesting bit in the command script is the exclamation point after $(QUIET). The purpose is to negate the exit status of egrep. That is, make should consider the command a failure if egrep *does* find one of the patterns.

```
$(OUTPUT_DIR)/chk_fixme: $(ALL_XML_OUT)
        # Looking for RM: and FIXME...
        $(QUIET)$(AWK)                                        \
                '/FIXME/ { printf "%s:%s: %s\n", FILENAME, NR, $$0 }  \
                /^ *RM:/  {                                   \
                          if ( $$0 !~ /RM: Done/ )            \
                          printf "%s:%s: %s\n", FILENAME, NR, $$0  \
                }' $(subst $(OUTPUT_DIR)/,$(SOURCE_DIR)/,$^)
        $(TOUCH) $@
```

This check is for unresolved notes to myself. Obviously, any text labeled FIXME should be fixed and the label removed. In addition, any occurrence of RM: that is not followed immediately by Done should be flagged. Notice how the format of the printf function follows the standard format for compiler errors. This way, standard tools that recognize compiler errors will properly process these warnings.

```
$(OUTPUT_DIR)/chk_duplicate_macros: $(SOURCE_DIR)/macros.m4
        # Looking for duplicate macros...
        $(QUIET)! $(EGREP) --only-matching                 \
              "\[^]+'," $< |                               \
        $(SORT) |                                          \
        uniq -c |                                          \
        $(AWK) '$$1 > 1 { printf "$>:0: %s\n", $$0 }' | \
        $(EGREP) "^"
        $(TOUCH) $@
```

This checks for duplicate macro definitions in the m4 macro file. The m4 processor does not consider redefinition to be an error, so I added a special check. The pipeline goes like this: grab the defined symbol in each macro, sort, count duplicates, filter out all lines with a count of one, then use egrep one last time purely for its exit status. Again, note the negation of the exit status to produce a make error only when something is found.

```
ALL_EXAMPLES := $(TMP)/all_examples

$(OUTPUT_DIR)/chk_orphaned_examples: $(ALL_EXAMPLES) $(DEPENDENCY_FILES)
        $(QUIET)$(AWK) -F/ '/(EXAMPLES|OUTPUT)_DIR/ { print $$3 }' \
              $(filter %.d,$^) |                            \
        $(SORT) -u |                                        \
        comm -13 - $(filter-out %.d,$^)
        $(TOUCH) $@

.INTERMEDIATE: $(ALL_EXAMPLES)
$(ALL_EXAMPLES):
        # Looking for unused examples...
        $(QUIET) ls -p $(EXAMPLES_DIR) |        \
        $(AWK) '/CVS/ { next }                  \
              /\// { print substr($$0, 1, length - 1) }' > $@
```

The final check looks for examples that are not referenced in the text. This target uses a funny trick. It requires two sets of input files: all the example directories, and all the XML dependency files. The prerequisites list is separated into these two sets using filter and filter-out. The list of example directories is generated by using ls -p (this appends a slash to each directory) and scanning for slashes. The pipeline first grabs the XML dependency files from the prerequisite list, outputs the example directories it finds in them, and removes any duplicates. These are the examples actually referenced in the text. This list is fed to comm's standard input, while the list of all known example directories is fed as the second file. The -13 option indicates that comm should print only lines found in column two (that is, directories that are not referenced from a dependency file).

The Linux Kernel Makefile

The Linux kernel *makefile* is an excellent example of using make in a complex build environment. While it is beyond the scope of this book to explain how the Linux kernel is structured and built, we can examine several interesting uses of make employed by the kernel build system. See *http://macarchive.linuxsymposium.org/ols2003/Proceedings/All-Reprints/Reprint-Germaschewski-OLS2003.pdf* for a more complete discussion of the 2.5/2.6 kernel build process and its evolution from the 2.4 approach.

Since the *makefile* has so many facets, we will discuss just a few features that are applicable to a variety of applications. First, we'll look at how single-letter make variables are used to simulate single-letter command-line options. We'll see how the source and binary trees are separated in a way that allows users to invoke make from the source tree. Next, we'll examine the way the *makefile* controls the verboseness of the output. Then we'll review the most interesting user-defined functions and see how they reduce code duplication, improve readability, and provide encapsulation. Finally, we'll look at the way the *makefile* implements a simple help facility.

The Linux kernel build follows the familiar configure, build, install pattern used by my most free software. While many free and open software packages use a separate *configure* script (typically built by autoconf), the Linux kernel *makefile* implements configuration with make, invoking scripts and helper programs indirectly.

When the configuration phase is complete, a simple make or make all will build the bare kernel, all the modules, and produce a compressed kernel image (these are the vmlinux, modules, and bzImage targets, respectively). Each kernel build is given a unique version number in the file *version.o* linked into the kernel. This number (and the *version.o* file) are updated by the *makefile* itself.

Some *makefile* features you might want to adapt to your own *makefile* are: the handling of command line options, analyzing command-line goals, saving build status between builds, and managing the output of make.

Command-Line Options

The first part of the *makefile* contains code for setting common build options from the command line. Here is an excerpt that controls the verbose flag:

```
# To put more focus on warnings, be less verbose as default
# Use 'make V=1' to see the full commands
ifdef V
  ifeq ("$(origin V)", "command line")
    KBUILD_VERBOSE = $(V)
  endif
endif
ifndef KBUILD_VERBOSE
  KBUILD_VERBOSE = 0
endif
```

The nested ifdef/ifeq pair ensures that the KBUILD_VERBOSE variable is set only if V is set on the command line. Setting V in the environment or *makefile* has no effect. The following ifndef conditional will then turn off the verbose option if KBUILD_VERBOSE has not yet been set. To set the verbose option from either the environment or *makefile*, you must set KBUILD_VERBOSE and not V.

Notice, however, that setting KBUILD_VERBOSE directly on the command line is allowed and works as expected. This can be useful when writing shell scripts (or aliases) to invoke the *makefile*. These scripts would then be more self-documenting, similar to using GNU long options.

The other command-line options, sparse checking (C) and external modules (M), both use the same careful checking to avoid accidentally setting them from within the *makefile*.

The next section of the *makefile* handles the output directory option (O). This is a fairly involved piece of code. To highlight its structure, we've replaced some parts of this excerpt with ellipses:

```
# kbuild supports saving output files in a separate directory.
# To locate output files in a separate directory two syntax'es are supported.
# In both cases the working directory must be the root of the kernel src.
# 1) O=
# Use "make O=dir/to/store/output/files/"
#
# 2) Set KBUILD_OUTPUT
# Set the environment variable KBUILD_OUTPUT to point to the directory
# where the output files shall be placed.
# export KBUILD_OUTPUT=dir/to/store/output/files/
# make
#
# The O= assigment takes precedence over the KBUILD_OUTPUT environment variable.
# KBUILD_SRC is set on invocation of make in OBJ directory
# KBUILD_SRC is not intended to be used by the regular user (for now)
ifeq ($(KBUILD_SRC),)

  # OK, Make called in directory where kernel src resides
  # Do we want to locate output files in a separate directory?
  ifdef O
    ifeq ("$(origin O)", "command line")
      KBUILD_OUTPUT := $(O)
    endif
  endif
  …
  ifneq ($(KBUILD_OUTPUT),)
    …
    .PHONY: $(MAKECMDGOALS)

    $(filter-out _all,$(MAKECMDGOALS)) _all:
            $(if $(KBUILD_VERBOSE:1=),@)$(MAKE) -C $(KBUILD_OUTPUT)      \
            KBUILD_SRC=$(CURDIR)          KBUILD_VERBOSE=$(KBUILD_VERBOSE) \
            KBUILD_CHECK=$(KBUILD_CHECK) KBUILD_EXTMOD="$(KBUILD_EXTMOD)"  \
```

```
            -f $(CURDIR)/Makefile $@
    # Leave processing to above invocation of make
    skip-makefile := 1
  endif # ifneq ($(KBUILD_OUTPUT),)
endif # ifeq ($(KBUILD_SRC),)

# We process the rest of the Makefile if this is the final invocation of make
ifeq ($(skip-makefile),)
  …the rest of the makefile here…
endif   # skip-makefile
```

Essentially, this says that if KBUILD_OUTPUT is set, invoke make recursively in the output directory defined by KBUILD_OUTPUT. Set KBUILD_SRC to the directory where make was originally executed, and grab the *makefile* from there as well. The rest of the *makefile* will not be seen by make, since skip-makefile will be set. The recursive make will reread this same *makefile* again, only this time KBUILD_SRC will be set, so skip-makefile will be undefined, and the rest of the *makefile* will be read and processed.

This concludes the processing of command-line options. The bulk of the *makefile* follows in the ifeq ($(skip-makefile),) section.

Configuration Versus Building

The *makefile* contains configuration targets and build targets. The configuration targets have the form menuconfig, defconfig, etc. Maintenance targets like clean are treated as configuration targets as well. Other targets such as all, vmlinux, and modules are build targets. The primary result of invoking a configuration target is two files: *.config* and *.config.cmd*. These two files are included by the *makefile* for build targets but are not included for configuration targets (since the configuration target creates them). It is also possible to mix both configuration targets and build targets on a single make invocation, such as:

```
$ make oldconfig all
```

In this case, the *makefile* invokes itself recursively handling each target individually, thus handling configuration targets separately from build targets.

The code controlling configuration, build, and mixed targets begins with:

```
# To make sure we do not include .config for any of the *config targets
# catch them early, and hand them over to scripts/kconfig/Makefile
# It is allowed to specify more targets when calling make, including
# mixing *config targets and build targets.
# For example 'make oldconfig all'.
# Detect when mixed targets is specified, and make a second invocation
# of make so .config is not included in this case either (for *config).
no-dot-config-targets := clean mrproper distclean \
                         cscope TAGS tags help %docs check%

config-targets := 0
mixed-targets  := 0
dot-config     := 1
```

The variable `no-dot-config-targets` lists additional targets that do not require a *.config* file. The code then initializes the `config-targets`, `mixed-targets`, and `dot-config` variables. The `config-targets` variable is 1 if there are any configuration targets on the command line. The `dot-config` variable is 1 if there are build targets on the command line. Finally, `mixed-targets` is 1 if there are both configuration and build targets.

The code to set `dot-config` is:

```
ifneq ($(filter $(no-dot-config-targets), $(MAKECMDGOALS)),)
  ifeq ($(filter-out $(no-dot-config-targets), $(MAKECMDGOALS)),)
    dot-config := 0
  endif
endif
```

The `filter` expression is non-empty if there are configuration targets in `MAKECMDGOALS`. The `ifneq` part is true if the `filter` expression is not empty. The code is hard to follow partly because it contains a double negative. The `ifeq` expression is true if `MAKECMDGOALS` contains only configuration targets. So, `dot-config` will be set to 0 if there are configuration targets and only configuration targets in `MAKECMDGOALS`. A more verbose implementation might make the meaning of these two conditionals more clear:

```
config-target-list := clean mrproper distclean \
                         cscope TAGS tags help %docs check%

config-target-goal := $(filter $(config-target-list), $(MAKECMDGOALS))
build-target-goal := $(filter-out $(config-target-list), $(MAKECMDGOALS))

ifdef config-target-goal
  ifndef build-target-goal
    dot-config := 0
  endif
endif
```

The `ifdef` form can be used instead of `ifneq`, because empty variables are treated as undefined, but care must be taken to ensure a variable does not contain merely a string of blanks (which would cause it to be defined).

The `config-targets` and `mixed-targets` variables are set in the next code block:

```
ifeq ($(KBUILD_EXTMOD),)
  ifneq ($(filter config %config,$(MAKECMDGOALS)),)
    config-targets := 1
    ifneq ($(filter-out config %config,$(MAKECMDGOALS)),)
      mixed-targets := 1
    endif
  endif
endif
```

`KBUILD_EXTMOD` will be non-empty when external modules are being built, but not during normal builds. The first `ifneq` will be true when `MAKECMDGOALS` contains a goal with the config suffix. The second ifneq will be true when MAKECMDGOALS contains nonconfig targets, too.

Once the variables are set, they are used in an if-else chain with four branches. The code has been condensed and indented to highlight its structure:

```
ifeq ($(mixed-targets),1)
  # We're called with mixed targets (*config and build targets).
  # Handle them one by one.
  %:: FORCE
        $(Q)$(MAKE) -C $(srctree) KBUILD_SRC= $@
else
  ifeq ($(config-targets),1)
    # *config targets only - make sure prerequisites are updated, and descend
    # in scripts/kconfig to make the *config target
    %config: scripts_basic FORCE
            $(Q)$(MAKE) $(build)=scripts/kconfig $@
  else
    # Build targets only - this includes vmlinux, arch specific targets, clean
    # targets and others. In general all targets except *config targets.
    ...

    ifeq ($(dot-config),1)
      # In this section, we need .config
      # Read in dependencies to all Kconfig* files, make sure to run
      # oldconfig if changes are detected.
      -include .config.cmd
      include .config

      # If .config needs to be updated, it will be done via the dependency
      # that autoconf has on .config.
      # To avoid any implicit rule to kick in, define an empty command
      .config: ;

      # If .config is newer than include/linux/autoconf.h, someone tinkered
      # with it and forgot to run make oldconfig
      include/linux/autoconf.h: .config
              $(Q)$(MAKE) -f $(srctree)/Makefile silentoldconfig
    else
      # Dummy target needed, because used as prerequisite
      include/linux/autoconf.h: ;
    endif

    include $(srctree)/arch/$(ARCH)/Makefile
    ... lots more make code ...
  endif #ifeq ($(config-targets),1)
endif #ifeq ($(mixed-targets),1)
```

The first branch, ifeq ($(mixed-targets),1), handles mixed command-line arguments. The only target in this branch is a completely generic pattern rule. Since there are no specific rules to handle targets (those rules are in another conditional branch), each target invokes the pattern rule once. This is how a command line with both configuration targets and build targets is separated into a simpler command line. The command script for the generic pattern rule invokes make recursively for each target, causing this same logic to be applied, only this time with no mixed command-line targets. The FORCE prerequisite is used instead of .PHONY, because pattern rules like:

```
%:: FORCE
```

cannot be declared .PHONY. So it seems reasonable to use FORCE consistently everywhere.

The second branch of the if-else chain, ifeq ($(config-targets),1), is invoked when there are only configuration targets on the command line. Here the primary target in the branch is the pattern rule %config (other targets have been omitted). The command script invokes make recursively in the *scripts/kconfig* subdirectory and passes along the target. The curious $(build) construct is defined at the end of the *makefile*:

```
# Shorthand for $(Q)$(MAKE) -f scripts/Makefile.build obj=dir
# Usage:
# $(Q)$(MAKE) $(build)=dir
build := -f $(if $(KBUILD_SRC),$(srctree)/)scripts/Makefile.build obj
```

If KBUILD_SRC is set, the -f option is given a full path to the *scripts makefile*, otherwise a simple relative path is used. Next, the obj variable is set to the righthand side of the equals sign.

The third branch, ifeq ($(dot-config),1), handles build targets that require including the two generated configuration files, *.config* and *.config.cmd*. The final branch merely includes a dummy target for *autoconf.h* to allow it to be used as a prerequisite, even if it doesn't exist.

Most of the remainder of the *makefile* follows the third and fourth branches. It contains the code for building the kernel and modules.

Managing Command Echo

The kernel *makefiles* use a novel technique for managing the level of detail echoed by commands. Each significant task is represented in both a verbose and a quiet version. The verbose version is simply the command to be executed in its natural form and is stored in a variable named cmd_*action*. The brief version is a short message describing the action and is stored in a variable named quiet_cmd_*action*. For example, the command to produce emacs tags is:

```
quiet_cmd_TAGS = MAKE $@
      cmd_TAGS = $(all-sources) | etags -
```

A command is executed by calling the cmd function:

```
# If quiet is set, only print short version of command
cmd = @$(if $($(quiet)cmd_$(1)),\
          echo '  $($(quiet)cmd_$(1))' &&) $(cmd_$(1))
```

To invoke the code for building emacs tags, the *makefile* would contain:

```
TAGS:
        $(call cmd,TAGS)
```

Notice the cmd function begins with an @, so the only text echoed by the function is text from the echo command. In normal mode, the variable quiet is empty, and the test in the if, $($(quiet)cmd_$(1)), expands to $(cmd_TAGS). Since this variable is not empty, the entire function expands to:

```
echo '  $(all-sources) | etags -' && $(all-sources) | etags -
```

If the quiet version is desired, the variable quiet contains the value quiet_ and the function expands to:

```
echo '  MAKE $@' && $(all-sources) | etags -
```

The variable can also be set to silent_. Since there is no command silent_cmd_TAGS, this value causes the cmd function to echo nothing at all.

Echoing the command sometimes becomes more complex, particularly if commands contain single quotes. In these cases, the *makefile* contains this code:

```
$(if $($(quiet)cmd_$(1)),echo '  $(subst ','\'',$($(quiet)cmd_$(1)))';)
```

Here the echo command contains a substitution that replaces single quotes with escaped single quotes to allow them to be properly echoed.

Minor commands that do not warrant the trouble of writing cmd_ and quiet_cmd_ variables are prefixed with $(Q), which contains either nothing or @:

```
ifeq ($(KBUILD_VERBOSE),1)
  quiet =
  Q =
else
  quiet=quiet_
  Q = @
endif

# If the user is running make -s (silent mode), suppress echoing of
# commands

ifneq ($(findstring s,$(MAKEFLAGS)),)
  quiet=silent_
endif
```

User-Defined Functions

The kernel *makefile* defines a number of functions. Here we cover the most interesting ones. The code has been reformatted to improve readability.

The check_gcc function is used to select a gcc command-line option.

```
# $(call check_gcc,preferred-option,alternate-option)
check_gcc =                                              \
```

```
$(shell if $(CC) $(CFLAGS) $(1) -S -o /dev/null    \
        -xc /dev/null > /dev/null 2>&1;            \
    then                                           \
        echo "$(1)";                               \
    else                                           \
        echo "$(2)";                               \
    fi ;)
```

The function works by invoking gcc on a null input file with the preferred command-line option. The output file, standard output, and standard error files are discarded. If the gcc command succeeds, it means the preferred command-line option is valid for this architecture and is returned by the function. Otherwise, the option is invalid and the alternate option is returned. An example use can be found in *arch/i386/Makefile*:

```
# prevent gcc from keeping the stack 16 byte aligned
CFLAGS += $(call check_gcc,-mpreferred-stack-boundary=2,)
```

The if_changed_dep function generates dependency information using a remarkable technique.

```
# execute the command and also postprocess generated
# .d dependencies file
if_changed_dep =                                            \
    $(if                                                    \
      $(strip $?                                            \
        $(filter-out FORCE $(wildcard $^),$^)               \
        $(filter-out $(cmd_$(1)),$(cmd_$@))                 \
        $(filter-out $(cmd_$@),$(cmd_$(1)))),               \
    @set -e;                                                \
    $(if $($(quiet)cmd_$(1)),                               \
      echo '  $(subst ','\'',$($(quiet)cmd_$(1)))';)        \
    $(cmd_$(1));                                            \
    scripts/basic/fixdep                                    \
      $(depfile)                                            \
      $@                                                    \
      '$(subst $$,$$$$,$(subst ','\'',$(cmd_$(1))))'        \
      > $(@D)/.$(@F).tmp;                                   \
    rm -f $(depfile);                                       \
    mv -f $(@D)/.$(@F).tmp $(@D)/.$(@F).cmd
```

The function consists of a single if clause. The details of the test are pretty obscure, but it is clear the intent is to be non-empty if the dependency file should be regenerated. Normal dependency information is concerned with the modification timestamps on files. The kernel build system adds another wrinkle to this task. The kernel build uses a wide variety of compiler options to control the construction and behavior of components. To ensure that command-line options are properly accounted for during a build, the *makefile* is implemented so that if command-line options used for a particular target change, the file is recompiled. Let's see how this is accomplished.

In essence, the command used to compile each file in the kernel is saved in a *.cmd* file. When a subsequent build is executed, make reads the *.cmd* files and compares the current compile command with the last command. If they are different, the *.cmd* dependency file is regenerated causing the object file to be rebuilt. The *.cmd* file usually contains two items: the dependencies that represent actual files for the target file and a single variable recording the command-line options. For example, the file *arch/i386/kernel/cpu/mtrr/if.c* yields this (abbreviated) file:

```
cmd_arch/i386/kernel/cpu/mtrr/if.o := gcc -Wp,-MD …; if.c

deps_arch/i386/kernel/cpu/mtrr/if.o := \
  arch/i386/kernel/cpu/mtrr/if.c \

  …

arch/i386/kernel/cpu/mtrr/if.o: $(deps_arch/i386/kernel/cpu/mtrr/if.o)
$(deps_arch/i386/kernel/cpu/mtrr/if.o):
```

Getting back to the if_changed_dep function, the first argument to the strip is simply the prerequisites that are newer than the target, if any. The second argument to strip is all the prerequisites other than files and the empty target FORCE. The really obscure bit is the last two filter-out calls:

```
$(filter-out $(cmd_$(1)),$(cmd_$@))
$(filter-out $(cmd_$@),$(cmd_$(1)))
```

One or both of these calls will expand to a non-empty string if the command-line options have changed. The macro $(cmd_$(1)) is the current command and $(cmd_$@) will be the previous command, for instance the variable cmd_arch/i386/kernel/cpu/mtrr/if.o just shown. If the new command contains additional options, the first filter-out will be empty, and the second will expand to the new options. If the new command contains fewer options, the first command will contain the deleted options and the second will be empty. Interestingly, since filter-out accepts a list of words (each treated as an independent pattern), the order of options can change and the filter-out will still accurately identify added or removed options. Pretty nifty.

The first statement in the command script sets a shell option to exit immediately on error. This prevents the multiline script from corrupting files in the event of problems. For simple scripts another way to achieve this effect is to connect statements with && rather than semicolons.

The next statement is an echo command written using the techniques described in the section "Managing Command Echo" earlier in this chapter, followed by the dependency generating command itself. The command writes $(depfile), which is then transformed by scripts/basic/fixdep. The nested subst function in the fixdep command line first escapes single quotes, then escapes occurrences of $$ (the current process number in shell syntax).

Finally, if no errors have occurred, the intermediate file $(depfile) is removed and the generated dependency file (with its *.cmd* suffix) is moved into place.

The next function, if_changed_rule, uses the same comparison technique as if_changed_dep to control the execution of a command:

```
# Usage: $(call if_changed_rule,foo)
# will check if $(cmd_foo) changed, or any of the prequisites changed,
# and if so will execute $(rule_foo)

if_changed_rule =                                    \
    $(if $(strip $?                                  \
            $(filter-out $(cmd_$(1)),$(cmd_$(@F)))   \
            $(filter-out $(cmd_$(@F)),$(cmd_$(1)))), \
        @$(rule_$(1)))
```

In the topmost *makefile*, this function is used to link the kernel with these macros:

```
# This is a bit tricky: If we need to relink vmlinux, we want
# the version number incremented, which means recompile init/version.o
# and relink init/init.o. However, we cannot do this during the
# normal descending-into-subdirs phase, since at that time
# we cannot yet know if we will need to relink vmlinux.
# So we descend into init/ inside the rule for vmlinux again.
…

quiet_cmd_vmlinux__ = LD $@
define cmd_vmlinux__
    $(LD) $(LDFLAGS) $(LDFLAGS_vmlinux) \

    …
endef

# set -e makes the rule exit immediately on error

define rule_vmlinux__
    +set -e;                                         \
    $(if $(filter .tmp_kallsyms%,$^),,               \
      echo ' GEN     .version';                      \
      . $(srctree)/scripts/mkversion > .tmp_version; \
      mv -f .tmp_version .version;                   \
      $(MAKE) $(build)=init;)                        \
    $(if $($(quiet)cmd_vmlinux__),                   \
      echo '  $($(quiet)cmd_vmlinux__)' &&)          \
    $(cmd_vmlinux__);                                \
    echo 'cmd_$@ := $(cmd_vmlinux__)' > $(@D)/.$(@F).cmd
endef

define rule_vmlinux
    $(rule_vmlinux__);          \
    $(NM) $@ |                  \
    grep -v '\(compiled\)\|…' | \
    sort > System.map
endef
```

The if_changed_rule function is used to invoke rule_vmlinux, which performs the link and builds the final *System.map*. As the comment in the *makefile* notes, the rule_vmlinux__ function must regenerate the kernel version file and relink *init.o* before relinking *vmlinux*. This is controlled by the first if in rule_vmlinux__. The second if controls the echoing of the link command, $(cmd_vmlinux__). After the link command, the actual command executed is recorded in a *.cmd* file for comparison in the next build.

## CHAPTER 12

Debugging Makefiles

Debugging *makefiles* is somewhat of a black art. Unfortunately, there is no such thing as a *makefile* debugger to examine how a particular rule is being evaluated or a variable expanded. Instead, most debugging is performed with simple print statements and by inspection of the *makefile*. GNU make provides some help with various built-in functions and command-line options.

One of the best ways to debug a *makefile* is to add debugging hooks and use defensive programming techniques that you can fall back on when things go awry. I'll present a few basic debugging techniques and defensive coding practices I've found most helpful.

Debugging Features of make

The warning function is very useful for debugging wayward *makefiles*. Because the warning function expands to the empty string, it can be placed anywhere in a *makefile*: at the top-level, in target or prerequisite lists, and in command scripts. This allows you to print the value of variables wherever it is most convenient to inspect them. For example:

```
$(warning A top-level warning)

FOO := $(warning Right-hand side of a simple variable)bar
BAZ = $(warning Right-hand side of a recursive variable)boo

$(warning A target)target: $(warning In a prerequisite list)makefile $(BAZ)
        $(warning In a command script)
        ls
$(BAZ):
```

yields the output:

```
$ make
makefile:1: A top-level warning
makefile:2: Right-hand side of a simple variable
makefile:5: A target
```

```
makefile:5: In a prerequisite list
makefile:5: Right-hand side of a recursive variable
makefile:8: Right-hand side of a recursive variable
makefile:6: In a command script
ls
makefile
```

Notice that the evaluation of the warning function follows the normal make algorithm for immediate and deferred evaluation. Although the assignment to BAZ contains a warning, the message does not print until BAZ is evaluated in the prerequisites list.

The ability to inject a warning call anywhere makes it an essential debugging tool.

Command-Line Options

There are three command-line options I find most useful for debugging: --just-print (-n), --print-data-base (-p), and --warn-undefined-variables.

--just-print

The first test I perform on a new *makefile* target is to invoke make with the --just-print (-n) option. This causes make to read the *makefile* and print every command it would normally execute to update the target but without executing them. As a convenience, GNU make will also echo commands marked with the silent modifier (@).

The option is supposed to suppress all command execution. While this may be true in one sense, practically speaking, you must take care. While make will not execute command scripts, it will evaluate shell function calls that occur within an immediate context. For instance:

```
REQUIRED_DIRS = ...
_MKDIRS := $(shell for d in $(REQUIRED_DIRS); \
            do                                 \
              [[ -d $$d ]] || mkdir -p $$d;    \
            done)

$(objects) : $(sources)
```

As we've seen before, the purpose of the _MKDIRS simple variable is to trigger the creation of essential directories. When this is executed with --just-print, the shell command will be executed as usual when the *makefile* is read. Then make will echo (without executing) each compilation command required to update the $(objects) file list.

--print-data-base

The --print-data-base (-p) option is another one you'll use often. It executes the *makefile*, displaying the GNU copyright followed by the commands as they are run by make, then it will dump its internal database. The data is collected into groups of

---

values: variables, directories, implicit rules, pattern-specific variables, files (explicit rules), and the vpath search path:

```
# GNU Make 3.80
# Copyright (C) 2002  Free Software Foundation, Inc.
# This is free software; see the source for copying conditions.
# There is NO warranty; not even for MERCHANTABILITY or FITNESS FOR A
# PARTICULAR PURPOSE.
normal command execution occurs here

# Make data base, printed on Thu Apr 29 20:58:13 2004

# Variables
…
# Directories
…
# Implicit Rules
…
# Pattern-specific variable values
…
# Files
…
# VPATH Search Paths
```

Let's examine these sections in more detail.

The variables section lists each variable along with a descriptive comment:

```
# automatic
<D = $(patsubst %/,%,$(dir $<))
# environment
EMACS_DIR = C:/usr/emacs-21.3.50.7
# default
CWEAVE = cweave
# makefile (from `../mp3_player/makefile', line 35)
CPPFLAGS = $(addprefix -I ,$(include_dirs))
# makefile (from `../ch07-separate-binaries/makefile', line 44)
RM := rm -f
# makefile (from `../mp3_player/makefile', line 14)
define make-library
  libraries += $1
  sources   += $2

  $1: $(call source-to-object,$2)
        $(AR) $(ARFLAGS) $$@ $$^
endef
```

Automatic variables are not printed, but convenience variables derived from them like $(<D) are. The comment indicates the type of the variable as returned by the origin function (see the section "Less Important Miscellaneous Functions" in Chapter 4). If the variable is defined in a file, the filename and line number of the definition is given. Simple and recursive variables are distinguished by the

assignment operator. The value of a simple variable will be displayed as the evaluated form of the righthand side.

The next section, labeled Directories, is more useful to make developers than to make users. It lists the directories being examined by make, including SCCS and RCS subdirectories that might exist, but usually do not. For each directory, make displays implementation details, such as the device number, inode, and statistics on file pattern matches.

The Implicit Rules section follows. This contains all the built-in and user-defined pattern rules in make's database. Again, for those rules defined in a file, a comment indicates the file and line number:

```
%.c %.h: %.y
# commands to execute (from `../mp3_player/makefile', line 73):
        $(YACC.y) --defines $<
        $(MV) y.tab.c $*.c
        $(MV) y.tab.h $*.h

%: %.c
#   commands to execute (built-in):
        $(LINK.c) $^ $(LOADLIBES) $(LDLIBS) -o $@

%.o: %.c
#   commands to execute (built-in):
        $(COMPILE.c) $(OUTPUT_OPTION) $<
```

Examining this section is a great way to become familiar with the variety and structure of make's built-in rules. Of course, not all built-in rules are implemented as pattern rules. If you don't find the rule you're looking for, check in the Files section where the old-style suffix rules are listed.

The next section catalogs the pattern-specific variables defined in the *makefile*. Recall that pattern-specific variables are variable definitions whose scope is precisely the execution time of their associated pattern rule. For example, the pattern variable YYLEXFLAG, defined as:

```
%.c %.h: YYLEXFLAG := -d
%.c %.h: %.y
        $(YACC.y) --defines $<
        $(MV) y.tab.c $*.c
        $(MV) y.tab.h $*.h
```

would be displayed as:

```
# Pattern-specific variable values

%.c :
# makefile (from `Makefile', line 1)
# YYLEXFLAG := -d
# variable set hash-table stats:
# Load=1/16=6%, Rehash=0, Collisions=0/1=0%
```

```
%.h :
#  makefile (from `Makefile', line 1)
#  YYLEXFLAG := -d
#  variable set hash-table stats:
#  Load=1/16=6%, Rehash=0, Collisions=0/1=0%

#  2 pattern-specific variable values
```

The Files section follows and lists all the explicit and suffix rules that relate to specific files:

```
#  Not a target:
.p.o:
#   Implicit rule search has not been done.
#   Modification time never checked.
#   File has not been updated.
#   commands to execute (built-in):
        $(COMPILE.p) $(OUTPUT_OPTION) $<

lib/ui/libui.a: lib/ui/ui.o
#   Implicit rule search has not been done.
#   Last modified 2004-04-01 22:04:09.515625
#   File has been updated.
#   Successfully updated.
#   commands to execute (from `../mp3_player/lib/ui/module.mk', line 3):
        ar rv $@ $^

lib/codec/codec.o: ../mp3_player/lib/codec/codec.c ../mp3_player/lib/codec/codec.c ..
/mp3_player/include/codec/codec.h
#   Implicit rule search has been done.
#   Implicit/static pattern stem: `lib/codec/codec'
#   Last modified 2004-04-01 22:04:08.40625
#   File has been updated.
#   Successfully updated.
#   commands to execute (built-in):
        $(COMPILE.c) $(OUTPUT_OPTION) $<
```

Intermediate files and suffix rules are labeled "Not a target"; the remainder are targets. Each file includes comments indicating how make has processed the rule. Files that are found through the normal vpath search have their resolved path displayed.

The last section is labeled VPATH Search Paths and lists the value of VPATH and all the vpath patterns.

For *makefiles* that make extensive use of user-defined functions and eval to create complex variables and rules, examining this output is often the only way to verify that macro expansion has generated the expected values.

--warn-undefined-variables

This option causes make to display a warning whenever an undefined variable is expanded. Since undefined variables expand to the empty string, it is common for typographical errors in variable names to go undetected for long periods. The problem with this option, and why I use it only rarely, is that many built-in rules include undefined variables as hooks for user-defined values. So running make with this option will inevitably produce many warnings that are not errors and have no useful relationship to the user's *makefile*. For example:

```
$ make --warn-undefined-variables -n
makefile:35: warning: undefined variable MAKECMDGOALS
makefile:45: warning: undefined variable CFLAGS
makefile:45: warning: undefined variable TARGET_ARCH
...
makefile:35: warning: undefined variable MAKECMDGOALS
make: warning: undefined variable CFLAGS
make: warning: undefined variable TARGET_ARCH
make: warning: undefined variable CFLAGS
make: warning: undefined variable TARGET_ARCH
...
make: warning: undefined variable LDFLAGS
make: warning: undefined variable TARGET_ARCH
make: warning: undefined variable LOADLIBES
make: warning: undefined variable LDLIBS
```

Nevertheless, this command can be extremely valuable on occasion in catching these kinds of errors.

The --debug Option

When you need to know how make analyzes your dependency graph, use the --debug option. This provides the most detailed information available other than by running a debugger. There are five debugging options and one modifier: basic, verbose, implicit, jobs, all, and makefile, respectively.

If the debugging option is specified as --debug, basic debugging is used. If the debugging option is given as -d, all is used. To select other combinations of options, use a comma separated list --debug=*option1*,*option2* where the option can be one of the following words (actually, make looks only at the first letter):

basic

>   Basic debugging is the least detailed. When enabled, make prints each target that is found to be out-of-date and the status of the update action. Sample output looks like:

```
    File all does not exist.
      File app/player/play_mp3 does not exist.
        File app/player/play_mp3.o does not exist.
      Must remake target app/player/play_mp3.o.
    gcc ... ../mp3_player/app/player/play_mp3.c
        Successfully remade target file app/player/play_mp3.o.
```

verbose

>   This option sets the basic option and includes additional information about which files where parsed, prerequisites that did not need to be rebuilt, etc.:

```
File all does not exist.
 Considering target file app/player/play_mp3.
  File app/player/play_mp3 does not exist.
   Considering target file app/player/play_mp3.o.
    File app/player/play_mp3.o does not exist.
     Pruning file ../mp3_player/app/player/play_mp3.c.
     Pruning file ../mp3_player/app/player/play_mp3.c.
     Pruning file ../mp3_player/include/player/play_mp3.h.
    Finished prerequisites of target file app/player/play_mp3.o.
   Must remake target app/player/play_mp3.o.
gcc ... ../mp3_player/app/player/play_mp3.c
   Successfully remade target file app/player/play_mp3.o.
   Pruning file app/player/play_mp3.o.
```

implicit

> This option sets the basic option and includes additional information about
> implicit rule searches for each target:

```
File all does not exist.
 File app/player/play_mp3 does not exist.
 Looking for an implicit rule for app/player/play_mp3.
 Trying pattern rule with stem play_mp3.
 Trying implicit prerequisite app/player/play_mp3.o.
 Found an implicit rule for app/player/play_mp3.
  File app/player/play_mp3.o does not exist.
  Looking for an implicit rule for app/player/play_mp3.o.
  Trying pattern rule with stem play_mp3.
  Trying implicit prerequisite app/player/play_mp3.c.
  Found prerequisite app/player/play_mp3.c as VPATH ../mp3_player/app/player/
play_mp3.c
  Found an implicit rule for app/player/play_mp3.o.
 Must remake target app/player/play_mp3.o.
gcc ... ../mp3_player/app/player/play_mp3.c
 Successfully remade target file app/player/play_mp3.o.
```

jobs

> This options prints the details of subprocesses invoked by make. It does not
> enable the basic option.

```
Got a SIGCHLD; 1 unreaped children.
gcc ... ../mp3_player/app/player/play_mp3.c
Putting child 0x10033800 (app/player/play_mp3.o) PID 576 on the chain.
Live child 0x10033800 (app/player/play_mp3.o) PID 576
Got a SIGCHLD; 1 unreaped children.
Reaping winning child 0x10033800 PID 576
Removing child 0x10033800 PID 576 from chain.
```

all

> This enables all the previous options and is the default when using the -d option.

makefile

> Normally, debugging information is not enabled until after the *makefiles* have
> been updated. This includes updating any included files, such as lists of depen-
> dencies. When you use this modifier, make will print the selected information

while rebuilding *makefiles* and include files. This option enables the basic option and is also enabled by the all option.

Writing Code for Debugging

As you can see, there aren't too many tools for debugging *makefiles*, just a few ways to dump make's internal data structures and a couple of print statements. When it comes right down to it, it is up to you to write your *makefiles* in ways that either minimize the chance of errors or provide your own scaffolding to help debug them.

The suggestions in this section are laid out somewhat arbitrarily as coding practices, defensive coding, and debugging techniques. While specific items, such as checking the exit status of commands, could be placed in either the good coding practice section or the defensive coding section, the three categories reflect the proper bias. Focus on coding your *makefiles* well without cutting too many corners. Include plenty of defensive coding to protect the *makefile* against unexpected events and environmental conditions. Finally, when bugs do arise, use every trick you can find to squash them.

The "Keep It Simple" Principle (*http://www.catb.org/~esr/jargon/html/K/KISS-Principle.html*) is at the heart of all good design. As you've seen in previous chapters, *makefiles* can quickly become complex, even for mundane tasks, such as dependency generation. Fight the tendency to include more and more features in your build system. You'll fail, but not as badly as you would if you simply include every feature that occurs to you.

Good Coding Practices

In my experience, most programmers do not see writing *makefiles* as programming and, therefore, do not take the same care as they do when writing in C++ or Java. But the make language is a complete nonprocedural language. If the reliability and maintainability of your build system is important, write it with care and use the best coding practices you can.

One of the most important aspects of programming robust *makefiles* is to check the return status of commands. Of course, make will check simple commands automatically, but *makefiles* often include compound commands that can fail quietly:

```
do:
        cd i-dont-exist; \
        echo *.c
```

When run, this *makefile* does not terminate with an error status, although an error most definitely occurs:

```
$ make
cd i-dont-exist; \
echo *.c
```

```
/bin/sh: line 1: cd: i-dont-exist: No such file or directory
*.c
```

Furthermore, the globbing expression fails to find any *.c* files, so it quietly returns the globbing expression. Oops. A better way to code this command script is to use the shell's features for checking and preventing errors:

```
SHELL = /bin/bash
do:
        cd i-dont-exist &&    \
        shopt -s nullglob && \
        echo *.c
```

Now the cd error is properly transmitted to make, the echo command never executes, and make terminates with an error status. In addition, setting the nullglob option of bash causes the globbing pattern to return the empty string if no files are found. (Of course, your particular application may prefer the globbing pattern.)

```
$ make
cd i-dont-exist && \
echo *.c
/bin/sh: line 1: cd: i-dont-exist: No such file or directory
make: *** [do] Error 1
```

Another good coding practice is formatting your code for maximum readability. Most *makefiles* I see are poorly formatted and, consequently, difficult to read. Which do you find easier to read?

```
_MKDIRS := $(shell for d in $(REQUIRED_DIRS); do [[ -d $$d \
]] || mkdir -p $$d; done)
```

or:

```
_MKDIRS := $(shell                              \
                for d in $(REQUIRED_DIRS);      \
                do                               \
                  [[ -d $$d ]] || mkdir -p $$d; \
                done)
```

If you're like most people, you'll find the first more difficult to parse, the semicolons harder to find, and the number of statements more difficult to count. These are not trivial concerns. A significant percentage of the syntax errors you will encounter in command scripts will be due to missing semicolons, backslashes, or other separators, such as pipe and logical operators.

Also, note that not all missing separators will generate an error. For instance, neither of the following errors will produce a shell syntax error:

```
TAGS:
        cd src \
        ctags --recurse

disk_free:
        echo "Checking free disk space..." \
        df . | awk '{ print $$4 }'
```

Formatting commands for readability will make these kinds of errors easier to catch. When formatting user-defined functions, indent the code. Occasionally, the extra spaces in the resulting macro expansion cause problems. If so, wrap the formatting in a strip function call. When formatting long lists of values, separate each value on its own line. Add a comment before each target, give a brief explanation, and document the parameter list.

The next good coding practice is the liberal use of variables to hold common values. As in any program, the unrestrained use of literal values creates code duplication and leads to maintenance problems and bugs. Another great advantage of variables is that you can get make to display them for debugging purposes during execution. I show a nice command line interface in the section "Debugging Techniques," later in this chapter.

Defensive Coding

Defensive code is code that can execute only if one of your assumptions or expectations is wrong — an if test that is never true, an assert function that never fails, or tracing code. Of course, the value of this code that never executes is that occasionally (usually when you least expect it), it does run and produce a warning or error, or you choose to enable tracing code to allow you to view the inner workings of make.

You've already seen most of this code in other contexts, but for convenience it is repeated here.

Validation checking is a great example of defensive code. This code sample verifies that the currently executing version of make is 3.80:

```
NEED_VERSION := 3.80
$(if $(filter $(NEED_VERSION),$(MAKE_VERSION)),,        \
  $(error You must be running make version $(NEED_VERSION).))
```

For Java applications, it is useful to include a check for files in the CLASSPATH.

Validation code can also simply ensure that something is true. The directory creation code from the previous section is of this nature.

Another great defensive coding technique is to use the assert functions defined in the section "Flow Control" in Chapter 4. Here are several versions:

```
# $(call assert,condition,message)
define assert
  $(if $1,,$(error Assertion failed: $2))
endef

# $(call assert-file-exists,wildcard-pattern)
define assert-file-exists
  $(call assert,$(wildcard $1),$1 does not exist)
endef

# $(call assert-not-null,make-variable)
define assert-not-null
```

```
         $(call assert,$($1),The variable "$1" is null)
       endef
```

I find sprinkling assert calls around the *makefile* to be a cheap and effective way of detecting missing and misspelled parameters as well as violations of other assumptions.

In Chapter 4, we wrote a pair of functions to trace the expansion of user-defined functions:

```
# $(debug-enter)
debug-enter = $(if $(debug_trace),\
              $(warning Entering $0($(echo-args))))

# $(debug-leave)
debug-leave = $(if $(debug_trace),$(warning Leaving $0))

comma := ,
echo-args   = $(subst ' ','$(comma) ',\
              $(foreach a,1 2 3 4 5 6 7 8 9,'$($a)'))
```

You can add these macro calls to your own functions and leave them disabled until they are required for debugging. To enable them, set debug_trace to any nonempty value:

```
$ make debug_trace=1
```

As noted in Chapter 4, these trace macros have a number of problems of their own but can still be useful in tracking down bugs.

The final defensive programming technique is simply to make disabling the @ command modifier easy by using it through a make variable, rather than literally:

```
QUIET := @
...
target:
        $(QUIET) some command
```

Using this technique, you can see the execution of the silent command by redefining QUIET on the command line:

```
$ make QUIET=
```

Debugging Techniques

This section discusses general debugging techniques and issues. Ultimately, debugging is a grab-bag of whatever works for your situation. These techniques have worked for me, and I've come to rely on them to debug even the simplest *makefile* problems. Maybe they'll help you, too.

One of the very annoying bugs in 3.80 is that when make reports problems in *makefiles* and includes a line number, I usually find that the line number is wrong. I haven't investigated whether the problem is due to include files, multiline variable assignments, or user-defined macros, but there it is. Usually the line number make reports is larger than the actual line number. In complex *makefiles*, I've had the line number be off by as much as 20 lines.

Often the easiest way to see the value of a make variable is to print it during the execution of a target. Although adding print statements using warning is simple, the extra effort of adding a generic debug target for printing variables can save lots of time in the long run. Here is a sample debug target:

```
debug:
        $(for v,$(V), \
          $(warning $v = $($v)))
```

To use it, just set the list of variables to print on the command line, and include the debug target:

```
$ make V="USERNAME SHELL" debug
makefile:2: USERNAME = Owner
makefile:2: SHELL = /bin/sh.exe
make: debug is up to date.
```

If you want to get really tricky, you can use the MAKECMDGOALS variable to avoid the assignment to the variable V:

```
debug:
        $(for v,$(V) $(MAKECMDGOALS), \
          $(if $(filter debug,$v),,$(warning $v = $($v))))
```

Now you can print variables by simply listing them on the command line. I don't recommend this technique, though, because you'll also get confusing make warnings indicating it doesn't know how to update the variables (since they are listed as targets):

```
$ make debug USERNAME SHELL
makefile:2: USERNAME = Owner
makefile:2: SHELL = /bin/sh.exe
make: debug is up to date.
make: *** No rule to make target USERNAME.  Stop.
```

In Chapter 10, I briefly mentioned using a debugging shell to help understand some of the activities make performs behind the scenes. While make echos commands in command scripts before they are executed, it does not echo the commands executed in shell functions. Often these commands are subtle and complex, particularly since they may be executed immediately or in a deferred fashion, if they occur in a recursive variable assignment. One way to see these commands execute is to request that the subshell enable debug printing:

```
DATE := $(shell date +%F)
OUTPUT_DIR = out-$(DATE)

make-directories := $(shell [ -d $(OUTPUT_DIR) ] || mkdir -p $(OUTPUT_DIR))

all: ;
```

When run with sh's debugging option, we see:

```
$ make SHELL="sh -x"
+ date +%F
+ '[' -d out-2004-05-11 ']'
+ mkdir -p out-2004-05-11
```

This even provides additional debugging information beyond make warning statements, since with this option the shell also displays the value of variables and expressions.

Many of the examples in this book are written as deeply nested expressions, such as this one that checks the PATH variable on a Windows/Cygwin system:

```
$(if $(findstring /bin/,                                  \
        $(firstword                                       \
          $(wildcard                                      \
            $(addsuffix /sort$(if $(COMSPEC),.exe),       \
              $(subst :, ,$(PATH))))))),,                 \
  $(error Your PATH is wrong, c:/usr/cygwin/bin should \
    precede c:/WINDOWS/system32))
```

There is no good way to debug these expressions. One reasonable approach is to unroll them, and print each subexpression:

```
$(warning $(subst :, ,$(PATH)))
$(warning /sort$(if $(COMSPEC),.exe))
$(warning $(addsuffix /sort$(if $(COMSPEC),.exe),    \
          $(subst :, ,$(PATH))))
$(warning $(wildcard                                 \
            $(addsuffix /sort$(if $(COMSPEC),.exe),  \
              $(subst :, ,$(PATH)))))
```

Although a bit tedious, without a real debugger, this is the best way (and sometimes the only way) to determine the value of various subexpressions.

Common Error Messages

The 3.81 GNU make manual includes an excellent section listing make error messages and their causes. We review a few of the most common ones here. Some of the issues described are not strictly make errors, such as syntax errors in command scripts, but are nonetheless common problems for developers. For a complete list of make errors, see the make manual.

Error messages printed by make have a standard format:

makefile:*n*: *** *message*. Stop.

or:

make:*n*: *** *message*. Stop.

The *makefile* part is the name of the *makefile* or include file in which the error occurred. The next part is the line number where the error occurred, followed by three asterisks and, finally, the error message.

Note that it is make's job to run other programs and that, if errors occur, it is very likely that problems in your *makefile* will manifest themselves as errors in these other programs. For instance, shell errors may result from badly formed command scripts, or compiler errors from incorrect command-line arguments. Figuring out what program produced the error message is your first task in solving the problem. Fortunately, make's error messages are fairly self-evident.

Syntax Errors

These are usually typographical errors: missing parentheses, using spaces instead of tabs, etc.

One of the most common errors for new make users is omitting parentheses around variable names:

```
foo:
        for f in $SOURCES; \
        do              \
          ...           \
        done
```

This will likely result in make expanding $S to nothing, and the shell executing the loop only once with f having a value of OURCES. Depending on what you do with f, you may get a nice shell error message like:

```
OURCES: No such file or directory
```

but you might just as easily get no message at all. Remember to surround your make variables with parentheses.

missing separator

The message:

```
makefile:2:missing separator. Stop.
```

or:

```
makefile:2:missing separator (did you mean TAB instead of 8 spaces?).  Stop.
```

usually means you have a command script that is using spaces instead of tabs.

The more literal interpretation is that make was looking for a make separator such as :, =, or a tab, and didn't find one. Instead, it found something it didn't understand.

commands commence before first target

The tab character strikes again!

This error message was first covered in the section "Parsing Commands" in Chapter 5. This error seems to appear most often in the middle of *makefiles* when a line outside of a command script begins with a tab character. make does its best to disambiguate this situation, but if the line cannot be identified as a variable assignment, conditional expression, or multiline macro definition, make considers it a misplaced command.

unterminated variable reference

This is a simple but common error. It means you failed to close a variable reference or function call with the proper number of parentheses. With deeply nested function calls and variable references, make files can begin to look like Lisp! A good editor that does parenthesis matching, such as Emacs, is the surest way to avoid these types of errors.

Errors in Command Scripts

There are three common types of errors in command scripts: a missing semicolon in multiline commands, an incomplete or incorrect path variable, or a command that simply encounters a problem when run.

We discussed missing semicolons in the section "Good Coding Practices," so we won't elaborate further here.

The classic error message:

```
bash: foo: command not found
```

is displayed when the shell cannot find the command foo. That is, the shell has searched each directory in the PATH variable for the executable and found no match. To correct this error, you must update your PATH variable, usually in your *.profile* (Bourne shell), *.bashrc* (bash), or *.cshrc* (C shell). Of course, it is also possible to set the PATH variable in the *makefile* itself, and export the PATH variable from make.

Finally, when a shell command fails, it terminates with a nonzero exit status. In this case, make reports the failure with the message:

```
$ make
touch /foo/bar
touch: creating /foo/bar: No such file or directory
make: *** [all] Error 1
```

Here the failing command is touch, which prints its own error message explaining the failure. The next line is make's summary of the error. The failing *makefile* target is shown in square brackets followed by the exit value of the failing program. Sometimes make will print a more verbose message if the program exits due to a signal, rather than simply a nonzero exit status.

Note also that commands executed silently with the @ modifier can also fail. In these cases, the error message presented may appear as if from nowhere.

In either of these cases, the error originates with the program make is running, rather than make itself.

No Rule to Make Target

This message has two forms:

```
make: *** No rule to make target XXX. Stop.
```

and:

```
make: *** No rule to make target XXX, needed by YYY. Stop.
```

It means that make decided the file *XXX* needed to be updated, but make could not find any rule to perform the job. make will search all the implicit and explicit rules in its database before giving up and printing the message.

There are three possible reasons for this error:

- Your *makefile* is missing a rule required to update the file. In this case, you will have to add the rule describing how to build the target.

- There is a typo in the *makefile*. Either make is looking for the wrong file or the rule to update the file specifies the wrong file. Typos can be hard to find in *makefile*s due to the use of make variables. Sometimes the only way to really be sure of the value of a complex filename is to print it out either by printing the variable directly or examining make's internal database.

- The file should exist but make cannot find it either, because it is missing or because make doesn't know where to look. Of course, sometimes make is absolutely correct. The file is missing—perhaps you forgot to check it out of CVS. More often, make simply can't find the file, because the source is placed somewhere else. Sometimes the source is in a separate source tree, or maybe the file is generated by another program and the generated file is in the binary tree.

Overriding Commands for Target

make allows only one command script for a target (except for double-colon rules, which are rarely used). If a target is given more than one command script, make prints the warning:

```
makefile:5: warning: overriding commands for target foo
```

It may also display the warning:

```
makefile:2: warning: ignoring old commands for target foo
```

The first warning indicates the line at which the second command script is found, while the second warning indicates the location of the original command script that is being overridden.

In complex *makefiles*, targets are often specified many times, each adding its own prerequisites. One of these targets usually includes a command script, but during development or debugging it is easy to add another command script without realizing you are actually overriding an existing set of commands.

For example, we might define a generic target in an include file:

```
# Create a jar file.
$(jar_file):
        $(JAR) $(JARFLAGS) -f $@ $^
```

and allow several separate *makefiles* to add their own prerequisites. Then in a *makefile* we could write:

```
# Set the target for creating the jar and add prerequisites
jar_file = parser.jar
$(jar_file): $(class_files)
```

If we were to inadvertently add a command script to this *makefile* text, make would produce the overriding warning.

## PART III

Appendixes

The final section of this book contains information that is not central to the goals of the book, but you might find it useful for unusual situations. Appendix A lists the options that the GNU make command accepts on the command line. Appendix B, which you will find amusing and possibly useful, stretches make to act as a general-purpose programming language with data structures and arithmetic operations. Appendix C contains the free license for the book.

Running make

GNU make has an impressive set of command-line options. Most command-line options include a short form and a long form. Short commands are indicated with a single dash followed by a single character, while long options begin with a double dash usually followed by whole words separated by dashes. The syntax of these commands is:

```
-o argument
--option-word=argument
```

The following are the most commonly used options to make. For a complete listing, see the GNU make manual or type make --help.

`--always-make`
`-B`

> Assume every target is out of date and update them all.

`--directory=directory`
`-C directory`

> Change to the given directory before searching for a *makefile* or performing any work. This also sets the variable CURDIR to *directory*.

`--environment-overrides`
`-e`

> Prefer environment variables to *makefile* variables when there is a choice. This command-line option can be overridden in the *makefile* for particular variables with the override directive.

`--file=makefile`
`-f makefile`

> Read the given file as the *makefile* rather than any of the default names (i.e., *makefile*, *Makefile*, or *GNUMakefile*).

`--help`

`-h`

> Print a brief summary of the command-line options.

`--include-dir=directory`

`-I directory`

> If an include file does not exist in the current directory, look in the indicated directories for include files before searching the compiled-in search path. Any number of `--include-dir` options can be given on the command line.

`--keep-going`

`-k`

> Do not terminate the make process if a command returns an error status. Instead, skip the remainder of the current target, and continue on with other targets.

`--just-print`

`-n`

> Display the set of commands that would be executed by make, but do not execute any commands from command scripts. This is very useful when you want to know what make will do before actually doing it. Be aware that this option does not prevent code in shell functions from executing, just commands in command scripts.

`--old-file=file`

`-o file`

> Treat *file* as if it were infinitely old, and perform the appropriate actions to update the goals. This can be very useful if a file has been accidentally touched or to determine the effect of one prerequisite on the dependency graph. This is the complement of `--new-file` (`-W`).

`--print-data-base`

`-p`

> Print make's internal database.

`--touch`

`-t`

> Execute the touch program on each out-of-date target to update its timestamp. This can be useful in bringing the files in a dependency graph up to date. For instance, editing a comment in a central header file may cause make to unnecessarily recompile an immense amount of code. Instead of performing the compile and wasting machine cycles, you can use the `--touch` option to force all files to be up to date.

`--new-file=file`

`-W file`

> Assume *file* is newer than any target. This can be useful in forcing an update on targets without having to edit or touch a file. This is the complement of `--old-file`.

```
--warn-undefined-variables
```
   Print a warning message if an undefined variable is expanded. This is a useful
   diagnostic tool since undefined variables quietly collapse into nothing. However, it is also common to include empty variables in *makefiles* for customization purposes. Any unset customization variables will be reported by this option
   as well.

APPENDIX B

The Outer Limits

As you've seen, GNU make can do some pretty incredible things, but I haven't seen very much that really pushes the limits of make 3.80 with its eval construct. In this exercise, we'll see if we can stretch it further than usual.

Data Structures

One of the limitations of make that occasionally chaffs when writing complex *makefiles* is make's lack of data structures. In a very limited way, you can simulate a data structure by defining variables with embedded periods (or even -> if you can stand it):

```
file.path = /foo/bar
file.type = unix
file.host = oscar
```

If pressed, you can even "pass" this file structure to a function by using computed variables:

```
define remote-file
  $(if $(filter unix,$($1.type)), \
    /net/$($1.host)/$($1.path),   \
    //$($1.host)/$($1.path))
endef
```

Nevertheless, this seems an unsatisfying solution for several reasons:

- You cannot easily allocate a instance of this "structure." Creating a new instance involves selecting a new variable name and assigning each element. This also means these pseudo-instances are not guaranteed to have the same fields (called *slots*).

- The structure exists only in the user's mind, and as a set of different make variables, rather than as a unified entity with its own name. And because the structure has no name, it is difficult to create a reference (or pointer) to a structure, so passing them as arguments or storing one in a variable is clumsy.

- There is no safe way to access a slot of the structure. Any typographical error in either part of the variable name yields the wrong value (or no value) with no warning from make.

But the remote-file function hints at a more comprehensive solution. Suppose we implement structure instances using computed variables. Early Lisp object systems (and even some today) used similar techniques. A structure, say file-info, can have instances represented by a symbolic name, such as file_info_1.

Another instance might be called file_info_2. The slots of this structure can be represented by computed variables:

```
file_info_1_path
file_info_1_type
file_info_1_host
```

Since the instance has a symbolic name, it can be saved in one or more variables (as usual, using recursive or simple variables is the choice of the programmer):

```
before_foo = file_info_1
another_foo = $(before_foo)
```

Elements of a file-info can be accessed using Lisp-like getters and setters:

```
path := $(call get-value,before_foo,path)
$(call set-value,before_foo,path,/usr/tmp/bar)
```

We can go further than this by creating a template for the file-info structure to allow the convenient allocation of new instances:

```
orig_foo := $(call new,file-info)
$(call set-value,orig_foo,path,/foo/bar)

tmp_foo := $(call new,file-info)
$(call set-value,tmp_foo,path,/tmp/bar)
```

Now, two distinct instances of file-info exist. As a final convenience, we can add the concept of default values for slots. To declare the file-info structure, we might use:

```
$(call defstruct,file-info,  \
  $(call defslot,path,),     \
  $(call defslot,type,unix), \
  $(call defslot,host,oscar))
```

Here, the first argument to the defstruct function is the structure name, followed by a list of defslot calls. Each defslot contains a single (*name*, *default value*) pair. Example B-1 shows the implementation of defstruct and its supporting code.

Example B-1. Structure definition in make

```
# $(next-id) - return a unique number
next_id_counter :=
define next-id
$(words $(next_id_counter))$(eval next_id_counter += 1)
endef
```

Example B-1. Structure definition in make (continued)

```
# all_structs - a list of the defined structure names
all_structs :=

value_sep := XxSepxX

# $(call defstruct, struct_name, $(call defslot, slot_name, value), ...)
define defstruct
  $(eval all_structs += $1)                                             \
  $(eval $1_def_slotnames :=)                                           \
  $(foreach v, $2 $3 $4 $5 $6 $7 $8 $9 $(10) $(11),                     \
    $(if $($v_name),                                                    \
      $(eval $1_def_slotnames             += $($v_name))                \
      $(eval $1_def_$($v_name)_default := $($v_value))))
endef

# $(call defslot,slot_name,slot_value)
define defslot
  $(eval tmp_id := $(next_id))
  $(eval $1_$(tmp_id)_name := $1)
  $(eval $1_$(tmp_id)_value := $2)
  $1_$(tmp_id)
endef

# all_instances - a list of all the instances of any structure
all_instances :=

# $(call new, struct_name)
define new
$(strip                                                                 \
  $(if $(filter $1,$(all_structs)),,                                    \
    $(error new on unknown struct '$(strip $1)'))                       \
  $(eval instance := $1@$(next-id))                                     \
  $(eval all_instances += $(instance))                                  \
  $(foreach v, $($(strip $1)_def_slotnames),                           \
    $(eval $(instance)_$v := $($(strip $1)_def_$v_default)))            \
  $(instance))
endef

# $(call delete, variable)
define delete
$(strip                                                                              \
  $(if $(filter $($(strip $1)),$(all_instances)),,                                   \
    $(error Invalid instance '$($(strip $1))'))                                      \
  $(eval all_instances := $(filter-out $($(strip $1)),$(all_instances)))  \
  $(foreach v, $($(strip $1)_def_slotnames),                                         \
    $(eval $(instance)_$v := )))
endef

# $(call struct-name, instance_id)
define struct-name
$(firstword $(subst @, ,$($(strip $1))))
endef
```

```
# $(call check-params, instance_id, slot_name)
define check-params
  $(if $(filter $($(strip $1)),$(all_instances)),,          \
    $(error Invalid instance '$(strip $1)'))                \
  $(if $(filter $2,$($(call struct-name,$1)_def_slotnames)),,  \
    $(error Instance '$($(strip $1))' does not have slot '$(strip $2)'))
endef

# $(call get-value, instance_id, slot_name)
define get-value
$(strip                         \
  $(call check-params,$1,$2)    \
  $($($(strip $1))_$(strip $2)))
endef

# $(call set-value, instance_id, slot_name, value)
define set-value
  $(call check-params,$1,$2) \
  $(eval $($(strip $1))_$(strip $2) := $3)
endef

# $(call dump-struct, struct_name)
define dump-struct
{ $(strip $1)_def_slotnames "$($(strip $1)_def_slotnames)"     \
  $(foreach s,                                                 \
    $($(strip $1)_def_slotnames),$(strip                       \
    $(strip $1)_def_$s_default "$($(strip $1)_def_$s_default)")) }
endef

# $(call print-struct, struct_name)
define print-struct
{ $(foreach s,                              \
    $($(strip $1)_def_slotnames),$(strip    \
    { "$s" "$($(strip $1)_def_$s_default)" })) }
endef

# $(call dump-instance, instance_id)
define dump-instance
{ $(eval tmp_name := $(call struct-name,$1))    \
  $(foreach s,                                  \
    $($(tmp_name)_def_slotnames),$(strip        \
    { $($(strip $1))_$s "$($($(strip $1))_$s)" })) }
endef

# $(call print-instance, instance_id)
define print-instance
{ $(foreach s,                                          \
    $($(call struct-name,$1)_def_slotnames),"$(strip    \
    $(call get-value,$1,$s))") }
endef
```

Examining this code one clause at a time, you can see that it starts by defining the function next-id. This is a simple counter:

```
# $(next-id) - return a unique number
next_id_counter :=
define next-id
$(words $(next_id_counter))$(eval next_id_counter += 1)
endef
```

It is often said that you cannot perform arithmetic in make, because the language is too limited. In general, this is true, but for limited cases like this you can often compute what you need. This function uses eval to redefine the value of a simple variable. The function contains two expressions: the first expression returns the number of words in next_id_counter; the second expression appends another word to the variable. It isn't very efficient, but for numbers in the small thousands it is fine.

The next section defines the defstruct function itself and creates the supporting data structures.

```
# all_structs - a list of the defined structure names
all_structs :=

value_sep := XxSepxX

# $(call defstruct, struct_name, $(call defslot, slot_name, value), ...)
define defstruct
  $(eval all_structs += $1)                               \
  $(eval $1_def_slotnames :=)                             \
  $(foreach v, $2 $3 $4 $5 $6 $7 $8 $9 $(10) $(11),       \
    $(if $($v_name),                                       \
      $(eval $1_def_slotnames         += $($v_name))      \
      $(eval $1_def_$($v_name)_default := $($v_value))))) 
endef

# $(call defslot,slot_name,slot_value)
define defslot
  $(eval tmp_id := $(next_id))
  $(eval $1_$(tmp_id)_name := $1)
  $(eval $1_$(tmp_id)_value := $2)
  $1_$(tmp_id)
endef
```

The variable all_structs is a list of all known structures defined with defstruct. This list allows the new function to perform type checking on the structures it allocates. For each structure, S, the defstruct function defines a set of variables:

```
S_def_slotnames
S_def_slotn_default
```

The first variable defines the set of slots for a structure. The other variables define the default value for each slot. The first two lines of the defstruct function append to all_structs and initialize the slot names list, respectively. The remainder of the function iterates through the slots, building the slot list and saving the default value.

Each slot definition is handled by defslot. The function allocates an id, saves the slot name and value in two variables, and returns the prefix. Returning the prefix allows the argument list of defstruct to be a simple list of symbols, each of which provides access to a slot definition. If more attributes are added to slots later, incorporating them into defslot is straightforward. This technique also allows default values to have a wider range of values (including spaces) than simpler, alternative implementations.

The foreach loop in defstruct determines the maximum number of allowable slots. This version allows for 10 slots. The body of the foreach processes each argument by appending the slot name to S_def_slotnames and assigning the default value to a variable. For example, our file-info structure would define:

```
file-info_def_slotnames := path type host
file-info_def_path_default :=
file-info_def_type_default := unix
file-info_def_host_default := oscar
```

This completes the definition of a structure.

Now that we can define structures, we need to be able to instantiate one. The new function performs this operation:

```
# $(call new, struct_name)
define new
$(strip                                                        \
  $(if $(filter $1,$(all_structs)),,                           \
    $(error new on unknown struct '$(strip $1)'))              \
  $(eval instance := $1@$(next-id))                            \
  $(eval all_instances += $(instance))                        \
  $(foreach v, $($(strip $1)_def_slotnames),                   \
    $(eval $(instance)_$v := $($(strip $1)_def_$v_default)))   \
  $(instance))
endef
```

The first if in the function checks that the name refers to a known structure. If the structure isn't found in all_structs, an error is signaled. Next, we construct a unique id for the new instance by concatenating the structure name with a unique integer suffix. We use an at sign to separate the structure name from the suffix so we can easily separate the two later. The new function then records the new instance name for type checking by accessors later. Then the slots of the structure are initialized with their default values. The initialization code is interesting:

```
$(foreach v, $($(strip $1)_def_slotnames),                 \
  $(eval $(instance)_$v := $($(strip $1)_def_$v_default)))
```

The foreach loop iterates over the slot names of the structure. Using strip around on the structure name allows the user to add spaces after commas in the call to new. Recall that each slot is represented by concatenating the instance name and the slot name (for instance, file_info@1_path). The righthand side is the default value computed from the structure name and slot name. Finally, the instance name is returned by the function.

Note that I call these constructs functions, but they are actually macros. That is, the symbol new is recursively expanded to yield a new piece of text that is inserted into the *makefile* for reparsing. The reason the defstruct macro does what we want is because all the work is eventually embedded within eval calls, which collapse to nothing. Similarly, the new macro performs its significant work within eval calls. It can reasonably be termed a function, because the expansion of the macro conceptually yields a single value, the symbol representing the new instance.

Next, we need to be able to get and set values within our structures. To do this, we define two new functions:

```
# $(call get-value, instance_id, slot_name)
define get-value
$(strip                               \
  $(call check-params,$1,$2)    \
  $($($(strip $1))_$(strip $2)))
endef

# $(call set-value, instance_id, slot_name, value)
define set-value
  $(call check-params,$1,$2) \
  $(eval $($(strip $1))_$(strip $2) := $3)
endef
```

To get the value of a slot, we simply need to compute the slot variable name from the instance id and the slot name. We can improve safety by first checking that the instance and slot name are valid strings with the check-params function. To allow more aesthetic formating and to ensure that extraneous spaces do not corrupt the slot value, we wrap most of these parameters in strip calls.

The set function also checks parameters before setting the value. Again, we strip the two function arguments to allow users the freedom to add spaces in the argument list. Note that we do not strip the slot value, because the user might actually need the spaces.

```
# $(call check-params, instance_id, slot_name)
define check-params
  $(if $(filter $($(strip $1)),$(all_instances)),,        \
    $(error Invalid instance '$(strip $1)'))               \
  $(if $(filter $2,$($(call struct-name,$1)_def_slotnames)),,  \
    $(error Instance '$($(strip $1))' does not have slot '$(strip $2)'))
endef

# $(call struct-name, instance_id)
define struct-name
$(firstword $(subst @, ,$($(strip $1))))
endef
```

The check-params function simply checks that the instance id passed to the setter and getter functions is contained within the known instances list. Likewise, it checks that the slot name is contained within the list of slots belonging to this structure. The structure name is computed from the instance name by splitting the symbol on the @ and taking the first word. This means that structure names cannot contain an at sign.

To round out the implementation, we can add a couple of print and debugging functions. The following print function displays a simple user-readable representation of a structure definition and a structure instance, while the dump function displays the implementation details of the two constructs. See Example B-1 for the implementations.

Here's an example defining and using our file-info structure:

```
include defstruct.mk

$(call defstruct, file-info,      \
  $(call defslot, path,),         \
  $(call defslot, type,unix),     \
  $(call defslot, host,oscar))

before := $(call new, file-info)
$(call set-value, before, path,/etc/password)
$(call set-value, before, host,wasatch)

after := $(call new,file-info)
$(call set-value, after, path,/etc/shadow)
$(call set-value, after, host,wasatch)

demo:
        # before       = $(before)
        # before.path  = $(call get-value, before, path)
        # before.type  = $(call get-value, before, type)
        # before.host  = $(call get-value, before, host)
        # print before = $(call print-instance, before)
        # dump before  = $(call dump-instance, before)
        #
        # all_instances  = $(all_instances)
        # all_structs    = $(all_structs)
        # print file-info = $(call print-struct, file-info)
        # dump file-info  = $(call dump-struct, file-info)
```

and the output:

```
$ make
# before       = file-info@0
# before.path  = /etc/password
# before.type  = unix
# before.host  = wasatch
# print before = { "/etc/password" "unix" "wasatch" }
# dump before  = {  { file-info@0_path "/etc/password" } { file-info@0_type "unix" }
{ file-info@0_host "wasatch" } }
#
# all_instances  = file-info@0 file-info@1
# all_structs    = file-info
# print file-info = { { "path" "" } { "type" "unix" } { "host" "oscar" } }
# dump file-info  = { file-info_def_slotnames " path type host" file-info_def_path_
default "" file-info_def_type_default "unix" file-info_def_host_default "oscar" }
```

Also note how illegal structure uses are trapped:

```
$ cat badstruct.mk
include defstruct.mk
$(call new, no-such-structure)
$ make -f badstruct.mk
badstruct.mk:2: *** new on unknown struct 'no-such-structure'.  Stop.

$ cat badslot.mk
include defstruct.mk
$(call defstruct, foo, defslot(size, 0))
bar := $(call new, foo)
$(call set-value, bar, siz, 10)
$ make -f badslot.mk
badslot.mk:4: *** Instance 'foo@0' does not have slot 'siz'.  Stop.
```

Of course, there are lots of improvements that can be made to the code, but the basic ideas are sound. Here is a list of possible enhancements:

- Add a validation check to the slot assignment. This could be done with a hook function that must yield empty after the assignment has been performed. The hook could be used like this:

```
# $(call set-value, instance_id, slot_name, value)
define set-value
  $(call check-params,$1,$2)                                      \
  $(if $(call $(strip $1)_$(strip $2)_hook, value),               \
    $(error set-value hook, $(strip $1)_$(strip $2)_hook, failed)) \
  $(eval $($(strip $1))_$(strip $2) := $3)
endef
```

- Support for inheritance. A defstruct could accept another defstruct name as a superclass, duplicating all the superclass's members in the subclass.

- Better support for structure references. With the current implementation, a slot can hold the ID of another structure, but accessing is awkward. A new version of the get-value function could be written to check for references (by looking for *defstruct@number*), and perform automatic dereferencing.

Arithmetic

In the previous section, I noted that it is not possible to perform arithmetic in make using only its native features. I then showed how you could implement a simple counter by appending words to a list and returning the length of the list. Soon after I discovered the increment trick, Michael Mounteney posted a cool trick for performing a limited form of addition on integers in make.

His trick manipulates the number line to compute the sum of two integers of size one or greater. To see how this works, imagine the number line:

```
2 3 4 5 6 7 8 9 10 11 12 13 14 15
```

Now, notice that (if we could get the subscripts right), we could add, say 4 plus 5, by first taking a subset of the line from the fourth element to the end then selecting the fifth element of the subset. We can do this with native make functions:

```
number_line = 2 3 4 5 6 7 8 9 10 11 12 13 14 15
plus = $(word $2, $(wordlist $1, 15, $(number_line)))
four+five = $(call plus, 4, 5)
```

Very clever, Michael! Notice that the number line starts with 2 rather than 0 or 1. You can see that this is necessary if you run the plus function with 1 and 1. Both subscripts will yield the first element and the answer must be 2, therefore, the first element of the list must be 2. The reason for this is that, for the word and wordlist functions, the first element of the list has subscript 1 rather than 0 (but I haven't bothered to prove it).

Now, given a number line, we can perform addition, but how do we create a number line in make without typing it in by hand or using a shell program? We can create all numbers between 00 and 99 by combining all possible values in the tens place with all possible values in the ones place. For example:

```
make -f - <<< '$(warning $(foreach i, 0 1 2, $(addprefix $i, 0 1 2)))'
/c/TEMP/Gm002568:1:  00 01 02  10 11 12  20 21 22
```

By including all digits 0 through 9, we would produce all numbers from 00 to 99. By combining the foreach again with a hundreds column, we would get the numbers from 000 to 999, etc. All that is left is to strip the leading zeros where necessary.

Here is a modified form of Mr. Mounteney's code to generate a number line and define the plus and gt operations:

```
# combine - concatentate one sequence of numbers with another
combine = $(foreach i, $1, $(addprefix $i, $2))

# stripzero - Remove one leading zero from each word
stripzero = $(patsubst 0%,%,$1)

# generate - Produce all permutations of three elements from the word list
generate = $(call stripzero,                            \
              $(call stripzero,                         \
                $(call combine, $1,                     \
                  $(call combine, $1, $1))))

# number_line - Create a number line from 0 to 999
number_line := $(call generate,0 1 2 3 4 5 6 7 8 9)
length      := $(word $(words $(number_line)), $(number_line))

# plus - Use the number line to add two integers
plus = $(word $2,                                       \
          $(wordlist $1, $(length),                     \
            $(wordlist 3, $(length), $(number_line))))

# gt - Use the number line to determine if $1 is greater than $2
gt = $(filter $1,                                       \
```

```
        $(wordlist 3, $(length),                              \
          $(wordlist $2, $(length), $(number_line)))))

all:
        @echo $(call plus,4,7)
        @echo $(if $(call gt,4,7),is,is not)
        @echo $(if $(call gt,7,4),is,is not)
        @echo $(if $(call gt,7,7),is,is not)
```

When run, the *makefile* yields:

```
$ make
11
is not
is
is not
```

We can extend this code to include subtraction by noting that subscripting a reversed list is just like counting backwards. For example, to compute 7 minus 4, first create the number line subset 0 to 6, reverse it, then select the fourth element:

```
number_line := 0 1 2 3 4 5 6 7 8 9...
1through6    := 0 1 2 3 4 5 6
reverse_it   := 6 5 4 3 2 1 0
fourth_item := 3
```

Here is the algorithm in make syntax:

```
# backwards - a reverse number line
backwards := $(call generate, 9 8 7 6 5 4 3 2 1 0)

# reverse - reverse a list of words
reverse    = $(strip                                       \
                 $(foreach f,                              \
                     $(wordlist 1, $(length), $(backwards)), \
                     $(word $f, $1)))

# minus - compute $1 minus $2
minus      = $(word $2,                                     \
                 $(call reverse,                            \
                     $(wordlist 1, $1, $(number_line)))))

minus:
        # $(call minus, 7, 4)
```

Multiplication and division are left as an exercise for the reader.

GNU Free Documentation License— GNU Project—Free Software Foundation (FSF)

Version 1.2, November 2002

Copyright © 2000,2001,2002 Free Software Foundation, Inc.
59 Temple Place, Suite 330, Boston, MA 02111-1307 USA

Everyone is permitted to copy and distribute verbatim copies of this license document, but changing it is not allowed.

0. PREAMBLE

The purpose of this License is to make a manual, textbook, or other functional and useful document "free" in the sense of freedom: to assure everyone the effective freedom to copy and redistribute it, with or without modifying it, either commercially or noncommercially. Secondarily, this License preserves for the author and publisher a way to get credit for their work, while not being considered responsible for modifications made by others.

This License is a kind of "copyleft", which means that derivative works of the document must themselves be free in the same sense. It complements the GNU General Public License, which is a copyleft license designed for free software.

We have designed this License in order to use it for manuals for free software, because free software needs free documentation: a free program should come with manuals providing the same freedoms that the software does. But this License is not limited to software manuals; it can be used for any textual work, regardless of subject matter or whether it is published as a printed book. We recommend this License principally for works whose purpose is instruction or reference.

1. APPLICABILITY AND DEFINITIONS

This License applies to any manual or other work, in any medium, that contains a notice placed by the copyright holder saying it can be distributed under the terms of this License. Such a notice grants a world-wide, royalty-free license, unlimited in duration, to use that work under the conditions stated herein. The "Document", below, refers to any such manual or work. Any member of the public is a licensee, and is addressed as "you". You accept the license if you copy, modify or distribute the work in a way requiring permission under copyright law.

A "Modified Version" of the Document means any work containing the Document or a portion of it, either copied verbatim, or with modifications and/or translated into another language.

A "Secondary Section" is a named appendix or a front-matter section of the Document that deals exclusively with the relationship of the publishers or authors of the Document to the Document's overall subject (or to related matters) and contains nothing that could fall directly within that overall subject. (Thus, if the Document is in part a textbook of mathematics, a Secondary Section may not explain any mathematics.) The relationship could be a matter of historical connection with the subject or with related matters, or of legal, commercial, philosophical, ethical or political position regarding them.

The "Invariant Sections" are certain Secondary Sections whose titles are designated, as being those of Invariant Sections, in the notice that says that the Document is released under this License. If a section does not fit the above definition of Secondary then it is not allowed to be designated as Invariant. The Document may contain zero Invariant Sections. If the Document does not identify any Invariant Sections then there are none.

The "Cover Texts" are certain short passages of text that are listed, as Front-Cover Texts or Back-Cover Texts, in the notice that says that the Document is released under this License. A Front-Cover Text may be at most 5 words, and a Back-Cover Text may be at most 25 words.

A "Transparent" copy of the Document means a machine-readable copy, represented in a format whose specification is available to the general public, that is suitable for revising the document straightforwardly with generic text editors or (for images composed of pixels) generic paint programs or (for drawings) some widely available drawing editor, and that is suitable for input to text formatters or for automatic translation to a variety of formats suitable for input to text formatters. A copy made in an otherwise Transparent file format whose markup, or absence of markup, has been arranged to thwart or discourage subsequent modification by readers is not Transparent. An image format is not Transparent if used for any substantial amount of text. A copy that is not "Transparent" is called "Opaque".

Examples of suitable formats for Transparent copies include plain ASCII without markup, Texinfo input format, LaTeX input format, SGML or XML using a publicly available DTD, and standard-conforming simple HTML, PostScript or PDF designed for human modification. Examples of transparent image formats include PNG, XCF and JPG. Opaque formats include proprietary formats that can be read and edited only by proprietary word processors, SGML or XML for which the DTD and/or processing tools are not generally available, and the machine-generated HTML, PostScript or PDF produced by some word processors for output purposes only.

The "Title Page" means, for a printed book, the title page itself, plus such following pages as are needed to hold, legibly, the material this License requires to appear in the title page. For works in formats which do not have any title page as such, "Title Page" means the text near the most prominent appearance of the work's title, preceding the beginning of the body of the text.

A section "Entitled XYZ" means a named subunit of the Document whose title either is precisely XYZ or contains XYZ in parentheses following text that translates XYZ in another language. (Here XYZ stands for a specific section name mentioned below, such as "Acknowledgements", "Dedications", "Endorsements", or "History".) To "Preserve the Title" of such a section when you modify the Document means that it remains a section "Entitled XYZ" according to this definition.

The Document may include Warranty Disclaimers next to the notice which states that this License applies to the Document. These Warranty Disclaimers are considered to be included by reference in this License, but only as regards disclaiming warranties: any other implication that these Warranty Disclaimers may have is void and has no effect on the meaning of this License.

2. VERBATIM COPYING

You may copy and distribute the Document in any medium, either commercially or noncommercially, provided that this License, the copyright notices, and the license notice saying this License applies to the Document are reproduced in all copies, and that you add no other conditions whatsoever to those of this License. You may not use technical measures to obstruct or control the reading or further copying of the copies you make or distribute. However, you may accept compensation in exchange for copies. If you distribute a large enough number of copies you must also follow the conditions in section 3.

You may also lend copies, under the same conditions stated above, and you may publicly display copies.

3. COPYING IN QUANTITY

If you publish printed copies (or copies in media that commonly have printed covers) of the Document, numbering more than 100, and the Document's license notice requires Cover Texts, you must enclose the copies in covers that carry, clearly and legibly, all these Cover Texts: Front-Cover Texts on the front cover, and Back-Cover Texts on the back cover. Both covers must also clearly and legibly identify you as the publisher of these copies. The front cover must present the full title with all words of the title equally prominent and visible. You may add other material on the covers in addition. Copying with changes limited to the covers, as long as they preserve the title of the Document and satisfy these conditions, can be treated as verbatim copying in other respects.

If the required texts for either cover are too voluminous to fit legibly, you should put the first ones listed (as many as fit reasonably) on the actual cover, and continue the rest onto adjacent pages.

If you publish or distribute Opaque copies of the Document numbering more than 100, you must either include a machine-readable Transparent copy along with each Opaque copy, or state in or with each Opaque copy a computer-network location from which the general network-using public has access to download using public-standard network protocols a complete Transparent copy of the Document, free of added material. If you use the latter option, you must take reasonably prudent steps, when you begin distribution of Opaque copies in quantity, to ensure that this Transparent copy will remain thus accessible at the stated location until at least one year after the last time you distribute an Opaque copy (directly or through your agents or retailers) of that edition to the public.

It is requested, but not required, that you contact the authors of the Document well before redistributing any large number of copies, to give them a chance to provide you with an updated version of the Document.

4. MODIFICATIONS

You may copy and distribute a Modified Version of the Document under the conditions of sections 2 and 3 above, provided that you release the Modified Version under precisely this License, with the Modified Version filling the role of the Document, thus licensing distribution and modification of the Modified Version to whoever possesses a copy of it. In addition, you must do these things in the Modified Version:

1. Use in the Title Page (and on the covers, if any) a title distinct from that of the Document, and from those of previous versions (which should, if there were any, be listed in the History section of the Document). You may use the same title as a previous version if the original publisher of that version gives permission.

2. List on the Title Page, as authors, one or more persons or entities responsible for authorship of the modifications in the Modified Version, together with at least five of the principal authors of the Document (all of its principal authors, if it has fewer than five), unless they release you from this requirement.

3. State on the Title page the name of the publisher of the Modified Version, as the publisher.

4. Preserve all the copyright notices of the Document.

5. Add an appropriate copyright notice for your modifications adjacent to the other copyright notices.

6. Include, immediately after the copyright notices, a license notice giving the public permission to use the Modified Version under the terms of this License, in the form shown in the Addendum below.

7. Preserve in that license notice the full lists of Invariant Sections and required Cover Texts given in the Document's license notice.

8. Include an unaltered copy of this License.

9. Preserve the section Entitled "History", Preserve its Title, and add to it an item stating at least the title, year, new authors, and publisher of the Modified Version as given on the Title Page. If there is no section Entitled "History" in the Document, create one stating the title, year, authors, and publisher of the Document as given on its Title Page, then add an item describing the Modified Version as stated in the previous sentence.

10. Preserve the network location, if any, given in the Document for public access to a Transparent copy of the Document, and likewise the network locations given in the Document for previous versions it was based on. These may be placed in the "History" section. You may omit a network location for a work that was published at least four years before the Document itself, or if the original publisher of the version it refers to gives permission.

11. For any section Entitled "Acknowledgements" or "Dedications", Preserve the Title of the section, and preserve in the section all the substance and tone of each of the contributor acknowledgements and/or dedications given therein.

12. Preserve all the Invariant Sections of the Document, unaltered in their text and in their titles. Section numbers or the equivalent are not considered part of the section titles.

13. Delete any section Entitled "Endorsements". Such a section may not be included in the Modified Version.

14. Do not retitle any existing section to be Entitled "Endorsements" or to conflict in title with any Invariant Section.

15. Preserve any Warranty Disclaimers.

If the Modified Version includes new front-matter sections or appendices that qualify as Secondary Sections and contain no material copied from the Document, you may at your option designate some or all of these sections as invariant. To do this, add their titles to the list of Invariant Sections in the Modified Version's license notice. These titles must be distinct from any other section titles.

You may add a section Entitled "Endorsements", provided it contains nothing but endorsements of your Modified Version by various parties—for example, statements of peer review or that the text has been approved by an organization as the authoritative definition of a standard.

You may add a passage of up to five words as a Front-Cover Text, and a passage of up to 25 words as a Back-Cover Text, to the end of the list of Cover Texts in the Modified Version. Only one passage of Front-Cover Text and one of Back-Cover Text may be added by (or through arrangements made by) any one entity. If the Document already includes a cover text for the same cover, previously added by you or by arrangement made by the same entity you are acting on behalf of, you may not add another; but you may replace the old one, on explicit permission from the previous publisher that added the old one.

The author(s) and publisher(s) of the Document do not by this License give permission to use their names for publicity for or to assert or imply endorsement of any Modified Version.

5. COMBINING DOCUMENTS

You may combine the Document with other documents released under this License, under the terms defined in section 4 above for modified versions, provided that you include in the combination all of the Invariant Sections of all of the original documents, unmodified, and list them all as Invariant Sections of your combined work in its license notice, and that you preserve all their Warranty Disclaimers.

The combined work need only contain one copy of this License, and multiple identical Invariant Sections may be replaced with a single copy. If there are multiple Invariant Sections with the same name but different contents, make the title of each such section unique by adding at the end of it, in parentheses, the name of the original author or publisher of that section if known, or else a unique number. Make the same adjustment to the section titles in the list of Invariant Sections in the license notice of the combined work.

In the combination, you must combine any sections Entitled "History" in the various original documents, forming one section Entitled "History"; likewise combine any sections Entitled "Acknowledgements", and any sections Entitled "Dedications". You must delete all sections Entitled "Endorsements."

6. COLLECTIONS OF DOCUMENTS

You may make a collection consisting of the Document and other documents released under this License, and replace the individual copies of this License in the various documents with a single copy that is included in the collection, provided that you follow the rules of this License for verbatim copying of each of the documents in all other respects.

You may extract a single document from such a collection, and distribute it individually under this License, provided you insert a copy of this License into the extracted document, and follow this License in all other respects regarding verbatim copying of that document.

7. AGGREGATION WITH INDEPENDENT WORKS

A compilation of the Document or its derivatives with other separate and independent documents or works, in or on a volume of a storage or distribution medium, is called an "aggregate" if the copyright resulting from the compilation is not used to limit the legal rights of the compilation's users beyond what the individual works permit. When the Document is included in an aggregate, this License does not apply to the other works in the aggregate which are not themselves derivative works of the Document.

If the Cover Text requirement of section 3 is applicable to these copies of the Document, then if the Document is less than one half of the entire aggregate, the Document's Cover Texts may be placed on covers that bracket the Document within the aggregate, or the electronic equivalent of covers if the Document is in electronic form. Otherwise they must appear on printed covers that bracket the whole aggregate.

8. TRANSLATION

Translation is considered a kind of modification, so you may distribute translations of the Document under the terms of section 4. Replacing Invariant Sections with translations requires special permission from their copyright holders, but you may include translations of some or all Invariant Sections in addition to the original versions of these Invariant Sections. You may include a translation of this License, and all the license notices in the Document, and any Warranty Disclaimers, provided that you also include the original English version of this License and the original versions of those notices and disclaimers. In case of a disagreement between the translation and the original version of this License or a notice or disclaimer, the original version will prevail.

If a section in the Document is Entitled "Acknowledgements", "Dedications", or "History", the requirement (section 4) to Preserve its Title (section 1) will typically require changing the actual title.

9. TERMINATION

You may not copy, modify, sublicense, or distribute the Document except as expressly provided for under this License. Any other attempt to copy, modify, sublicense or distribute the Document is void, and will automatically terminate your rights under this License. However, parties who have received copies, or rights, from you under this License will not have their licenses terminated so long as such parties remain in full compliance.

10. FUTURE REVISIONS OF THIS LICENSE

The Free Software Foundation may publish new, revised versions of the GNU Free Documentation License from time to time. Such new versions will be similar in spirit to the present version, but may differ in detail to address new problems or concerns. See *http://www.gnu.org/copyleft/*.

Each version of the License is given a distinguishing version number. If the Document specifies that a particular numbered version of this License "or any later version" applies to it, you have the option of following the terms and conditions either of that specified version or of any later version that has been published (not as a draft) by the Free Software Foundation. If the Document does not specify a version number of this License, you may choose any version ever published (not as a draft) by the Free Software Foundation.

Index

Symbols

* (asterisk) wildcard, 12
{ } (curly braces) in variables, 41
+= (append) operator, 45
$% automatic variable, 16
$+ automatic variable, 17
$< automatic variable, 16
$? automatic variable, 16
$@ automatic variable, 16
$^ automatic variable, 17
$* automatic variables, 17
[ ] (brackets) wildcard, 12
@ command prefix, echo and, 92
?= (conditional variable assignment)
    operator, 44
- (dash) command prefix, 93
= operator, 42
:= operator, 43
?= operator, environment variables, 52
( ) (parentheses) in variables, 41
^ in patterns, 12
% (percent) character, pattern rules, 22
+ (plus) command modifier, 93
? (question mark) wildcard, 12
@ sign, performance and, 188
~ (tilde) wildcard, 12

A

add-manifest function, jars, 176
addprefix function, 75
addsuffix function, 74
all target, 15
ALL_TREES variable, 155

--always-make option, 249
Ant (Java), 160
    build files, 160
        mkdir program, 162
    portability, 162
    tasks, 161
append operator (+=), 45
ar command, archive libraries, 34
archive libraries, 34
archive members, automatic variables
        and, 16
arguments, patterns as built-in functions, 65
arithmetic, performing with make, 260
arrays, files array and command-line
        limits, 102
assert function, 76
automake tool, 139
automatic variables, 16, 53
    archive members, 16
    empty targets and, 16
    prerequisites, 16
    targets and, 16
    VPATH and, 19
    vpath and, 19

B

basename function, 73
bash shell, benchmarking and, 183
benchmarking, 182
    bash shell, 183
    Cygwin and, 184
    subst function calls and, 185
    variable assignment speed, 185

We'd like to hear your suggestions for improving our indexes. Send email to *index@oreilly.com*.

no-op commands, 95
notdir function, 73

O

object files, updates, 27
$(OBJECTS) variable, 23
--old-file option, 250
options
    commands, errors and, 94
    portability and, 130
origin function, 79
output, book makefile example, 213

P

packages, Java, 159
parallelism
    --jobs option, 190
    performance and, 190
    pmake, 194
parameters
    passing to functions, 86
    user-defined functions, 62
parentheses, variables and, 41, 78
parsing
    commands, 88
        command scripts and, 89
        editors and, 90
    eval function and, 83
partial source trees, 156
passing parameters to functions, 86
passing variables, recursive make and, 111
paths, portability and, 130
patsubst function, 68
pattern rules, 10, 21
    % (percent) character, 22
    implicit rules and, 10
    static pattern rules, 23
    suffix rules, 24
        deleting, 24
patterns, 22
    as arguments in built-in functions, 65
    filter function, 65
pattern-specific variables, 50
performance
    @ sign and, 188
    benchmarking and, 182
    bottlenecks, 186
    distribution and, 194
    initialization and, 188
    introduction, 182
    parallelism and, 190

recursive variables, 187
    simple variables, 187
.PHONY target modifier, 13
phony targets, 13
    interfaces and, 15
    nonrecursive make and, 117
    output
        debugging, 14
        reading, 14
    prerequisites, 13
    special targets, 30
    standard, 15
pmake, 194
portability, 129
    Ant (Java), 162
    Cygwin, 131
    nonportable tools, 137
    options and, 130
    paths and, 130
    program behavior and, 130
    program names and, 130
    shell and, 130, 139
.PRECIOUS target modifier, 30
prefixes
    on commands
        @, 92
        - (dash), 93
        + (plus), 93
    pattern rules, 23
prerequisites
    automatic variables and, 16
    libraries as, 38
    phony targets, 13
    rules and, 4
    saving, 39
    targets
        chaining, 6
        .INTERMEDIATE modifier and, 30
        .SECONDARY modifier, 30
    updates, ordering and, 110
--print-data-base option, 250
    debugging and, 230
program behavior, portability and, 130
program management, 134
program names, portability and, 130
program-variables macro, 82

R

RCS source control, implicit rules and, 28
read-only source, 149
rebuilds, minimizing, 7
recursion, 107

About the Author

Robert Mecklenburg began using Unix as a student in 1977 and has been programming professionally for 23 years. His make experience started in 1982 at NASA with Unix Version 7. Robert received his PhD in computer science from the University of Utah in 1991. Since then, he has worked in many fields ranging from mechanical CAD to bioinformatics, and brings his extensive experience in C++, Java, and Lisp to bear on the problems of project management with make.

Colophon

Our look is the result of reader comments, our own experimentation, and feedback from distribution channels. Distinctive covers complement our distinctive approach to technical topics, breathing personality and life into potentially dry subjects.

The animal on the cover of *Managing Projects with GNU Make*, Third Edition is a potto, a member of the loris family. A small primate native to the tropical forests of West Africa, the potto is 17 inches long and covered with dense, wooly, reddish-brown fur. Its opposable thumbs give it an excellent grasp, leaving it well adapted to its life in the trees. The potto spends its days sleeping in crevices or holes in trees, emerging at night to hunt for food (insects, snails, and bats). Unlike many primates, the potto generally lives alone.

Matt Hutchinson was the production editor for *Managing Projects with GNU Make*, Third Edition. Octal Publishing, Inc. provided production services. Johnna Dinse wrote the index. Adam Witwer, Jamie Peppard, and Darren Kelly provided quality control.

Edie Freedman designed the cover of this book. The cover image is a 19th-century engraving from the Dover Pictorial Archive. Clay Fernald produced the cover layout with QuarkXPress 4.1 using Adobe's ITC Garamond font.

David Futato designed the interior layout. This book was converted by Joe Wizda to FrameMaker 5.5.6 with a format conversion tool created by Erik Ray, Jason McIntosh, Neil Walls, and Mike Sierra that uses Perl and XML technologies. The text font is Linotype Birka; the heading font is Adobe Myriad Condensed; and the code font is LucasFont's TheSans Mono Condensed. The illustrations that appear in the book were produced by Robert Romano and Jessamyn Read using Macromedia FreeHand MX and Adobe Photoshop CS.